HOW
Boat Things
WORK

HOW
Boat Things
WORK

AN ILLUSTRATED GUIDE

CHARLIE WING

INTERNATIONAL MARINE / McGRAW-HILL
Camden, Maine • New York • Chicago • San Francisco •
Lisbon • London • Madrid • Mexico City • Milan • New Delhi •
San Juan • Seoul • Singapore • Sydney • Toronto

This slim volume is dedicated to Bill Fulton who,
more than any other, shares my childish enthusiasm
for how boat things work.

The McGraw·Hill Companies

3 4 5 6 7 8 9 0 QPD QPD 0 9

© 2004, 2007 by Charlie Wing

All rights reserved. The name "International Marine" and the International Marine logo are trademarks of The McGraw-Hill Companies. Printed in the United States of America.

The Library of Congress has cataloged the cloth edition as follows:

Wing, Charles, 1929–
    How boat things work: an illustrated guide / Charlie Wing.
        p.   cm.
    ISBN 0-07-137754-9
    1. Motorboats—Equipment and supplies—Handbooks, manuals, etc. 2. Motorboats—Maintenance and repair—Amateurs' manuals. 3. Sailboats—Maintenance and repair—Handbooks, manuals, etc. I. Title.
VM341.W54 2004
623.82—dc22   2003108314

Paperback ISBN-13: 978-0-07-149344-4
Paperback ISBN-10: 0-07-149344-1

Questions regarding the content of this book should be addressed to
    International Marine
    P.O. Box 220
    Camden, ME 04843
    www.internationalmarine.com

Questions regarding the ordering of this book should be addressed to
    The McGraw-Hill Companies
    Customer Service Department
    P.O. Box 547
    Blacklick, OH 43004
    Retail customers: 1-800-262-4729
    Bookstores: 1-800-722-4726

Illustrations by Charlie Wing

Contents

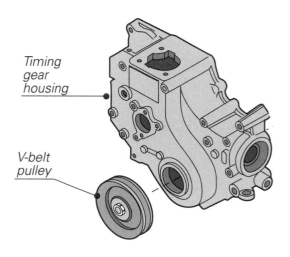

Timing gear housing

V-belt pulley

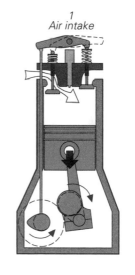

1
Air intake

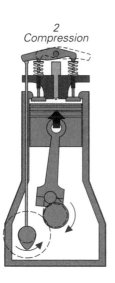

2
Compression

3
Fuel injection

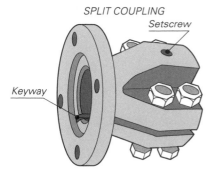

SPLIT COUPLING

Setscrew

Keyway

CHAPTER 2   *Steering and Controls*

CHAPTER 3   *Standing Rigging*

CHAPTER 4   *Line Handling*

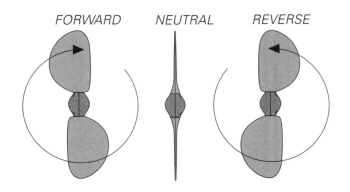

FORWARD   NEUTRAL   REVERSE

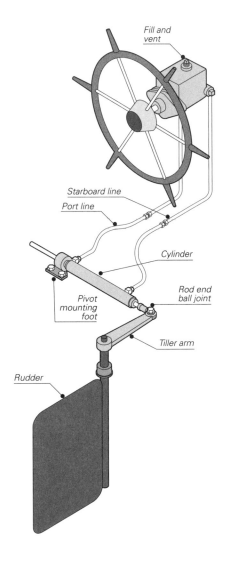

Fill and vent

Starboard line

Port line

Cylinder

Pivot mounting foot

Rod end ball joint

Tiller arm

Rudder

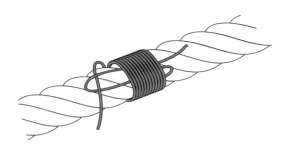

CHAPTER 5   *Ground Tackle*

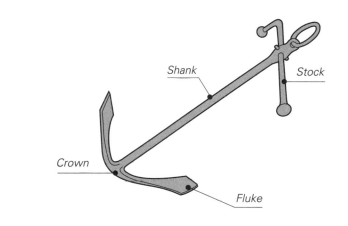

CHAPTER 6   *Electrical*

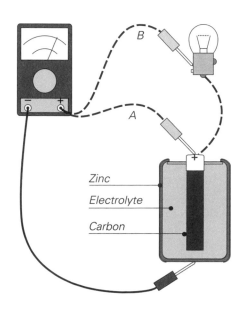

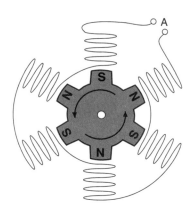

CHAPTER 7 *Plumbing*

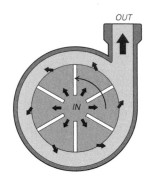

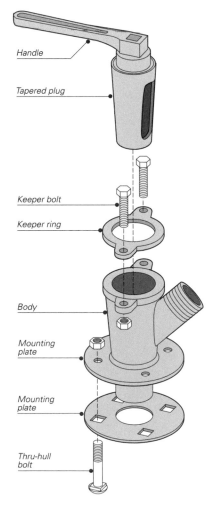

Introduction

We moved aboard *Puffin*, our 39-foot Southern Cross cutter, in 1986. In October of that year, my wife and I departed Portland, Maine to follow the sun to the Caribbean. In retrospect we neither knew what we were doing, nor what lay over the horizon. Experienced sailors won't be surprised to hear that we made it barely to Long Island Sound before a problem arose.

We were motoring through The Race when we became aware of a new and different sound, a sound from the engine compartment not unlike that of ball bearings being thrown about in a washing machine. It didn't sound dangerous, but neither did it sound healthy. In an instant my position as captain was reduced to that of incompetent engineer. I didn't have a clue.

As I stared at the mass of metal from which the sound emanated, I tried to picture what was happening inside. Does it need oil? How can one tell? And what kind of oil if it does? Maybe I should stop the engine. If I don't stop it, will the damage increase? After we reached port I considered unbolting the transmission and taking a look inside. What stopped me was the fear that, once unbolted from the engine, all of the oil, gears, clutches, shafts and who-knows-what-else would literally spill into the bilge. Of course we called a certified diesel mechanic who, at great expense, unbolted the transmission and took it away to the transmission hospital. And no, nothing fell out—not even a drop of oil.

This sort of scene played out several more times on our journey south. A guest attempted to flush the better part of a roll of Bounty paper towels down the head. She nearly succeeded, but the fibrous mass finally hung up somewhere within the bowels of the Crown Imperial and, once again, I found myself trying to imagine the inner workings of the china throne.

Another time we were backing out of a marina slip, perilously close to a million-dollar yacht, when the shift linkage parted. The 22,000-pound *Puffin* was making several knots astern straight at the yacht, while I flipped the now-useless shift lever back and forth. In my panic I worsened the situation by shifting the adjacent throttle lever to full-on. Fortunately our little fiberglass dinghy cushioned the blow so the only thing hurt was my pride—once again. And, again, because I hadn't a clue about steering pedestals, throttle cables and shift cables, we paid a mechanic a month's cruising kitty to perform a simple repair.

I began to see that boat things weren't really that complicated and that, were we to continue cruising, either a rich relative would have to bequeath us a fortune or I was going to have to overcome my fear of mechanical devices. Actually, not fear of machines, but fear of the unknown. What was inside? If I could only see what was inside, I could probably figure out how the thing worked and, therefore, fix it.

This is the book I wish I had then—a collection of exploded views and explanations of how the mechanical gizmos on boats work. I hope it helps to diminish your fear of the unknown.

CHARLIE WING
Falmouth, Maine

1

Propulsion

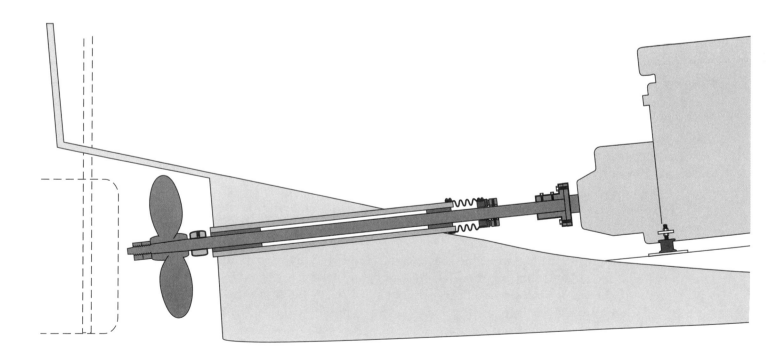

Drivetrain

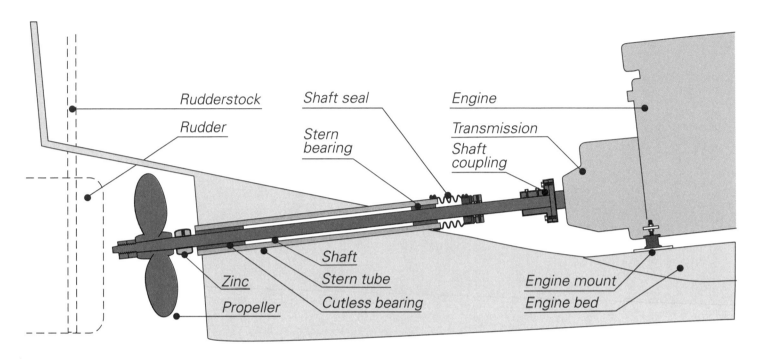

Drivetrain on a typical powerboat.

The drivetrain is the assemblage of components that move a boat through the water under power. The engine supplies mechanical power in the form of a rotating output shaft. Bolted to the engine is a transmission (also known as a gearbox or reverse gear), which is used to reverse the output shaft's direction of rotation when the operator wants to move astern. Very often the gearbox steps down the shaft revolutions per minute (rpm).

Integral with the hull are a pair of fore-and-aft engine beds, spaced and inclined to align the output shaft of the transmission with the propeller shaft. The engine sits on four adjustable engine mounts that provide a degree of vibration isolation, but, more importantly, permit final alignment of the two shafts.

A shaft coupling (pages 46–47) connects the propeller shaft to the output shaft of the transmis-

sion. The propeller shaft penetrates the hull through a stern tube and is supported by a stern bearing at the inboard end of the stern tube and a Cutless bearing (page 45) at the outboard end. The Cutless bearing is cooled by seawater. Some boats let seawater into the stern tube through a hole and out through the Cutless bearing. Water is prevented from entering the boat by a shaft seal or a stuffing box (pages 48–49), which forms a nearly watertight seal around the rotating shaft.

Finally, a propeller (pages 50–56) converts shaft rotation to thrust by engaging the water around it. When water is thrown to the rear, an equal and opposite reaction thrusts the boat forward, and vice versa.

The drivetrain is much more than a collection of individual parts. The components must be matched to the boat and to each other. The engine horsepower must be matched to the hull to achieve desired

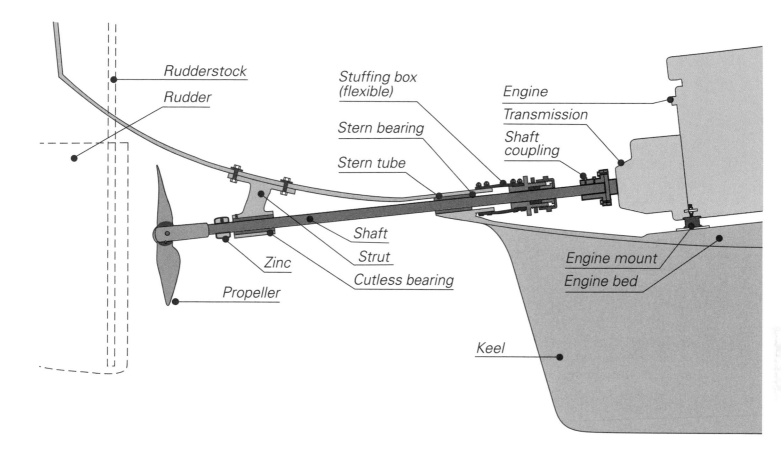

Nearly identical to the drivetrain on a powerboat, the typical drivetrain on a sailboat often includes a flexible stuffing box.

speed. A planing hull with an engine that is too small can never climb out of the displacement mode, severely disappointing its owner. On the other hand, an engine that is too large will often have to be run at low rpm, a practice particularly harmful to diesel engines.

The two halves of the shaft coupling must be precisely aligned. Misalignment results in vibration, rapid wear of the stern bearing and, worse, wear of the transmission shaft and bearings.

The propeller must be sized to match the engine's rated horsepower and rpm, the gearbox ratio, hull waterline length, hull displacement, and propeller style. If the propeller size (diameter in inches) and/or pitch (inches of advance per revolution) are too great, the engine will never reach its rated rpm. Too small a propeller will allow the full-rated rpm but will not utilize the full-rated power. Finally, if the combined area of the propeller blades is too small, excessive suction on the blades' leading edges will produce vapor bubbles (cavitation), which will erode the blades.

In a powerboat with twin engines, the two propellers rotate in opposite directions in order to balance the sideways thrusts and torque (see page 50). Since the engines are invariably identical, the rotation change is accomplished in the gearboxes.

The following pages will illustrate a variety of engines, transmissions, shaft couplings, stuffing boxes, and propellers, but the function of each component is always the same. The one thing to remember is that each is part of an overall drivetrain system and must be matched to the whole.

Principles of the Diesel Engine

All internal combustion engines convert the chemical energy of a fuel to mechanical energy through combustion. The primary difference between gasoline and diesel engines is the manner in which the combustion occurs.

In the gasoline engine, gasoline and air premixed in a carburetor are introduced into the cylinders. An electric spark causes the mixture to ignite at a precise time in the piston cycle, driving the piston down in a power stroke.

In a diesel engine, air in the cylinder is compressed by the piston by a factor of about 20 (the compression ratio). Since the temperature of air is a measure of its energy per volume, quickly reducing its volume by a factor of 20 or more raises its temperature to about 1,000°F. Diesel fuel sprayed into the hot, compressed air ignites, further increasing both temperature and pressure and pushing the piston down in a power stroke. By metering the amount and duration of the spray, the fuel injector produces a controlled combustion.

The principal parts of a diesel engine are shown here. The cylinders are machined in the cast-iron engine block. The pistons slide up and down inside the cylinders and are linked to the crankshaft by connecting rods. The point of connection to the crankshaft (the crank end bearing) is offset from the main bearing, so up-and-down motion of the piston produces rotation in the crankshaft. Expandable piston rings in grooves in the piston seal the cylinder against leakage.

In the bottom of the engine block (the crankcase), a camshaft is linked to the crankshaft by a timing chain or gears, as shown. The camshaft incorporates lobed cams, which, in a four-stroke engine, rotate at half the rate of the crankshaft. Tappets, riding on the cams, drive steel push rods up and down through holes in the block to the engine head. Rocker arms, driven alternately by the push rods and valve springs, actuate intake and exhaust valves, letting air into the cylinder and combustion products out at the proper times. The cams and push rods force the valves open, while the valve springs cause them to close. Note that the illustration, for purposes of clarity, shows intake and exhaust valves on opposite sides. In a real engine the valves are in line.

A fuel injection pump, driven by the camshaft, delivers pulses of diesel fuel to the injectors, which spray the fuel into the hot, compressed air at precisely the right moment and in the right amount.

An engine has a single crankshaft but can have any number of cylinders. The timing of each cylinder is controlled by the relative positions of its cams on the camshaft and its crankshaft throw.

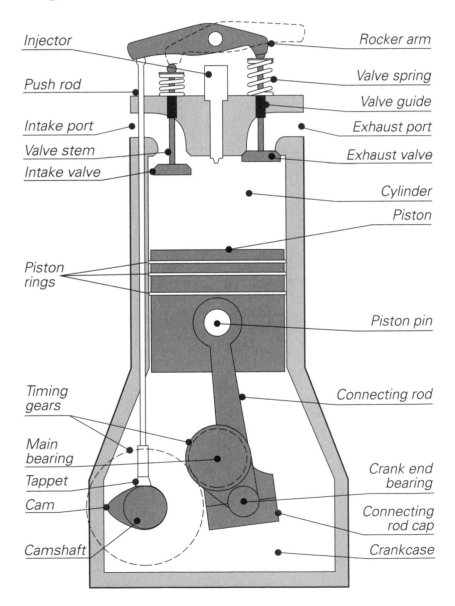

Four-Stroke Diesel Cycle

Most small marine diesels are of the four-stroke variety. The sequence of air intake, compression, fuel injection, and exhaust requires two upstrokes and two downstrokes, for a total of four strokes, in two complete revolutions of the crankshaft:

1. *Air Intake.* On a downstroke the inlet valve opens. The suction created by the piston draws fresh air into the cylinder.

2. *Compression.* Shortly after the piston reaches the bottom of its stroke, the intake valve closes, trapping the air in the cylinder. The closing of the intake valve is delayed just enough to take advantage of the momentum of the inrushing air. The piston then rises to the top of its stroke, compressing the enclosed air to about $1/20$ of the cylinder volume and raising its temperature above the 750°F ignition temperature of diesel fuel.

3. *Fuel Injection.* At the top of the stroke (usually called the power stroke), the injector begins spraying fuel into the hot air, which immediately burns. The combustion raises both the temperature and pressure in the cylinder, forcing the piston down in a power stroke. The amount of fuel injected determines the power delivered by the engine. The maximum useful amount is limited, however, by the amount of oxygen available for combustion. Excess, unburned fuel is exhausted as a black, oily soot.

4. *Exhaust.* In the following upstroke the exhaust valve opens, allowing the rising piston to flush the products of combustion out of the cylinder. At the end of the exhaust stroke, the exhaust valve closes, readying the cylinder for the next complete cycle.

In the following pages we will examine the major subassemblies of the two-cylinder Yanmar 2GM diesel engine. While it has only two cylinders and is rated at just 13 horsepower at 3,400 rpm, it shares the same basic diesel principles with all other four-stroke marine diesel engines.

1 Air intake	*2* Compression	*3* Fuel injection	*4* Exhaust

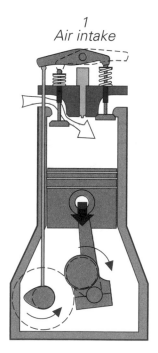 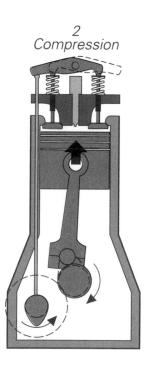 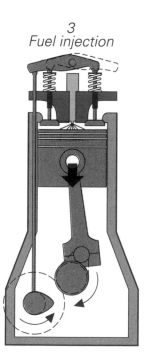 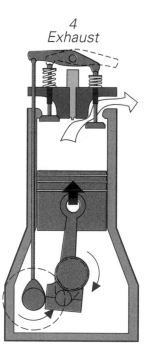

The ubiquitous four-stroke marine diesel carries its name to indicate the four distinct moves in its combustion cycle.

Yanmar 2GM

Yanmar diesel engines are popular because sophisticated engineering has reduced their weight per horsepower and levels of vibration. In addition they have earned a reputation for both reliability and worldwide availability of parts.

The small marine series includes engines with one, two, and three cylinders (1GM through 3GM). Many parts are interchangeable between models, reducing the parts inventory a service center must stock.

In the pages that follow, each of the subassemblies below is shown in exploded view with accompanying discussion of function and operation.

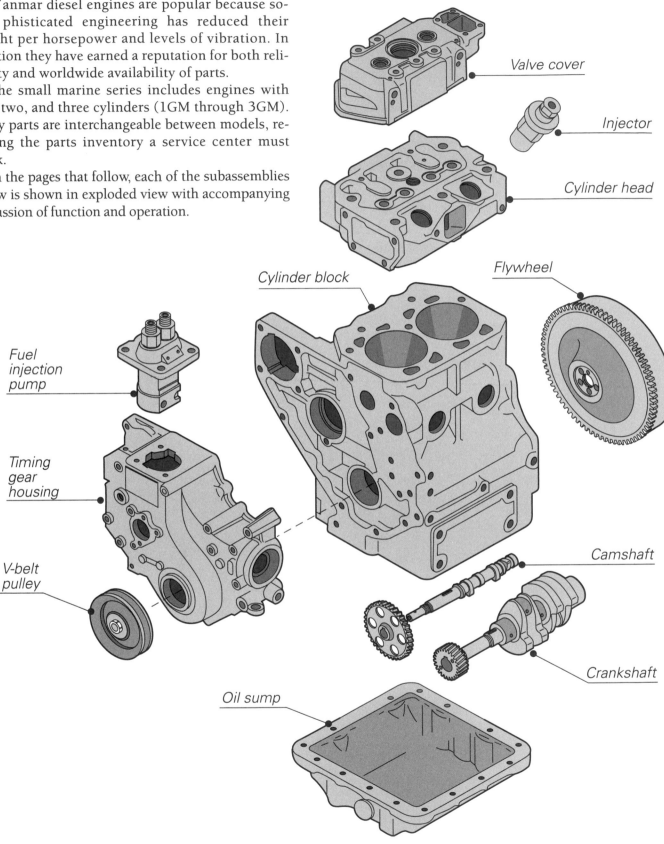

Valve cover

Injector

Cylinder head

Cylinder block

Flywheel

Fuel injection pump

Timing gear housing

V-belt pulley

Camshaft

Crankshaft

Oil sump

Cylinder Block

The central part of the engine is the cylinder block, a massive, complex iron casting containing chambers for crankshaft, camshaft, and push rods; large, cylindrical holes for the cylinders; and numerous passages for air, water, and lubricating oil.

Cast iron is heavy, but resists warping from overheating better than most other metals. While weight might not seem an issue in a boat weighing 10,000 or more pounds, Yanmar has engineered their blocks for maximum power-to-weight ratio.

In older Yanmar engines the cylinders are actually cylindrical cast-iron liners (shown below), pressed into cast and bored cylinder holes. Liners are often employed because they can be replaced when worn, without having to throw away the whole block. Wet-type liners contact the block only at top and bottom, allowing engine cooling water to circulate between liner and block. The Yanmar's dry liners fit in direct contact with the block, dissipating the heat of combustion by conduction to the block. Newer Yanmar diesels dispense with liners entirely.

Water freezing in a block's cooling passages can crack even a massive iron block, requiring removal of the engine and an expensive overhaul. The replaceable cup plugs ("freeze plugs") are, in reality, just plugs for the holes used to remove the molding sand from the casting.

Seawater-cooled engines are most vulnerable to cracked blocks, since they must either be kept warm or flushed with antifreeze after each use in cold climates. Freshwater-cooled engines circulate a mixture of antifreeze and freshwater through the block. A separate heat exchanger transfers the heat of this coolant mixture to raw seawater circulated by an engine-driven pump. Even so, the seawater side of the heat exchanger and exhaust manifold cooling jacket must be flushed with antifreeze or thoroughly drained.

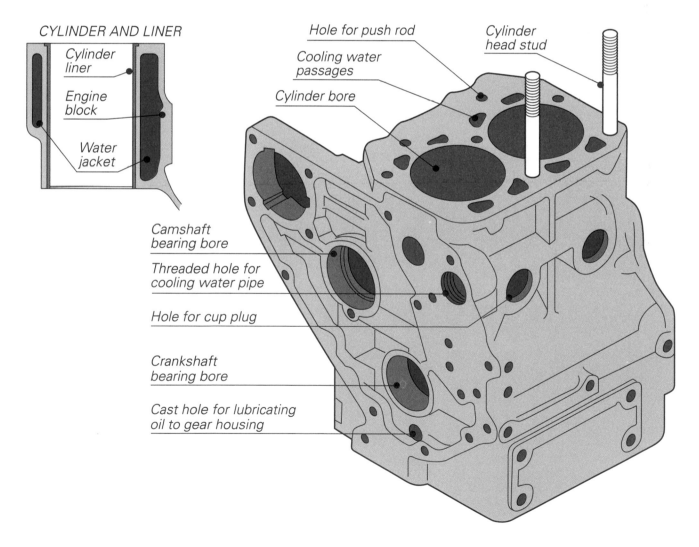

CYLINDER AND LINER

Cylinder liner

Engine block

Water jacket

Hole for push rod

Cooling water passages

Cylinder bore

Cylinder head stud

Camshaft bearing bore

Threaded hole for cooling water pipe

Hole for cup plug

Crankshaft bearing bore

Cast hole for lubricating oil to gear housing

Piston

A piston may travel 500,000 miles and experience a billion power strokes in its lifetime. And this is no leisure cruise. During the intake stroke it experiences room-temperature air and negative pressure. Just a few hundredths of a second later it is exposed to a temperature of several thousand degrees and pressure of 1,000 pounds per square inch. Incredibly, it does this while maintaining a perfect seal.

The seal is effected by a set of three rings. The sliding contact face of each ring is plated with chromium for wear resistance, but each ring has a different cross section. The top ring is exposed to the worst conditions, so it has a rugged barrel-shaped face. The second ring has a tapered face to minimize contact area and effect the tightest seal. The third ring (the oil ring) distributes lubricating oil to the cylinder face.

The crankpin bearings are lubricated by oil forced through holes drilled axially in the crankshaft. Oil exiting the bearings splashes onto the piston and cylinder liner walls.

CONNECTING ROD

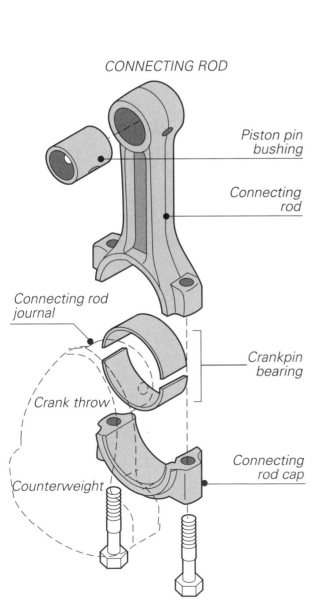

Piston pin bushing

Connecting rod

Connecting rod journal

Crankpin bearing

Crank throw

Counterweight

Connecting rod cap

PISTON AND RINGS

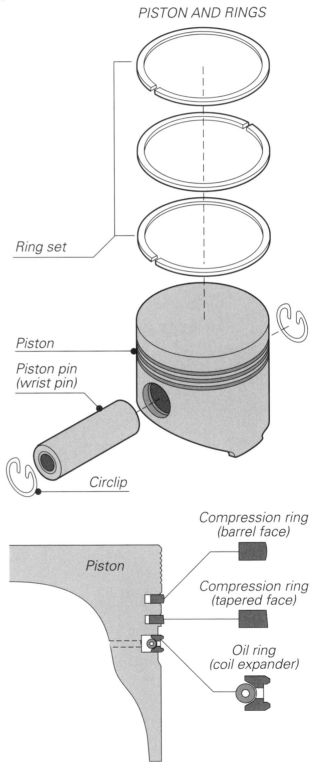

Ring set

Piston

Piston pin (wrist pin)

Circlip

Compression ring (barrel face)

Compression ring (tapered face)

Piston

Oil ring (coil expander)

Crankshaft

The crankshaft is the workhorse of the engine, converting the up-and-down motion of the pistons and connecting rods to rotary motion. The ends of the crankshaft are set in fixed main bearings. In this two-cylinder engine, the crankshaft is also supported by an intermediate bearing. Between the main bearings are the crank throws, or crank arms, which offset the connecting rod journals, or crankpins, to form a crank (rotational lever arm). The crank throws have rather large lobes, or counterweights, opposite the connecting rod journals, which balance the crankshaft and minimize engine vibration. For clarity, only one of the two pistons is ghosted into this drawing.

The crankshaft is drilled, allowing lubricating oil to be forced into it through holes in each of the bearings.

At one end of the crankshaft are keyed the crankshaft timing gear and a pulley. The crankshaft gear drives the camshaft timing gear (page 20), which controls the timing of the valves and fuel injection pump. The pulley drives a belt that turns the water pumps and the alternator.

The opposite end of the crankshaft—the power output end—is bolted to the flywheel, which supports the ring gear and provides rotational inertia.

The most common cause of failure of a crankshaft is poor lubrication. The journals can be remachined, however, to provide new bearing surfaces. Like cylinder liners, replacement bearings are available in several precision-ground sizes to match the remachined journals.

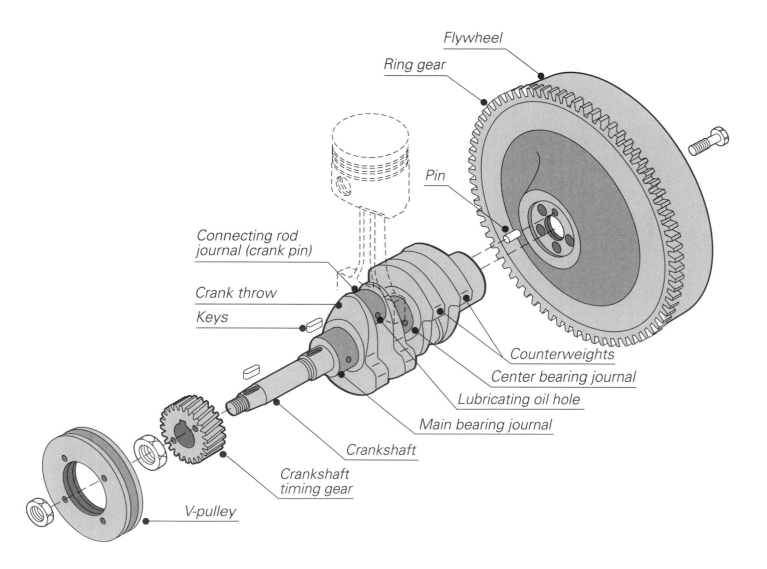

Flywheel

Ring gear

Pin

Connecting rod journal (crank pin)

Crank throw

Keys

Counterweights

Center bearing journal

Lubricating oil hole

Main bearing journal

Crankshaft

Crankshaft timing gear

V-pulley

Camshaft

The camshaft resides in the crankcase portion of the engine block. It is driven by the camshaft gear, which engages the crankshaft gear. In four-stroke engines the camshaft gear always has twice as many teeth as the crankshaft gear, so it turns at half the rotation rate of the crankshaft.

The shaft contains four eccentric cams for driving the four valves (two intake, two exhaust) of the two-cylinder 2GM engine. A fifth cam drives the fuel feed pump, which delivers fuel from the tank to the injection pump. Because the injection pump is in turn required to deliver fuel to the injectors in synch with the opening and closing of the valves, it is driven by a sixth cam (the fuel cam) keyed onto the opposite end of the camshaft.

Four tappets ride on the four intake and exhaust valve cams and lift the push rods, which extend into the head to actuate the valves. The tappets serve as large feet for the push rods in order to minimize wear of rods and cams. The tappets are guided in the block to resist the side thrust of the cams.

The camshaft is subjected to much smaller unbalanced loads than the crankshaft, so no counterbalancing lobes or intermediate bearings are required.

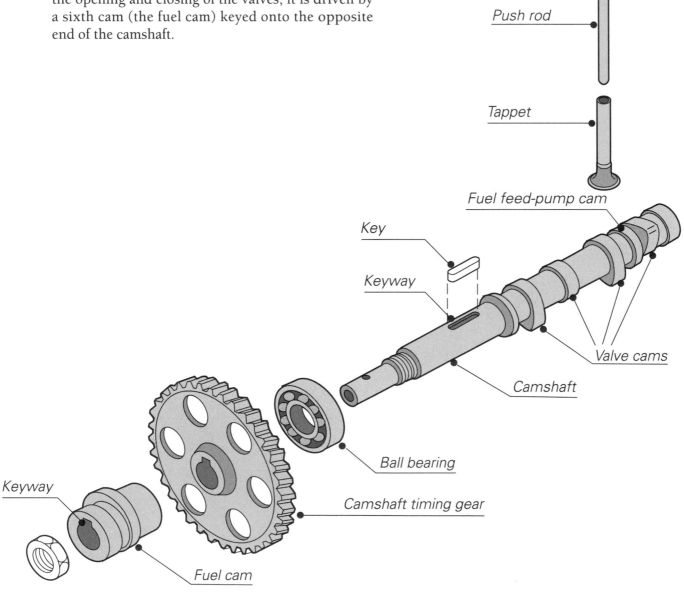

Cylinder Head

The cylinder head is an intricate casting mated to the top of the cylinder block. It forms the tops of the cylinders, contains intake and exhaust ports plus cooling water passages, and houses the valves and injectors. The integrity of both the head casting and the gasketed seal between head and cylinder block are critical. If the head cracks or warps, or if the gasket fails, coolant is likely to leak into the cylinders and the crankcase.

The head is second only to the block in expense to replace. For this reason the surfaces subject to wear—valves, valve guides, and valve seats—are all replaceable, although replacement requires removal of the head.

The head also supports the rocker arm assembly—the linkage between the push rods from the camshaft in the crankcase to the valves in the head.

When closed, there is a small clearance (valve clearance) between the top of the valve stem and the rocker. If the clearance is too small, the valve will be partially open during part of the burn cycle, which will "burn" or erode the valve and valve seat. If the clearance is too great, the engine will suffer power loss. For this reason valve clearance adjust screws are provided on the rockers.

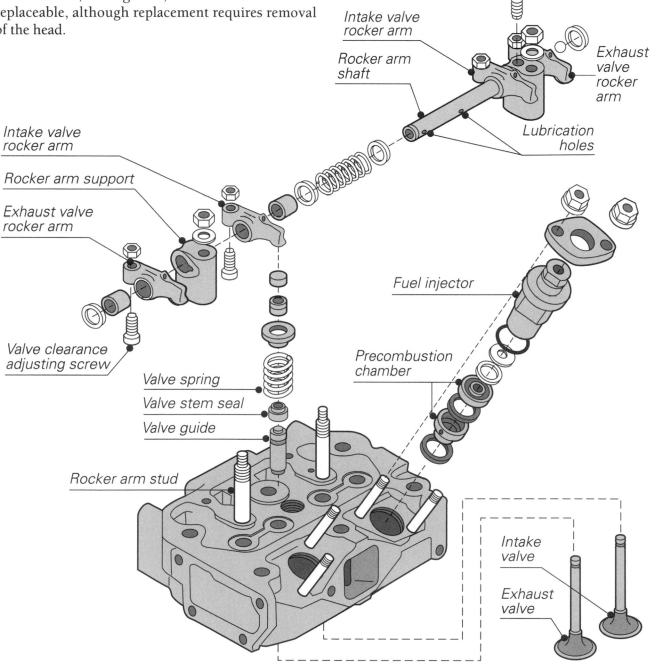

Timing Gear Housing

The timing gear housing contains the gears that link the camshaft and fuel injection pump to the crankshaft. Gears are employed because the timing of the inlet and exhaust valve openings and fuel injection is critical to engine efficiency. An error of a single gear tooth (or chain link in a timing chain) can reduce power output by 10 percent. An error of three or more teeth or links can stop the engine.

The mating surfaces (flanges) of the cylinder block and gear housing are machined flat and sealed against oil leakage with a gear housing gasket. An oil seal prevents lubricating oil from leaking around the output end of the crankshaft.

The gears are lubricated by dipping into the oil in the crankcase—the bottom chamber of the cylinder block.

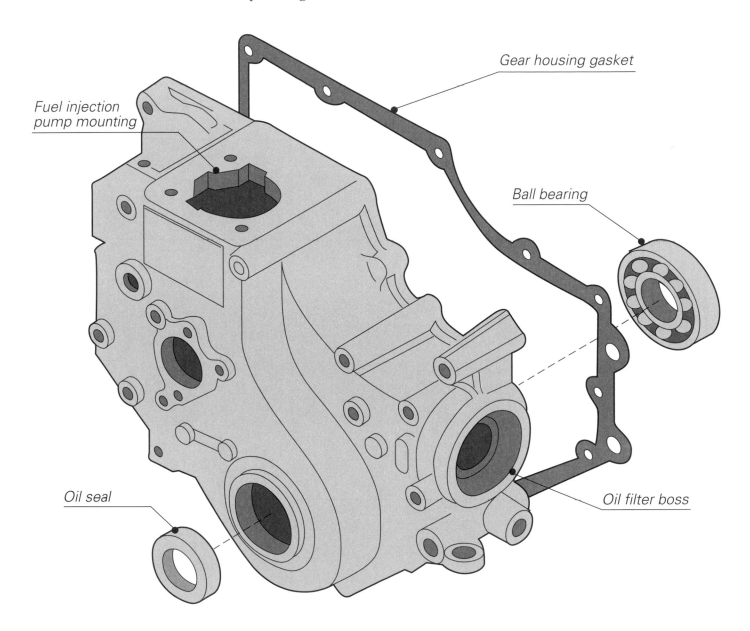

Gear housing gasket

Fuel injection pump mounting

Ball bearing

Oil seal

Oil filter boss

See page 16 for locations of V-belt pulley, flywheel, and fuel injection pump.

Flywheel Housing

As its name implies, the flywheel housing covers the flywheel. In the Yanmar it also provides mating flanges for mounting the transmission and the starter motor.

The heavy, cast-iron flywheel has two functions. First, its great mass (28 pounds on the Yanmar 2GM) acts to smooth the rotation of the engine's output shaft. With each piston delivering a power stroke less than a quarter of the time, it is as if you were punching a weight rather than pushing on it steadily. The greater the number of cylinders, the greater the percentage of "push time" and the smoother the output, but regardless of the number of cylinders, the flywheel makes the engine run more smoothly.

The second function of the flywheel is to serve as a mount for the ring gear. The ring gear is a large-diameter ring of 97 teeth pressed onto the circumference of the flywheel. When starting the engine, the small pinion gear (9 teeth) of the starter motor engages the ring gear to turn the crankshaft. The large gear ratio allows the small starter to turn over the massive diesel, even when cold.

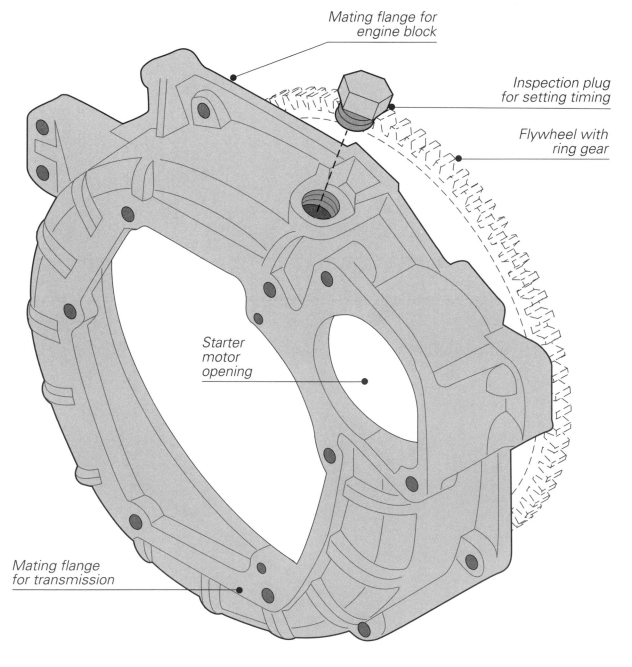

Mating flange for engine block

Inspection plug for setting timing

Flywheel with ring gear

Starter motor opening

Mating flange for transmission

Valve Cover

Like the lube oil sump, the valve cover is under no positive pressure, so it is made of lighter metal than the cylinder block and head. However, because the rocker arm assembly is continuously and generously lubricated, the entire top surface of the head is covered with oil. A valve cover gasket prevents the oil from escaping.

Lubricating oil pumped up to the rocker arm assembly returns easily to the crankcase, so the easiest way to add oil to the engine is through the oil fill cap.

The cover is bolted down to the head by screwing the two knobs (cap nuts) down onto the ends of the rocker arm support studs.

Ports on the side of the valve cover are for the decompression levers. When activated, the valves are forced open, and the engine can be turned over easily. This allows turning the crankshaft by hand for servicing, prelubrication of the engine after a long layup, or building flywheel momentum for cold-weather starting.

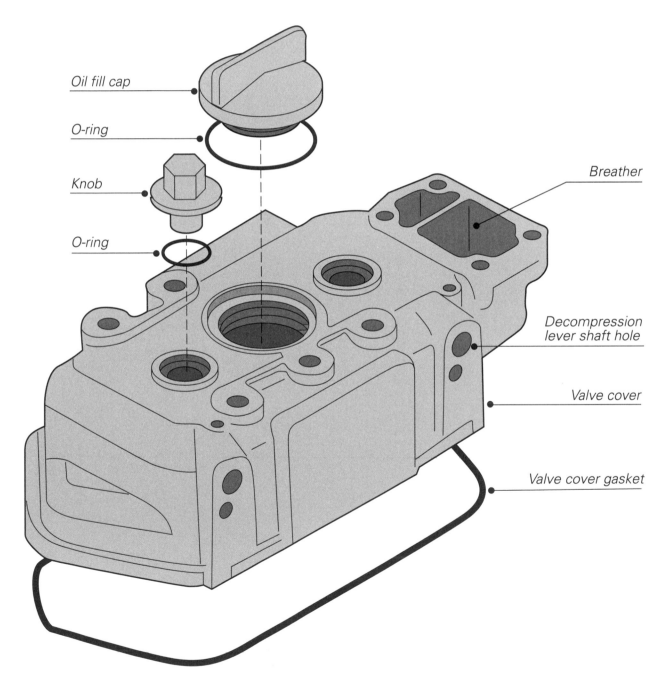

Oil fill cap

O-ring

Knob

O-ring

Breather

Decompression lever shaft hole

Valve cover

Valve cover gasket

Air Intake and Breather

Dirt is the enemy of the diesel engine. Because of the high compression ratio—up to 24:1 as opposed to 8:1 for a gasoline engine—extreme tolerances must be maintained.

Dirt can enter an engine in the fuel, lubricating oil, and combustion air. Each fluid is, therefore, filtered.

The air filter/silencer for the Yanmar engine is an open-cell polyurethane foam cone, mounted on a perforated metal cylinder. The filter can be washed with ordinary detergent, but Yanmar recommends the filter be replaced when it shows any sign of deterioration.

Some diesels have separate air filters for each cylinder, but the Yanmar has a single air intake of 3-inch diameter. As a backup measure, a runaway engine can be stopped simply by placing a hand over the air inlet.

The breather allows the crankcase to operate at atmospheric pressure without venting oil fumes. Hot oil vapor rising to the cylinder head passes through the breather chamber and is then fed into the air intake, to be burned along with the diesel fuel. Oil that condenses out drains back to the head.

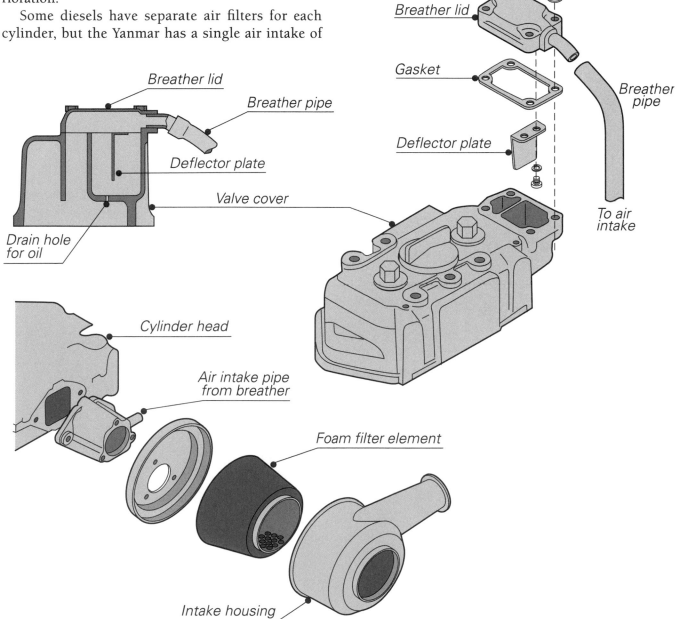

Breather lid

Breather pipe

Deflector plate

Valve cover

Drain hole for oil

Breather lid

Gasket

Deflector plate

Breather pipe

To air intake

Cylinder head

Air intake pipe from breather

Foam filter element

Intake housing

Fuel System

Because of the requirements for extreme cleanliness and precise fuel injection, the fuel system of a diesel is more complicated than that of a gasoline engine. Water, dirt, and biological growth in the fuel can all stop a diesel quickly, in addition to damaging the engine.

Yanmar diesels come equipped with fuel filters, but these should be considered secondary to one or more large-capacity filter/water separators (primary fuel filter in illustration). The primary fuel filter is placed in an accessible location for easy replacement. The fuel is sucked through the primary filter by the engine's fuel lift pump, which is mechanically driven by the fuel cam on the camshaft. (A priming lever on the pump allows the pump to be operated by hand when bleeding the engine.) After passing through the finer secondary filter, the fuel enters the fuel injection pump, where it is pressurized to 2,500 pounds per square inch (psi) and metered precisely to each of the fuel injection valves.

As you will see, the fuel injectors don't utilize all of the fuel sent to them. The excess fuel bleeds back to the fuel tank through the fuel return line.

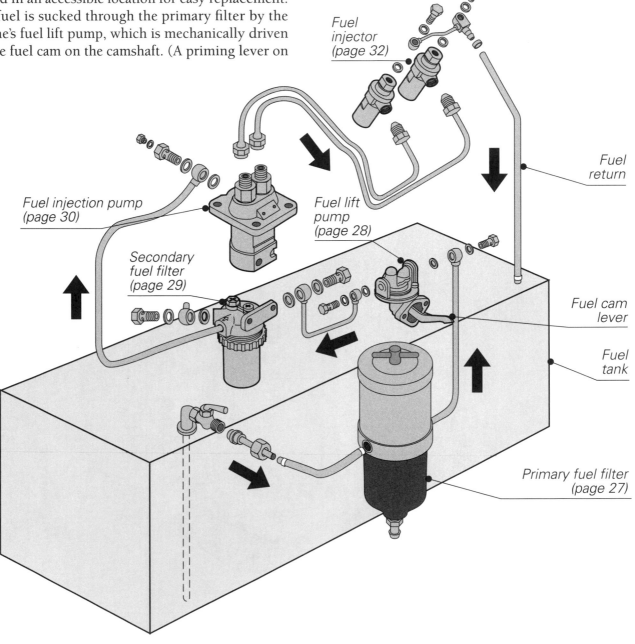

Fuel system (engine block not shown).

Primary Fuel Filter

Diesel fuel is notoriously variable. It is easy to get a healthy dose of water along with fuel in remote areas. Water vapor in the air of a partially filled fuel tank can condense over the winter to liquid water. The greater the air volume, the greater the condensation. Finally, there are microscopic bacteria that thrive on the hydrocarbons in fuel, sometimes growing into a gel-like mass in the fuel tank and lines.

The small Yanmar fuel filter can be easily overwhelmed by these contaminants, so a much larger capacity primary fuel filter is recommended—particularly one with a clear bowl that can be easily monitored and drained.

The illustration shows a typical Racor "turbine" filter/water separator. Fuel is drawn into the airtight filter by the suction of the fuel feed pump. The pump can lift fuel a maximum of about 30 inches. At greater heights, a positive-pressure pump should be employed at tank level.

In the Racor, contaminants are separated in three stages:

1. The fuel spins like a centrifuge, throwing the heavier water and sediments outward against the bowl.

2. Finely dispersed water is attracted to and coalesces on the surfaces of the baffle, then falls to the bottom of the bowl.

3. The fuel finally passes through a replaceable filter element, available in three degrees of filtration: 2, 10, or 30 microns (1 micron = 1 millionth of a meter). Most diesel manufacturers recommend filtration to the 10-micron level.

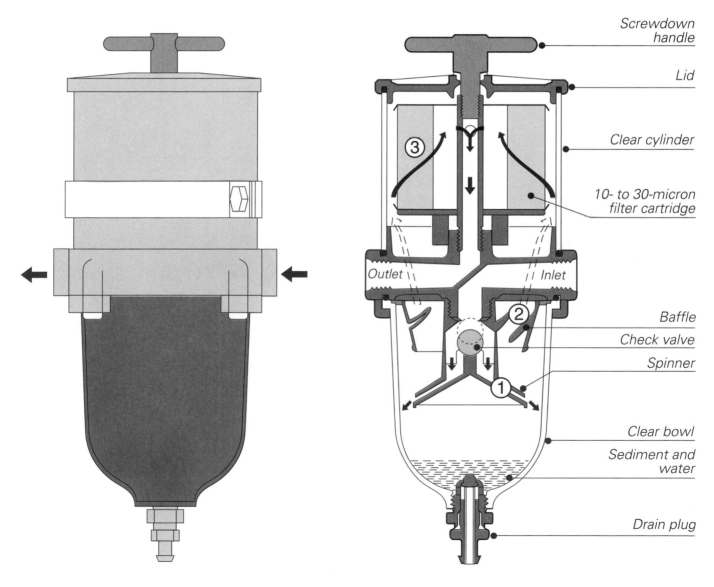

Screwdown handle

Lid

Clear cylinder

10- to 30-micron filter cartridge

Outlet   Inlet

Baffle

Check valve

Spinner

Clear bowl

Sediment and water

Drain plug

Fuel Feed Pump

The fuel lift pump lifts the diesel fuel from the fuel tank through the primary filter and feeds it to the secondary fuel filter. It is a simple diaphragm pump with a single large rubberized fabric diaphragm and spring-loaded inlet and outlet valves. Unless the diaphragm is worn, or unless debris prevents one of the valves from seating completely, the pump is capable of lifting the fuel 31.5 inches.

The diaphragm is actuated by the fuel feed-pump cam lever, which moves up and down with the rotation of the eccentric fuel feed-pump cam. It can also be actuated manually, without the engine turning over, by the external manual, or priming, lever. This is useful when bleeding air from the fuel lines.

The most common failure is of the fabric diaphragm, so a spare should be carried. Fortunately, the pump is easily removed from the engine while at sea.

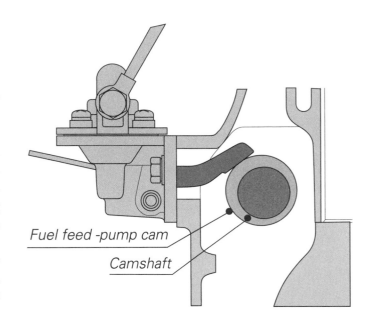

Fuel feed -pump cam

Camshaft

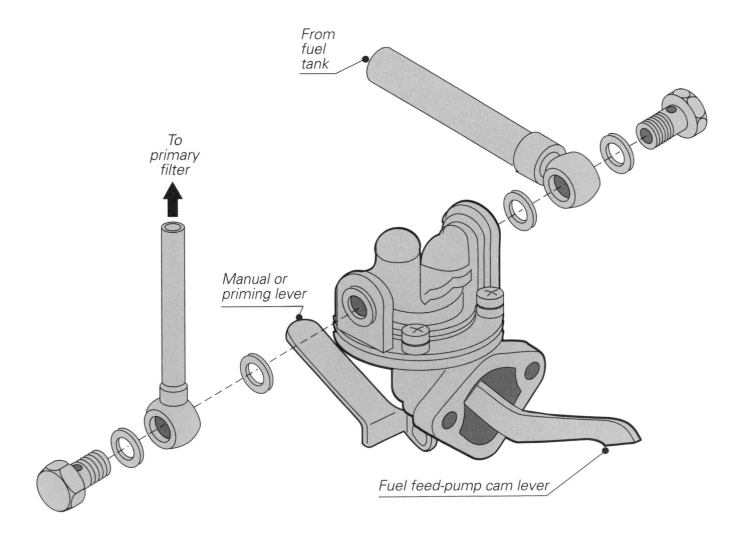

From fuel tank

To primary filter

Manual or priming lever

Fuel feed-pump cam lever

Secondary Fuel Filter

The Yanmar fuel filter is intended to remove fuel impurities to the manufacturer's recommended specification: 10 microns (0.0004 inch). Its capacity is minuscule, however. Worse, it has no clear bowl to indicate its status, nor does it have a bottom drain. It is highly recommended, therefore, that a larger-capacity primary filter be installed ahead of it. Nevertheless, the filter will trap some impurities and should be inspected and cleaned every 250 hours.

Resist the impulse to clean and recycle the paper filter. Rinsing it, even in clean diesel fuel, will change its micron rating. Instead, carry a supply of new filters aboard.

After replacing the filter, you should bleed the fuel system of air. Bleeding the air from a Yanmar diesel's fuel lines is a simple two-step process. First, loosen the air-bleed bolt at the top of the fuel filter while flipping the manual lever of the fuel feed pump up and down. When the bubbles at the air-bleed bolt are replaced by pure fuel, tighten the bolt. Second, with the engine decompression levers engaged, turn over the engine rapidly with a similar air-bleed bolt on the fuel injection pump loosened. Again, when the bubbles stop, tighten the bolt, return the decompression levers to their normal position, and start the engine. You rarely have to bleed the injector lines at the injectors.

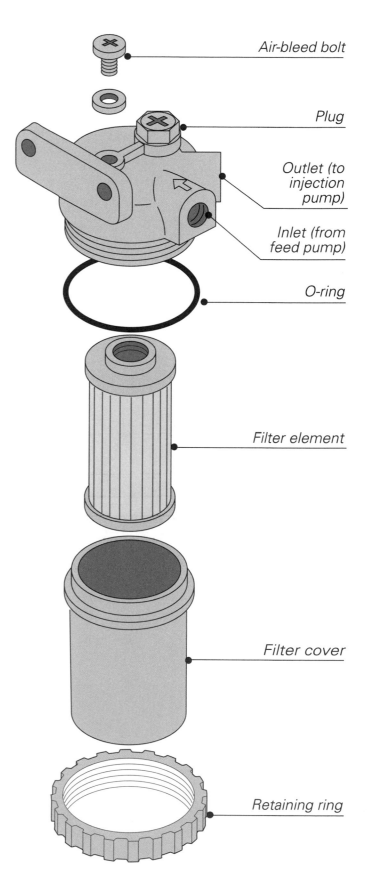

Air-bleed bolt

Plug

Outlet (to injection pump)

Inlet (from feed pump)

O-ring

Filter element

Filter cover

Retaining ring

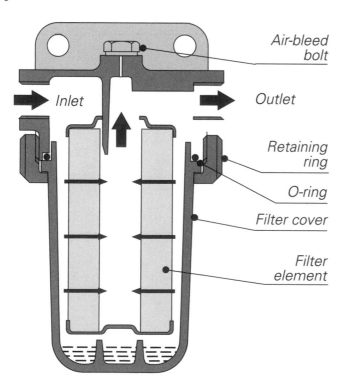

Air-bleed bolt

Inlet

Outlet

Retaining ring

O-ring

Filter cover

Filter element

Fuel Injection Pump

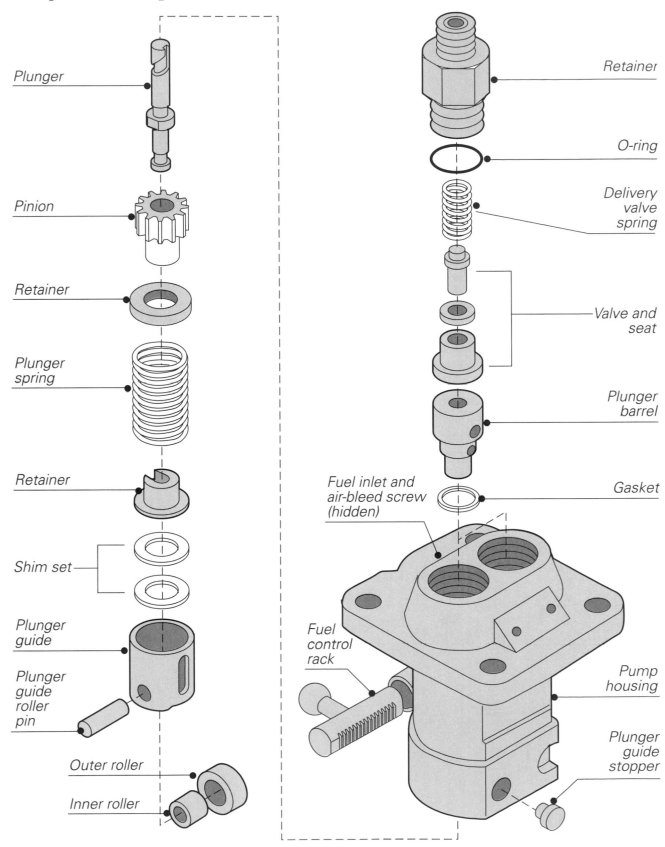

Plunger

Pinion

Retainer

Plunger spring

Retainer

Shim set

Plunger guide

Plunger guide roller pin

Outer roller

Inner roller

Retainer

O-ring

Delivery valve spring

Valve and seat

Plunger barrel

Gasket

Fuel inlet and air-bleed screw (hidden)

Fuel control rack

Pump housing

Plunger guide stopper

Fuel Metering

The function of the injection pump is to force metered amounts of fuel at the correct times to the injectors. It is the most precise part of the entire engine. Operating at pressures of up to 2,500 psi, the pistons (here called the plungers—one for each cylinder of the engine) and their cylinders (barrels) are lapped to a tolerance of closer than 0.0001 inch. In fact, if damaged they must be replaced as matched sets.

Pump parts may be grouped by function:

1. Pressurizing and delivering fuel: plunger and plunger barrel
2. Stroking the plunger: camshaft, plunger guide roller, and plunger spring
3. Controlling volume of fuel delivered: fuel control rack and pinion.

Here is how the pump works. As the camshaft rotates, the plunger guide rollers riding on the fuel cam (page 20) rise and fall, in turn forcing the plungers up and down. The plungers have a diameter of approximately 1/4 inch and a stroke of 1/4 inch, so the maximum amount of fuel that can be pumped per stroke is 0.012 cubic inch. The amount of fuel delivered per stroke is actually about 10 percent of that, or 0.000005 gallon (0.004 teaspoon).

Each plunger has a spiral channel (lead) and

groove connecting the lead to the top of the plunger. The barrel contains a fuel inlet hole (the oil hole). When the plunger is at the bottom of its stroke, fuel flows through the oil hole, filling the delivery chamber. On the upstroke the plunger cuts off the oil hole, and the fuel is forced at 2,500 psi past the delivery valve, through the high-pressure fuel line to the injector. When the pressure at the injector reaches 2,200 psi, the injector nozzle opens, spraying fuel into the combustion chamber.

As soon as the spiral plunger lead reaches the oil hole, however, the pressurized fuel is vented through the lead back to the oil hole, ending the injection of fuel. Due to the spiral shape of the plunger lead (see below), rotating the plunger effectively changes the length of the fuel delivery stroke and the amount of fuel delivered to the injector.

This is the mechanism by which the power output of the engine is controlled. The plunger is keyed to a pinion gear that engages a linear gear called the fuel control rack. All of the plungers—one for each cylinder of the engine—are geared to the single rack, so all operate together.

Repairing fuel injection pumps and injectors requires expensive test equipment and specialized training. Even a certified diesel mechanic should attempt repairs to these components only when necessary.

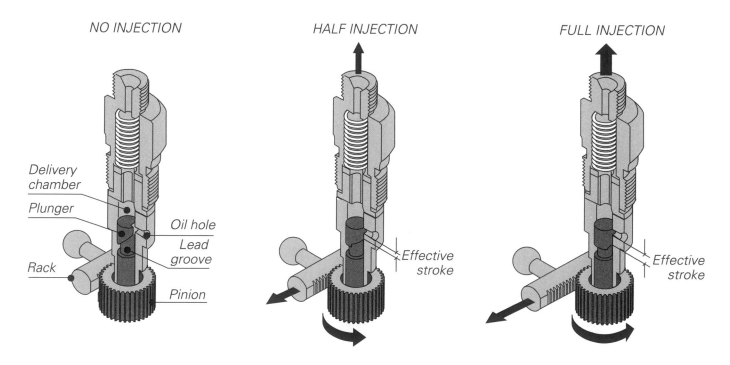

NO INJECTION

HALF INJECTION

FULL INJECTION

Delivery chamber

Plunger

Oil hole

Lead groove

Rack

Pinion

Effective stroke

Effective stroke

Fuel Injectors

The fuel injectors atomize the fuel sent at 2,500 psi from the fuel injector pump and inject it into the pre-heated combustion chambers in a pattern designed for optimum fuel/air mixing and complete combustion.

Before combustion, the nozzle valve is held down against the valve seat of the nozzle body by the nozzle spring. When the injection pump pressurizes the fuel to 2,500 psi, the fuel enters a pressure chamber at the bottom of the nozzle body. This pressure overcomes the force of the spring, the nozzle valve is lifted off its seat, and the fuel is sprayed into the combustion chamber.

When the pressure from the injection pump drops, the spring again pushes the nozzle valve down against the valve seat, and the fuel flow stops.

With clean fuel and not too much running under load at low rpm, fuel injectors ordinarily require no attention for thousands of hours. The injectors are easily removed, however, and can be serviced at any of the many shops servicing diesel truck engines.

FUEL INJECTION SYSTEM

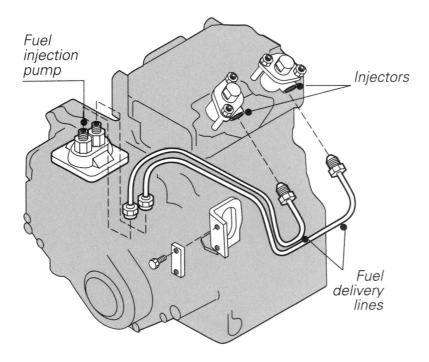

Fuel injection pump

Injectors

Fuel delivery lines

INDIVIDUAL FUEL INJECTOR

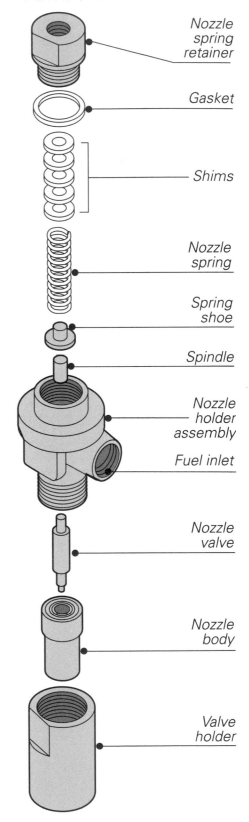

Nozzle spring retainer

Gasket

Shims

Nozzle spring

Spring shoe

Spindle

Nozzle holder assembly

Fuel inlet

Nozzle valve

Nozzle body

Valve holder

Lubrication System

Lubricating oil is added to the engine through the oil filler cap in the valve cover. From there it flows down through the tappet holes in the cylinder block to the oil pan at the bottom of the engine.

With the engine running, oil is drawn from the oil pan through the suction pipe by an oil pump that is gear-driven off the crankshaft gear. The pump forces oil through a replaceable filter cartridge to remove impurities. The oil pressure is monitored by a pressure switch with an alarm light (which lights when the pressure drops to 7 psi) and regulated by the oil pressure regulator (relief valve), which spills excess oil back into the pan.

The oil is then fed to each of the crankshaft bearings and through holes drilled in the cylinder block and head to the rocker arm shaft. Holes drilled in the crankshaft feed oil from the crankshaft bearings to the piston crank pins (page 19).

A hole drilled through the rocker arm shaft feeds oil to the rocker arms and the push rods. Oil returning from the rocker arm chamber flows down the push rod holes and lubricates the tappets, cams, and cam bearings. Finally, the oil drips back into the oil pan to be recycled.

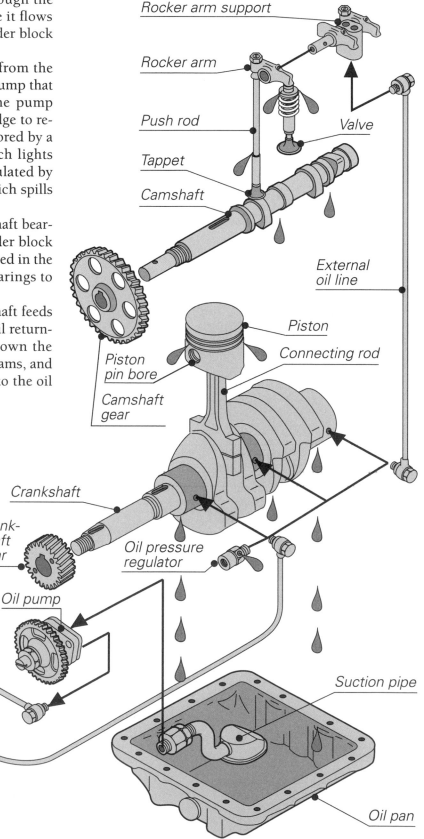

Rocker arm support

Rocker arm

Push rod

Valve

Tappet

Camshaft

External oil line

Piston

Connecting rod

Piston pin bore

Camshaft gear

Crankshaft

Crankshaft gear

Oil pressure regulator

Oil pump

Pressure switch

Oil filter

External oil lines

Suction pipe

Oil pan

Lubricating Oil Pump

The oil pump is bolted to the timing-gear end of the cylinder block and is driven by a gear that engages the crankshaft gear. Inlet and outlet holes are drilled through the block, and the pump is sealed to the block with a gasket.

The trochoid pump has remarkably few moving parts—just inner and outer rotors—so it ordinarily requires no maintenance for the life of the engine. In spite of its simplicity, however, it pumps about 14 quarts per minute at a pressure of 43 to 57 psi.

The illustrations at bottom show how a trochoid pump works. The pump consists of a five-lobed, shaftless outer rotor revolving freely within the cylindrical pump body. A second, four-lobed rotor rotates on a shaft inside the outer rotor. The shaft of the inner rotor is off-center, so that when one of its four lobes is fully engaged between the lobes of the outer rotor, the opposite lobe just clears the inner rotor. As the inner rotor turns, it thus forces the outer rotor to turn, but at $4/5$ of its rate. Steps 1–3 below show how this results in a pumping action.

STEP 1. The cavity over the inlet port between the two rotors is increasing in volume.

STEP 2. One-eighth of a turn later the cavity is at maximum volume and is over neither inlet nor outlet.

STEP 3. Another $1/8$ of a turn later the cavity is over the outlet port and is becoming smaller.

The net result is that fluid is suctioned in during Step 1 and forced out during Step 3. The same sequence occurs with each of the four lobes.

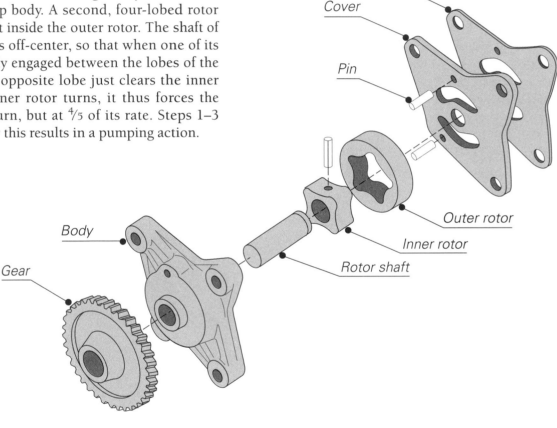

Gasket
Cover
Pin
Outer rotor
Inner rotor
Rotor shaft
Body
Gear

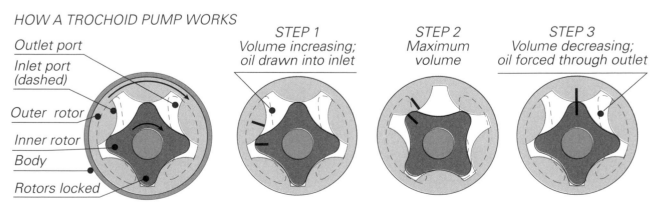

HOW A TROCHOID PUMP WORKS

Outlet port
Inlet port (dashed)
Outer rotor
Inner rotor
Body
Rotors locked

STEP 1
Volume increasing; oil drawn into inlet

STEP 2
Maximum volume

STEP 3
Volume decreasing; oil forced through outlet

Seawater Cooling System

The basic Yanmar engine is cooled by seawater (often called *raw water*). Due to the increased corrosion seen with this system and the high cost of maintenance, however, most owners purchase the engine with the optional heat exchanger, which allows the engine to be cooled by a mixture of freshwater and antifreeze. The seawater-cooled version is described on this page and the freshwater option on the following page.

Seawater is first drawn through the seacock (and a strainer, if there is one) by the seawater pump, which is driven by a belt from a pulley on the end of the crankshaft.

From the pump the flow splits into two paths:

1. Through a rubber hose to the pipe on the end of the thermostat housing, then to the mixing elbow, where it mixes with and cools the engine exhaust.
2. Into the engine block, where it flows through a series of cavities known collectively as the cylinder jacket (see page 17), then up through the similar cavities in the cylinder head, then to the thermostat housing.

Before the engine reaches its operating temperature, the thermostat (a temperature-sensitive valve) remains closed, retaining the water in the engine. As soon as the engine temperature reaches 107°F, the thermostat starts to open, letting seawater flow out of the engine and to the mixing elbow. The thermostat opens fully at 125°F, providing enough cooling to maintain the engine at that temperature under full load conditions.

If, for any reason, the engine overheats, the temperature switch in the thermostat housing turns on a warning light on the instrument panel.

Replaceable, sacrificial zincs are screwed into both the cylinder block and the cylinder head to prevent electrolytic corrosion.

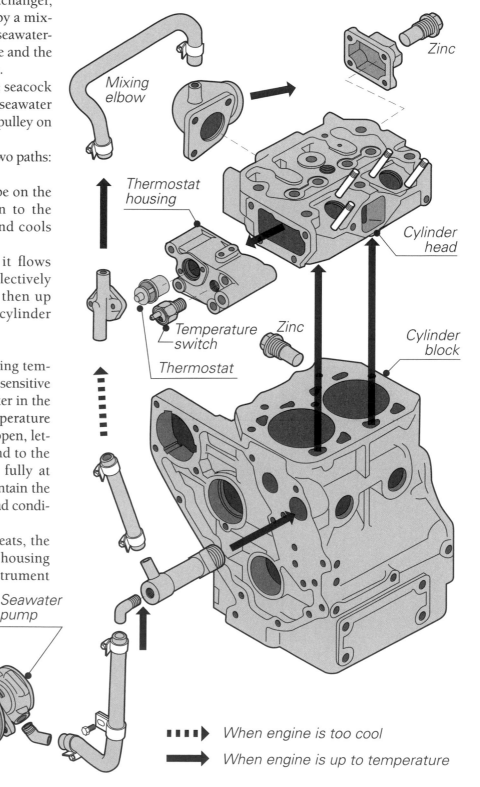

Mixing elbow

Zinc

Thermostat housing

Cylinder head

Temperature switch

Zinc

Thermostat

Cylinder block

Seawater pump

Seacock

▪▪▪▪▶ When engine is too cool

➤ When engine is up to temperature

Freshwater Cooling System

The freshwater-cooled engine is cooled directly by a captive mixture of freshwater and antifreeze that contains corrosion inhibitors, the heat of the coolant being transferred to seawater through a heat exchanger (page 40).

Seawater is pumped continuously from the seacock (and strainer, if there is one) through the heat exchanger by the seawater pump. Like the seawater pump, the freshwater pump runs continuously.

However, when the engine is cool, the thermostat (page 37) directs the coolant from the cylinder head through the pump and back to the cylinder block for further heating. At 160°F the thermostat begins to open and send the heated freshwater instead to the heat exchanger, where the heat is passed to the seawater, which then flows out with the exhaust. The thermostat is fully open and flow through the heat exchanger is complete at 185°F.

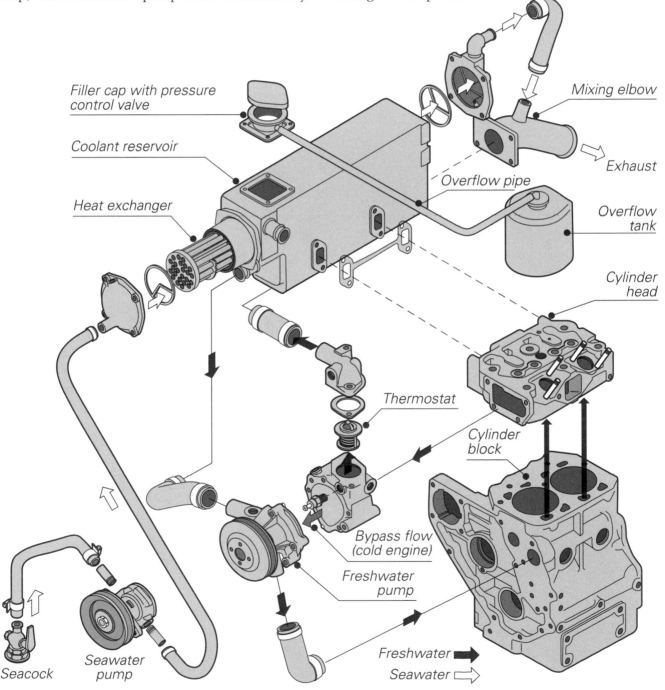

Filler cap with pressure control valve

Coolant reservoir

Heat exchanger

Mixing elbow

Exhaust

Overflow pipe

Overflow tank

Cylinder head

Thermostat

Cylinder block

Bypass flow (cold engine)

Freshwater pump

Seacock

Seawater pump

Freshwater ➤
Seawater ⇨

Freshwater Thermostat

The freshwater thermostat controls the temperature of the engine block and head. Before the engine reaches operating temperature, the thermostat directs the coolant exiting the head back to the pump and block for further heating. After the engine reaches operating temperature, the coolant is directed to the heat exchanger, where the excess heat is then transferred to seawater (freshwater-cooled engines). The heated seawater is then fed to the mixing elbow, where it further cools and silences the exhaust before exiting the boat.

As shown below, the thermostat is a simple valve operated by an encapsulated volume of wax. When cool, the bypass valve is retracted, allowing the coolant entering from the cylinder head to be pulled into the freshwater pump and sent back to the cylinder block.

When the coolant reaches 160°F, however, the wax begins to melt and expand. Its increased volume forces the bypass valve to close, redirecting the coolant to the heat exchanger. The suction of the freshwater pump now pulls the coolant through the exchanger, where it gives up its heat before being sent back to the block.

The bypass valve reaches total closure at 185°F. Thus the engine's normal operating temperature range is between 160°F and 185°F.

BELOW OPERATING TEMPERATURE

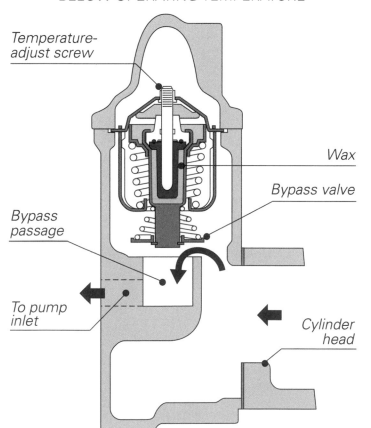

Temperature-adjust screw

Wax

Bypass valve

Bypass passage

To pump inlet

Cylinder head

AT OPERATING TEMPERATURE

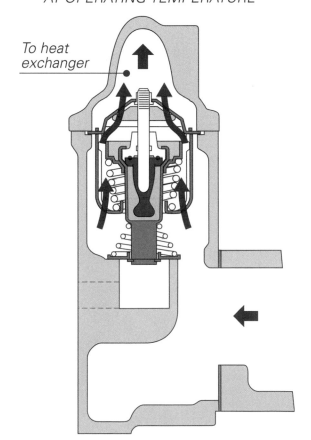

To heat exchanger

Seawater Pump

The seawater pump is powered by a belt driven by a pulley on the end of the crankshaft. It is of the rubber impeller type, which is not easily harmed or fouled by sea life sucked into the system.

The illustration at right shows the principle of the impeller pump. As the impeller turns, the cavities between impeller blades at the bottom are squeezed by a cam plate. At the same time the cavities between the blades at the top are diminished only slightly by contact with the pump body. The difference in volumes of the top and bottom cavities is the net amount pumped in the direction of the arrows.

While simple, there are two caveats with this type of pump:

1. If the pump is run dry, the rubber impeller will be destroyed within a few minutes by the heat of friction.

2. The impeller should be replaced every few years or every 1,000 hours, whichever occurs first, because pieces of the rubber blades may clog cooling passages in the engine or the thermostat.

When replacing an impeller, don't worry about the direction of rotation because the blades will be oriented properly the first time around.

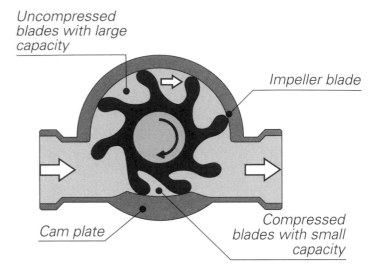

Uncompressed blades with large capacity

Impeller blade

Cam plate

Compressed blades with small capacity

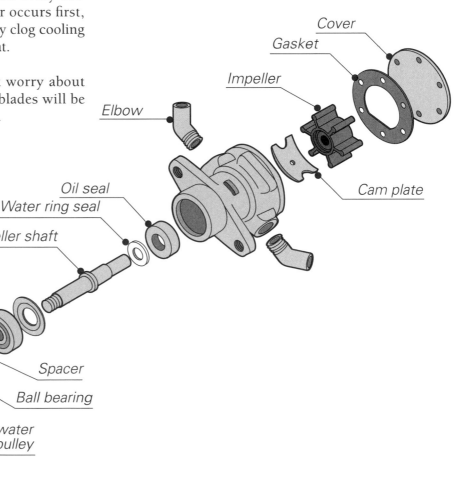

Cover

Gasket

Impeller

Elbow

Cam plate

Oil seal

Water ring seal

Impeller shaft

Ball bearing

Spacer

Ball bearing

Cooling water V-pulley

Freshwater Pump

The freshwater (actually a mixture of freshwater and antifreeze) pump is powered by a second belt driven by a pulley on the crankshaft. It is of the centrifugal type, which, except for replacement of seals, is generally maintenance free for the life of the engine.

The illustration at right shows how a centrifugal pump works. The rigid, spinning vanes throw water outward in a rotating spiral. When the spinning water encounters the outlet at the perimeter, it exits the pump. Lower pressure pulls water into the inlet at the center.

Since there is no foreign material in a freshwater cooling system, there is nothing to damage the impeller.

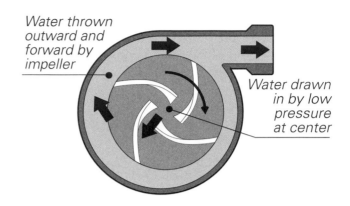

Water thrown outward and forward by impeller

Water drawn in by low pressure at center

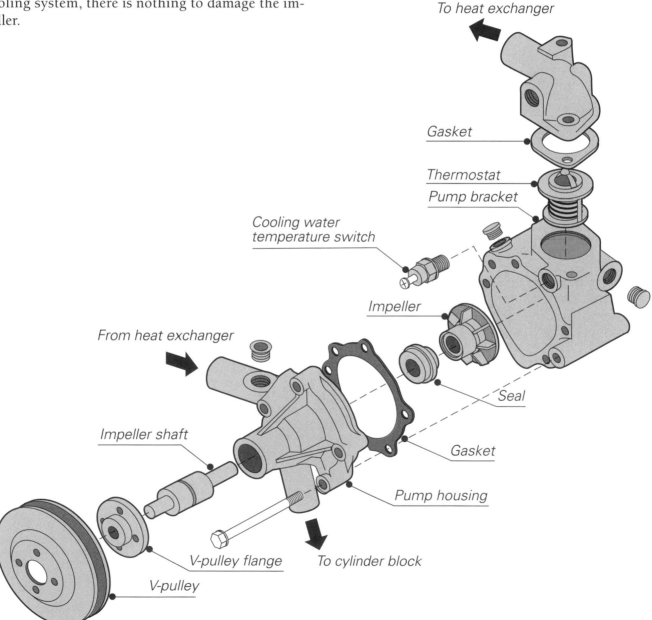

To heat exchanger

Gasket

Thermostat

Pump bracket

Cooling water temperature switch

Impeller

From heat exchanger

Seal

Impeller shaft

Gasket

Pump housing

V-pulley flange

To cylinder block

V-pulley

Heat Exchanger

The heat exchanger consists of twenty-four slender tubes passing through seven baffle plates and housed in a cylindrical tube (the cooling tube).

Seawater enters one end cap and is directed by the divider in the end cap into a subset of eight tubes. When the seawater reaches the opposite end, it is directed back through a second set of eight tubes and then back in the original direction through a third set.

Heated freshwater from the cylinder head enters one end of the cooling tube and flows between the twenty-four tubes, passing its excess heat to the seawater. As it flows toward the opposite end of the cooling tube, it is forced in a serpentine pattern by the baffle plates.

The cooled freshwater exits the opposite end of the cooling tube and flows into the freshwater reservoir below the cooling tube.

The filler cap on the top of the reservoir contains both pressure-relief and a vacuum-relief valves. When the pressure exceeds the limit, the pressure valve releases coolant vapor to an overflow tank, where the vapor condenses. When the heat exchanger pressure drops below atmospheric pressure, the vacuum valve opens, allowing coolant to be drawn back into the freshwater reservoir.

The heat exchanger end caps are easily removed, allowing deposits in the tubes to be rodded out with a wooden dowel.

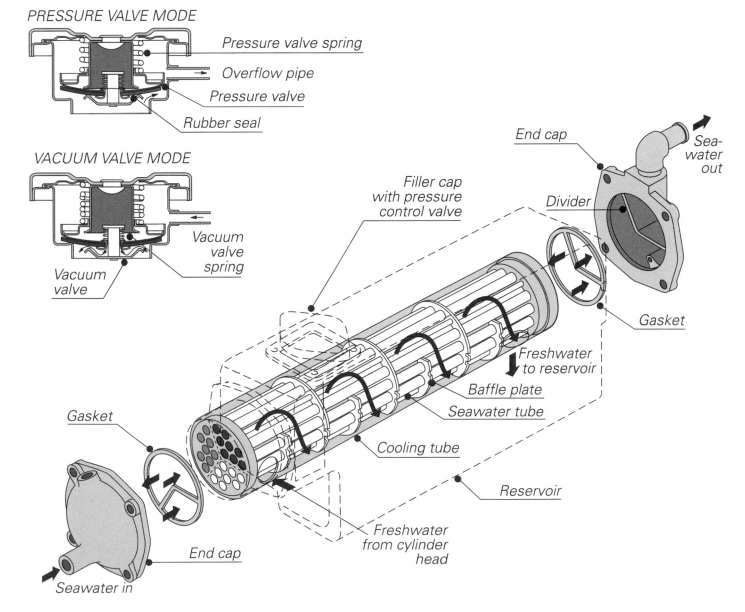

PRESSURE VALVE MODE
- Pressure valve spring
- Overflow pipe
- Pressure valve
- Rubber seal

VACUUM VALVE MODE
- Vacuum valve spring
- Vacuum valve

- Filler cap with pressure control valve
- End cap
- Seawater out
- Divider
- Gasket
- Freshwater to reservoir
- Baffle plate
- Seawater tube
- Cooling tube
- Reservoir
- Gasket
- End cap
- Seawater in
- Freshwater from cylinder head

Starter Motor

The starter motor is mounted on the flywheel housing so its drive gear (the pinion) can engage the flywheel ring gear to start the engine. The torque required to turn the engine over is reduced by the flywheel/pinion gear ratio of 97 ÷ 9 = 10.8.

The starting sequence is as follows:

1. The ignition key is switched on, and the start button depressed, sending current to the magnetic switch (solenoid).
2. The solenoid plunger overcomes the force of the torsion spring and activates the shift lever.
3. The shift lever thrusts the pinion gear forward to engage the flywheel ring gear.
4. At the same time the plunger closes the contacts of the main switch to the starter motor.
5. The starter motor rotates, turning the engine over until it starts or until the start button is released.
6. Releasing the start button stops the current to the solenoid.
7. With no force on the plunger, the torsion spring returns the plunger to its normal position, retracting the pinion and cutting current flow to the starter motor.

So that the started engine does not overspeed the starter motor and burn it out, the pinion is mounted on an overrunning clutch, which allows the pinion to freewheel when the engine is running.

Starter cables must be heavy and short, and contact resistance at both battery and solenoid must be low for the starter to develop enough torque to turn the engine over. To give an idea of the requirements, the current at peak output is roughly 230 amps, and 460 amps when stalled. With a battery voltage of 12 volts, the resistance of the motor is effectively 0.05 ohm. If the resistance of either cable or contacts approaches the figure, the motor won't turn over the engine. When the starter loses its "punch," the culprit is usually loose or corroded connections, not the cable.

The high starting-torque requirement of the engine is due to compression resistance, not friction. When starting the engine in cold weather, the compression-release lever can be actuated to reduce resistance. Once the engine is turning over, the lever is released, and the inertia of the flywheel aids in starting.

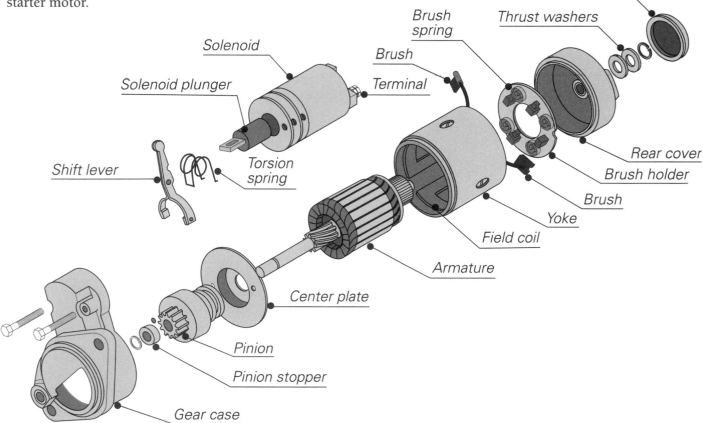

Transmissions

Yanmar KM2-A Two-Shaft Reduction and Reverse Gear

The Yanmar KM2-A reduction and reverse gear is of the two-shaft variety. The input shaft connects to the engine flywheel through a damper disk (not shown) to reduce shock-loading and vibration and features drive gears for forward and reverse operation. Bearings on the output shaft support the two larger output gears, forward and reverse.

The forward output gear is driven directly by the forward drive gear, so its rotation is opposite that of the engine. The reverse output gear is driven through an intermediate gear, so its rotation is in the same direc-

tion as the engine's. Since both output gears have more teeth than their input counterparts, engine rpm is reduced and torque increased in both forward and reverse. Depending on the model number, forward reduction ratios are 2.21:1, 2.62:1, or 3.22:1. Reverse reduction ratio is 3.06:1 on all models.

The direction of output rotation—forward or reverse—is determined by the drive cone (clutch), which slides back and forth between the output gears on the splined output shaft. When the gear shift lever forces the drive cone against the conical inside face of the for-

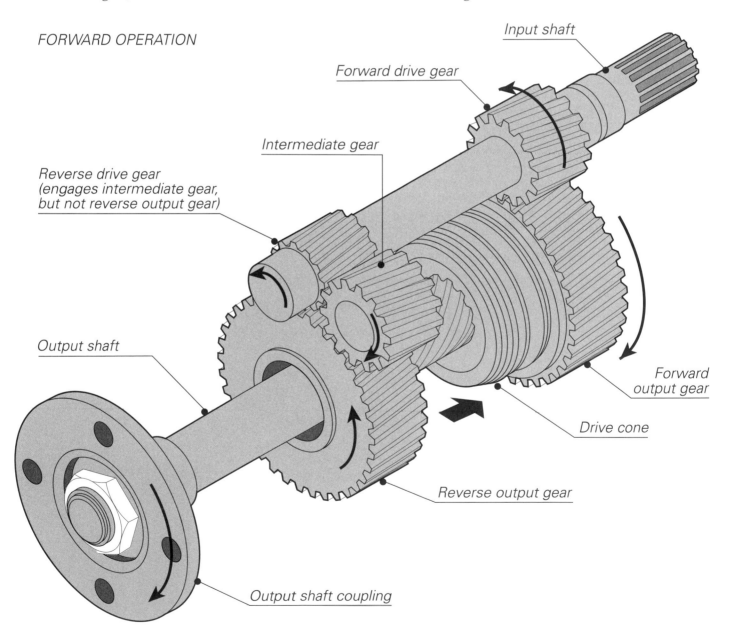

FORWARD OPERATION

Input shaft

Forward drive gear

Intermediate gear

Reverse drive gear
(engages intermediate gear,
but not reverse output gear)

Output shaft

Forward output gear

Drive cone

Reverse output gear

Output shaft coupling

ward output gear (opposite), the cone engages the gear and the output shaft turns in the forward direction, while the reverse output gear freewheels.

With the gear shift in neutral, the drive cone engages neither output gear, and the output shaft freewheels.

When the shift lever pushes the drive cone against the face of the reverse output gear (below), the output shaft is locked to the reverse output gear and the output shaft turns in the reverse direction.

The engine is protected from shock loads (due to shifting quickly from forward to reverse and to the propeller striking an object) by the clutch and the damper disk. The damper disk consists of two disks: one attached to the engine flywheel, the other to the transmission input shaft. Between the two disks are two sets of springs: a weak set designed to absorb the torsional vibration of the engine from piston action and a stronger set to absorb shock loads.

REVERSE OPERATION

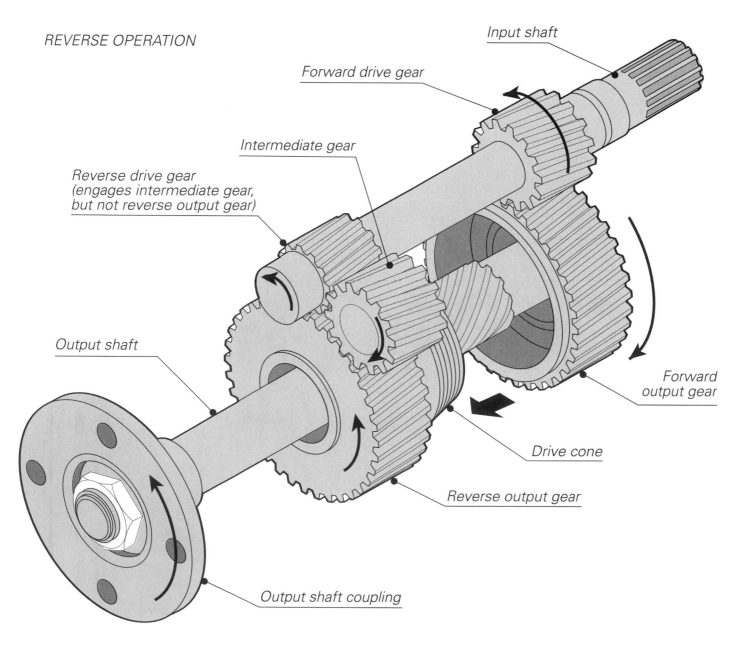

Input shaft

Forward drive gear

Intermediate gear

Reverse drive gear
(engages intermediate gear,
but not reverse output gear)

Output shaft

Forward output gear

Drive cone

Reverse output gear

Output shaft coupling

Planetary-Type Transmission

Another popular type of transmission is the epicyclic, or planetary, shown schematically at right. In this type of reverse gear the input gear is keyed directly to the engine, so it is always turning. Concentric with the input gear shaft is a gear carrier assembly, carrying four or more small planetary gears and directly coupled to the transmission's output shaft. Around the outside is a geared hub. Outside the hub is a brake band, which can clamp onto the hub to prevent its rotation.

In forward gear (bottom left) the forward clutch (not shown) locks the input drive gear to the gear carrier assembly, forcing the transmission output shaft to rotate in the same direction as the engine output shaft. At this time the brake band is loose, allowing the geared hub to rotate along with the carrier assembly.

In neutral the forward clutch disengages and the input gear, planetary gears, and geared hub freewheel. When the transmission is shifted to reverse (bottom right), the reverse clutch clamps the brake band, locking the geared hub. Now the input drive gear turns the planetary gears, which engage the locked hub gear, forcing the carrier assembly to rotate in the opposite direction.

This type of transmission only reverses shaft rotation and does not reduce forward rpm.

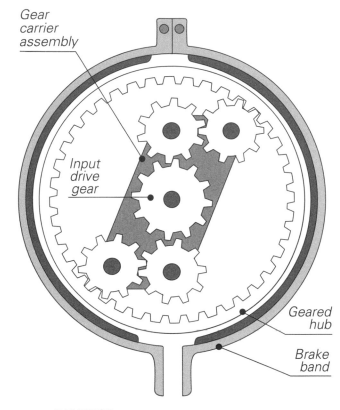

Gear carrier assembly

Input drive gear

Geared hub

Brake band

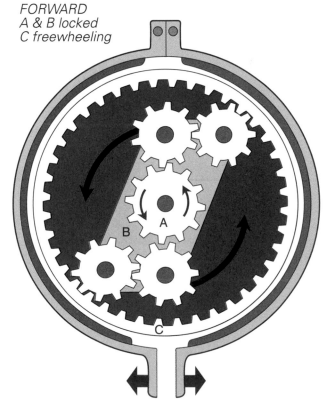

FORWARD
A & B locked
C freewheeling

REVERSE
A & B unlocked
C locked

Cutless Bearings

The Cutless bearing (trademarked version of a water-lubricated rubber bearing) supports the propeller end of the shaft. It is a long cylinder of stainless steel, naval brass, or fiberglass, with or without a flange, that fits snugly inside the stern tube or shaft strut.

The bearing surface consists of longitudinally ribbed nitrile rubber, the grooves between the ribs serving to admit seawater that both lubricates and cools the bearing surfaces. To increase flow, a hole is often drilled through the keel into the stern tube, admitting water to the forward end of the bearing.

Both shaft and Cutless bearing sleeve are designed to fit snugly without forcing. The bearing sleeve is held in the stern tube or strut by setscrews set into dimples in the sleeve.

If the shaft is properly aligned with both engine and stern tube, the rubber bearing surfaces should last for several thousand hours. Misalignment will cause the ribs to wear unevenly. Once they begin to wear, the shaft will begin to vibrate and wear will accelerate. If the shaft vibration becomes too great, misalignment stresses will be transmitted to the output shaft of the transmission, causing early failure of bearings and seals.

Another cause of accelerated wear is operating in silty or sandy water. Sand that enters the Cutless bearing along with cooling water will "sandpaper" both bearing and shaft. And once shaft diameter is reduced, no Cutless bearing will fit properly.

Another, and catastrophic, failure can result from running the engine in gear with the boat out of water. Without lubricating water, the rubber bearing surfaces heat rapidly and actually melt. Remember: the engine is not the only component that requires cooling water.

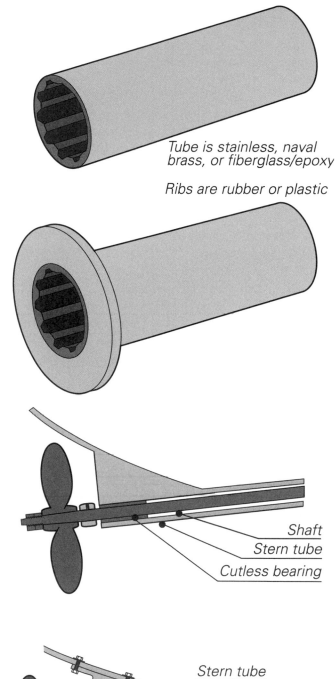

Tube is stainless, naval brass, or fiberglass/epoxy

Ribs are rubber or plastic

Shaft
Stern tube
Cutless bearing

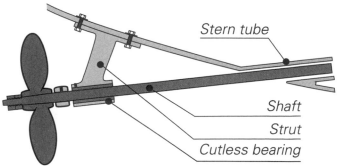

Stern tube

Shaft
Strut
Cutless bearing

Shaft Couplings

The shaft coupling mates the propeller shaft to the output shaft of the transmission, allowing the propeller shaft to be removed for servicing or replacement of engine, transmission, shaft, stuffing box, or Cutless bearing.

Since the coupling is solid steel, if the two shafts aren't aligned perfectly, something has to give. If you're lucky, what gives is the relatively inexpensive stern bearing or, even better, the Cutless bearing. If you're less fortunate, you are looking at a very expensive transmission repair.

What constitutes perfect alignment?

1. First, the coupling must be concentric with, and its face perpendicular to, the centerline of the shaft. It is a good idea to have a machine shop fit the coupling to the shaft to be certain.

2. Next, the diameters of the coupling faces must match, and when brought together without bolting, the edges must match (dimension A below). If the shaft is long and unsupported at the coupling end, its end should be supported by a fishing scale tensioned to the weight of the coupling half plus half of the unsupported shaft.

3. Finally, with the two couplings nearly touching, the gap between faces (dimension B below) should be the same all around. The difference should be no more than 0.001 inch per inch of diameter.

Shaft alignment should be checked once per year. Since a hull changes shape when placed in the water and, in the case of a sailboat, when the rigging is tensioned, alignment should be delayed until the boat is ready to go.

Aside from misalignment, the weak point in most shaft couplings is the method of attaching the coupling to the shaft. Were the shaft to slip out of the coupling, nothing except possibly the propeller running up against the rudder would stop the shaft from exiting the boat and leaving a considerable hole for water to enter.

All couplings have keyways that match an identical keyway machined into the end of the shaft. The purpose of the bronze or stainless key is to transmit torque, not hold the coupling on the shaft. Inexpensive couplings may have a single setscrew that seats in a dimple in the shaft. At the least, the head of the setscrew should be drilled, and a stainless wire passed through the head and wrapped around the

coupling to prevent the screw from loosening. Much better would be a solid pin through both coupling and shaft plus two or three setscrews set deeply into the shaft, with all screw heads wired together.

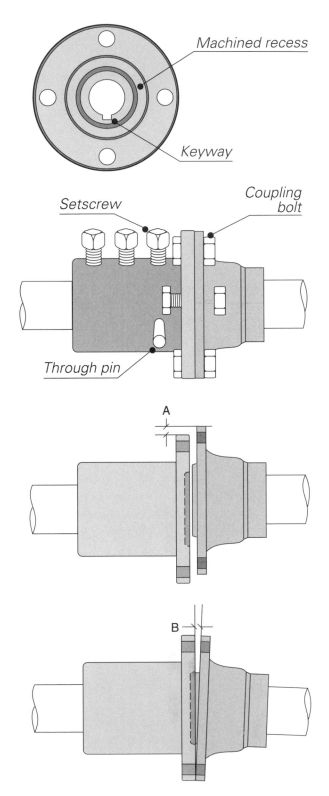

Machined recess

Keyway

Setscrew

Coupling bolt

Through pin

A

B

Standard couplings have solid cylinders with a machined keyway and threaded holes to accept setscrews.

In the split coupling the cylindrical body is split. First the shaft and key are inserted into the coupling. When the four or more bolts are tightened, the coupling grips the shaft as in a vise. Then a pilot dimple is drilled through the setscrew hole into the shaft, and the setscrew is inserted and tightened.

After years in a saltwater environment it is often difficult to remove a standard coupling from its shaft. The split coupling tends to separate itself when its bolts are loosened.

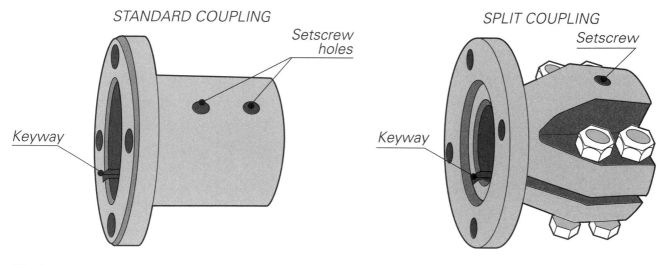

STANDARD COUPLING

Setscrew holes

Keyway

SPLIT COUPLING

Setscrew

Keyway

Drivesaver

Globe Rubber Works' Drivesaver is one of a class of plastic or rubber disks inserted between the two halves of a coupling. Frustrated by the difficulty of aligning engine and shaft, some boaters install these devices in the hopes of converting a standard coupling to a flexible coupling. There are such devices as flexible couplings, but the Drivesaver is not one of them.

The Drivesaver does, however, offer three features:

1. If the propeller were to strike a truly immovable object, a *properly sized* Drivesaver would shear and save the rest of the drivetrain components from serious damage.

2. It isolates the shaft and propeller galvanically from the transmission and engine—a benefit in marinas with stray electric currents.

3. It reduces vibration and noise slightly by decoupling the shaft and propeller from the transmission and engine.

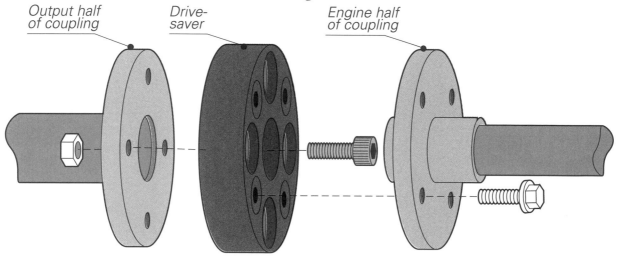

Output half of coupling

Drive-saver

Engine half of coupling

Stuffing Boxes

Rigid Stuffing Box

The stuffing box is a seal where the propeller shaft exits the hull that prevents incursion of water. Since the shaft rotates while the hull is stationary, the stuffing box necessarily requires a seal material (the packing) sliding over the shaft.

In the rigid stuffing box, the shaft passes through the stern tube, which is bolted to the hull. At the engine end the cylinder is enlarged to hold rings of packing material—grease-saturated flax of various diameters to fit the gap around the shaft.

The packing is wrapped around the shaft. Tightening the packing nut forces the concentric compression spacer against the packing, which squeezes the packing against the shaft, effecting the seal. Lubricating the seal requires that a few drops of water (perhaps one drop per 10 seconds) be allowed through. After seating the packing by turning the shaft for a minute, adjust the drip rate and tighten the locknut to prevent the packing nut from backing out.

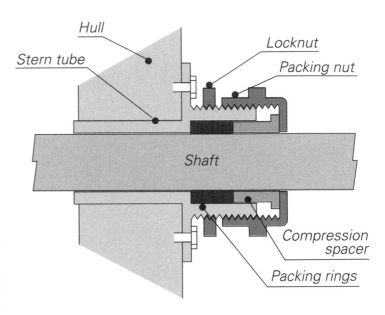

Flexible Stuffing Box

In a flexible stuffing box, the stuffing box and stern tube are connected by a short length of rubber hose. Double stainless hose clamps are used at both ends of the hose.

Single hose clamps would work and are sometimes used, but if the hose comes loose at either end an unattended boat will quickly sink. An attended boat suffering the same failure may not sink, but the crew will certainly experience anxiety—if not hysteria—at the resulting flood of water!

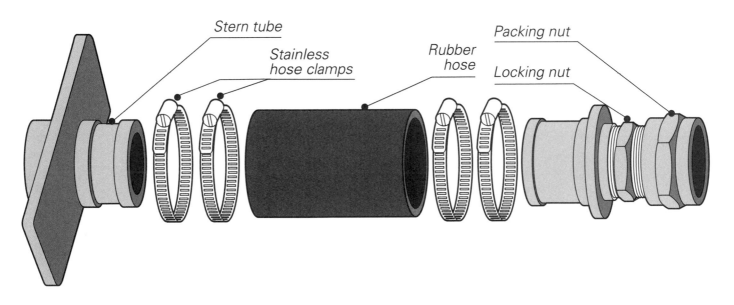

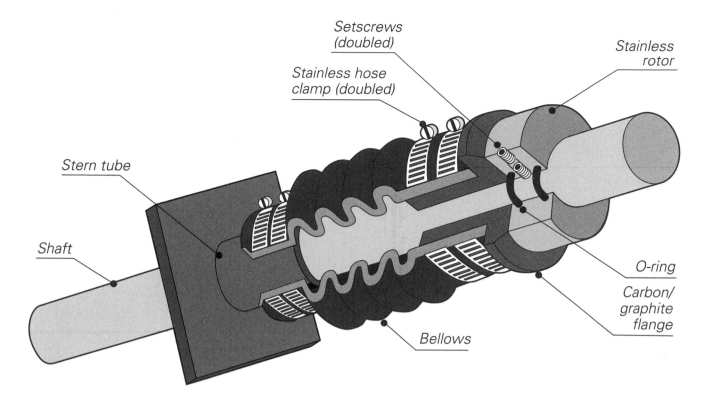

Setscrews (doubled)

Stainless hose clamp (doubled)

Stainless rotor

Stern tube

Shaft

O-ring

Carbon/ graphite flange

Bellows

Shaft Seals

Shaft seals serve the same purpose as stuffing boxes, but contain no packing to wear out and be replaced. As with the flexible stuffing box, the propeller end is clamped to the stern tube with double stainless hose clamps. A rubber bellows substitutes for the straight rubber hose.

At the engine end, the bellows clamps to a carbon/ graphite flange with a polished face. A cylindrical stainless rotor with a similarly polished face slides down the shaft to mate with the flange. Pressing the rotor against the flange before tightening its setscrews compresses the bellows, which then provides the pressure to maintain the seal. Note that the setscrews are doubled, effectively locking them in place.

The graphite flange remains fixed, while the stainless rotor rotates with the shaft. The combination of the natural lubricant, graphite, and a thin film of water provides a seal that never requires repacking.

In high-speed versions (see right), where friction might cause the seal to heat up, a hose barb allows water from the engine seawater pump to be injected into the seal. The water exits by way of the stern tube.

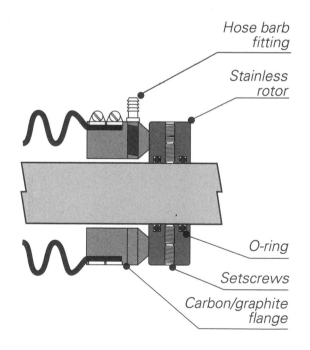

Hose barb fitting

Stainless rotor

O-ring

Setscrews

Carbon/graphite flange

Propellers

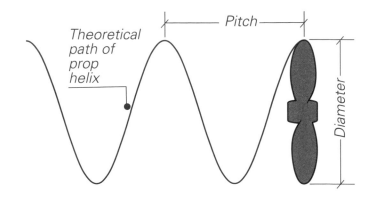

The "size" of a propeller consists of two numbers:

1. Diameter, the diameter of the circle traced by the rotating tips
2. Pitch, the theoretical forward advance of the propeller's helix in a single revolution assuming no slippage in the water (which of course is impossible).

In addition, the direction of rotation must be specified as viewed from astern in forward gear. For example, a 12RH17 propeller has a diameter of 12 inches, a pitch of 17 inches, and rotates clockwise when moving forward.

The propeller converts shaft rotation to thrust by engaging the water around it. The mass of water thrown to the rear causes an equal and opposite reaction, thrusting the boat forward. It is a mistake to think of the "screw" (propeller) *threading* its way through the water. The action requires that a mass of water be thrust relative to the still water around it. Propeller slip, the difference between theoretical pitch and the distance actually traveled in one revolution, is not only inevitable but necessary.

Most propellers are designed primarily to produce maximum thrust when going forward. However, all propellers produce reverse thrust when rotated in reverse. Some feathering props produce as much thrust in reverse as in forward, but most are less efficient.

As any boater knows, propellers also produce sideways forces. These are most apparent when the boat is dead in the water and there is no current past the rudder. Simply put, a propeller blade gets more "bite" at the bottom of its swing, and the result is a tendency to "walk" in the direction of rotation.

Thus, when landing or leaving a dock, a right-hand propeller in forward kicks the stern to starboard; a left-hand propeller kicks it to port. In reverse gear the thrusts are just the opposite. The experienced skipper with a right-hand propeller approaches a dock on the port side at an angle, because shifting into reverse will both stop the boat and pull the stern neatly into the dock. In a twin-engine boat, the starboard prop should be right-hand and the port prop left-hand so that their side thrusts cancel and each is outward-turning for best efficiency.

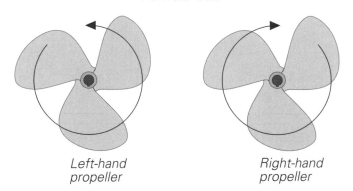

VIEWED FROM STERN
Forward Gear

Left-hand propeller

Right-hand propeller

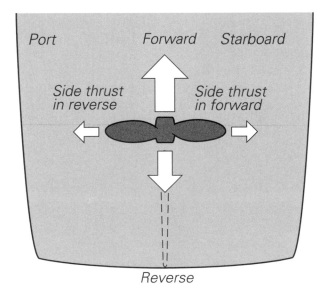

Direction and relative magnitude of forces generated by a right-hand prop.

The *drag* of an unrotating propeller is of no concern to the powerboater. But to the sailor trying to squeeze an extra fraction of a knot out of a 10-knot breeze, propeller drag is—well—a drag.

With a fixed propeller, thrust and drag are necessarily a tradeoff. The greater the total area of blade, the greater the thrust under power, but the greater the drag under sail. Sailors unwilling to go the folding or feathering route often settle for a small two-bladed propeller and line up the blades with the keel when sailing to minimize the exposed area. Others allow the propeller to freewheel, although the drag reduction from freewheeling is highly questionable, and wear on Cutless bearing, stuffing box, and transmission seals is increased.

Folding propellers solve the problem of drag by hinging the blades, which fold back into a streamlined shape when dragged through the water. When the engine is put in forward gear, centrifugal force opens the blades partway, then propeller thrust forces the blades fully open. Unfortunately things don't work as well in reverse. Although centrifugal force again works to open the blades, the thrust in reverse works to close them. Efficiency in reverse is notoriously poor.

The only way to achieve both high efficiency and low drag is to feather the propeller blades. The two- and three-blade Max-Prop propellers are the best known example of this genre. With the shaft not turning, the pressure of water flowing past the blades forces the blades to feather into an a streamlined profile. When the shaft is engaged, however, gears at the base of each blade force the blades to open fully. Turning the shaft in the reverse direction causes the blades to flip 180 degrees, so the efficiency is identical in forward and reverse.

Another example of a feathering propeller is the three-bladed Autoprop.

Each type of propeller is examined more fully in the following pages.

UNDER POWER   UNDER SAIL

Typical powerboat three-blade

Typical sail three-blade

Fixed sail two-blade

Folding sail two-blade

Feathering Max-Prop two-blade

Feathering Max-Prop three-blade

Feathering Autoprop three-blade

Fixed Propellers

Fixed propellers generally have two, three or four blades. The more blades, the smoother the operation, and the greater the blade area, the more thrust developed, given sufficient engine power.

While a propeller with two narrow blades allows "parking" the blade in the shadow of the keel for minimum drag under sail, there is a danger in having a total blade area too small for the horsepower of the engine. This can lead to the formation and collapse of water vapor bubbles (cavitation) on the forward face and tips, resulting in erosion of the metal.

Propeller shafts are tapered, with a machined keyway (rectangular slot) and threaded end. Propellers are bored with a taper and keyway matching those of the shaft. The propeller slides over the shaft and key. A large propeller nut drives the propeller tightly onto the shaft, followed by a locknut. A cotter pin is often passed through the locknut and shaft for added security.

If the taper was greased with antiseizing compound before the propeller was mounted, removal usually requires only loosening the nuts and a smart rap on the propeller hub with a hammer. If the propeller is seized to the shaft, special propeller pullers are available to put a strain on the prop while the hub is heated and struck with repeated blows.

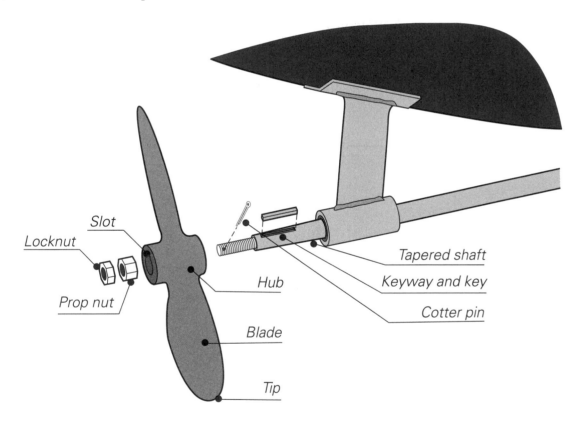

Locknut
Slot
Prop nut
Hub
Blade
Tip
Tapered shaft
Keyway and key
Cotter pin

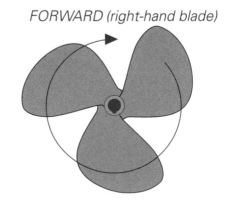

FORWARD (right-hand blade)

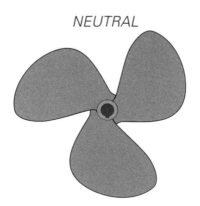

NEUTRAL

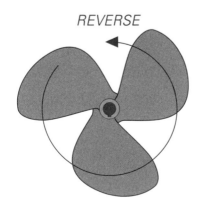

REVERSE

Folding Propellers

The Martec folding propeller, long a favorite of avid racing sailors, has three advantages:

- It is the least expensive nonfixed propeller
- It offers the least drag under sail
- It will not catch lobster and crab buoys when folded

On the other side of the equation:

- Its blade design is inefficient
- Performance in reverse is virtually nil
- The blades may not open at all if mussels and barnacles foul the pivot slot

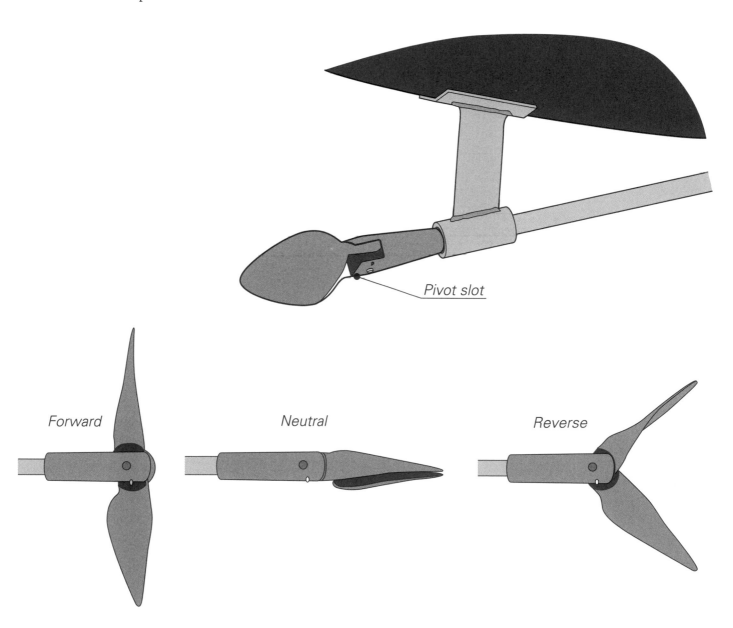

Pivot slot

Forward　　　　　*Neutral*　　　　　*Reverse*

Two-Blade, Feathering Max-Prop

Max-Prop feathering propellers are of a class of propellers that offer the advantages of:

- full feathering for minimum drag under sail
- large, efficient blade design
- identical efficiency in forward and reverse

Max-Props are expensive, however. In addition, early models required total disassembly for pitch adjustment (not recommended underwater due to possible loss of small parts) and at least partial disassembly for annual greasing. Newer models offer external grease fittings and pitch adjustment.

The basic principle of the Max-Prop is simple. Bevel gears on each blade engage a central bevel gear, the rotation of which is limited in both directions by stops in the hub. The pitch of the blades is changed by matching the teeth of the blade bevel gears to specified teeth in the central bevel gear. When the shaft is not turning, the pressure of water against the unbalanced blades forces them to feather. As soon as the shaft turns, however, the pressure twists the blades to either the full-forward or full-reverse pitch.

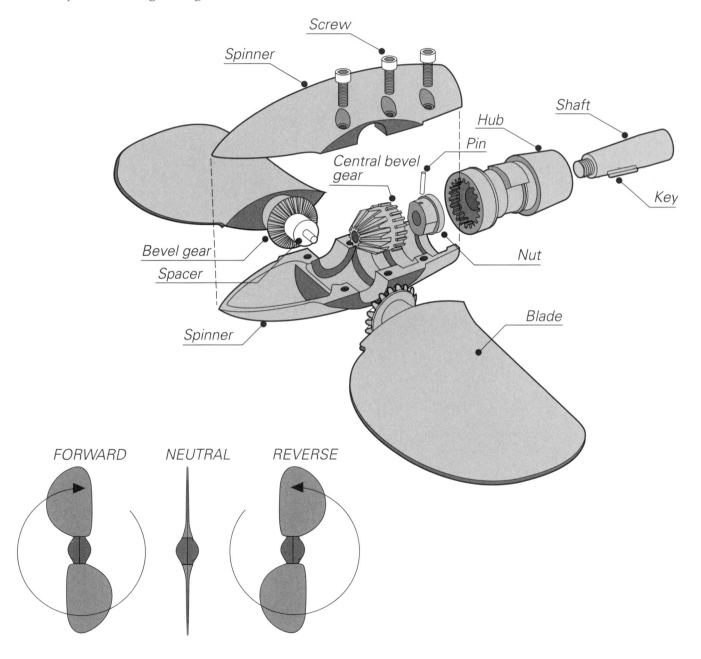

Three-Blade, Feathering Max-Prop

The principle behind the three-blade Max-Prop is identical to that of the two-blade and it functions the same way, except for the third blade and bevel gear.

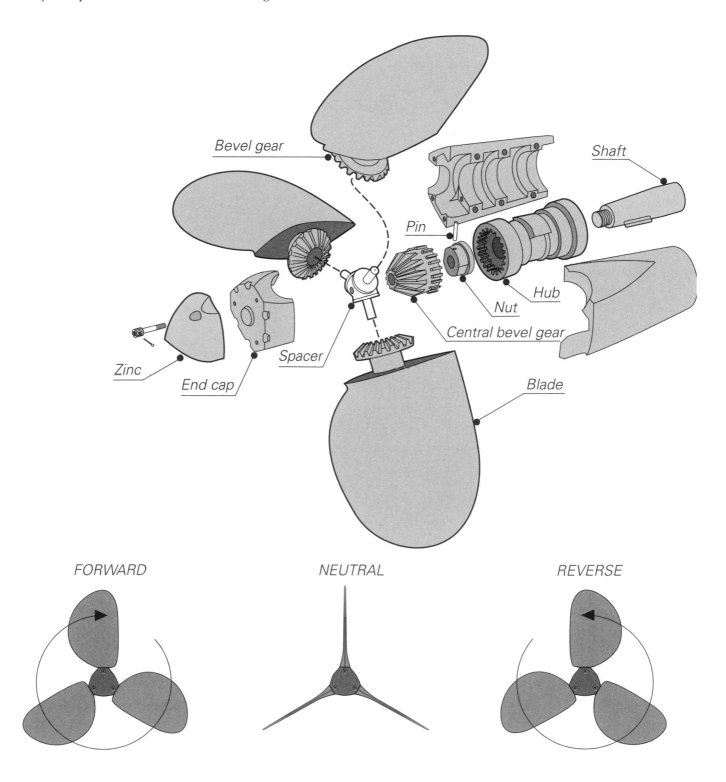

Bevel gear

Shaft

Pin

Hub

Nut

Central bevel gear

Zinc

End cap

Spacer

Blade

FORWARD   NEUTRAL   REVERSE

Automatic, Variable-Pitch Autoprop

The Max-Prop deploys from feathered position to maximum pitch against hard stops. It thus acts like a fixed prop in both forward and reverse. The Autoprop has no fixed stops, but varies its pitch according to load and rpm. Each Autoprop is custom-designed to match engine power, maximum shaft rpm, and boat speed.

The feathering action is shown below. First, with no stops, each blade is free to rotate about its pivot 360 degrees. Second, the blades' centers of area and thrust are offset from their pivots. When the boat is put into forward, the thrust forces the blades to move against the thrust to a position forward of the pivot. When the engine is stopped and the shaft locked (either by leaving the engine in gear or with a shaft lock), the blades trail back to a feathered position. And when the boat is put into reverse, the backward thrust forces the blades to positions behind the pivot point.

The pitch assumed by the blades depends on boat speed (water flow) and shaft rpm. Centrifugal force causes pitch to decrease with increasing rpm; the flow of water causes pitch to increase with boat speed. When starting at high rpm and low boat speed, the pitch is small, but as the boat (and water) speed increases, so does the pitch. The result is that the pitch automatically adjusts for maximum thrust efficiency.

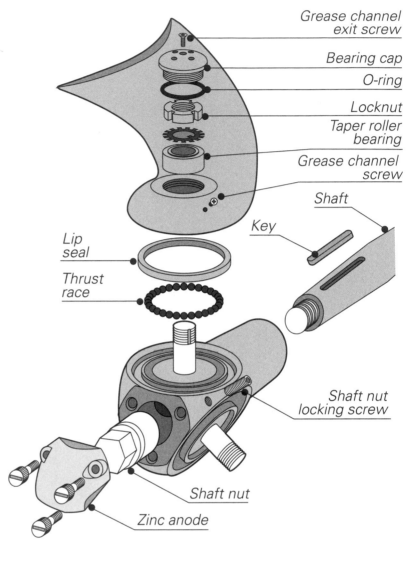

Grease channel exit screw
Bearing cap
O-ring
Locknut
Taper roller bearing
Grease channel screw
Shaft
Key
Lip seal
Thrust race
Shaft nut locking screw
Shaft nut
Zinc anode

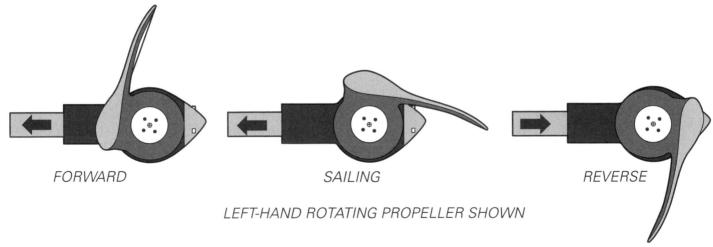

FORWARD   SAILING   REVERSE

LEFT-HAND ROTATING PROPELLER SHOWN

2

Steering and Controls

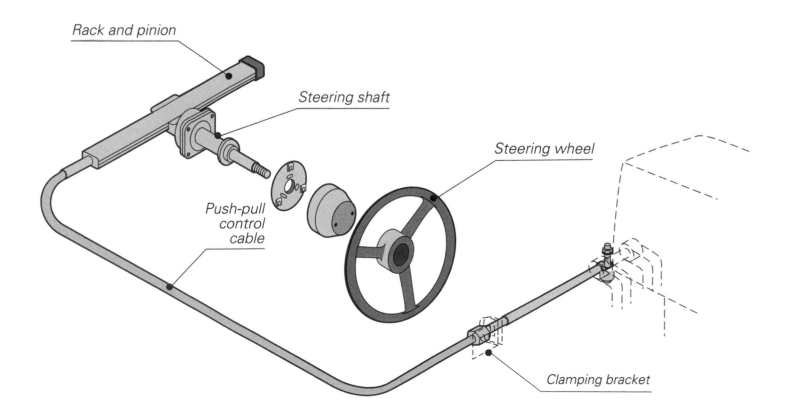

Rack and pinion

Steering shaft

Steering wheel

Push-pull control cable

Clamping bracket

Cables and Contols

Control cables are used to transmit linear (push-pull) forces between a steering station and an engine or steering. The waterproof cables can be routed anywhere through the hull, including the bilge, can be of virtually any length, and may be formed into curves of small radii.

The Morse 33C Red-Jaket cable is the most widely used control cable. It consists of a solid stainless steel wire core, sliding inside a polyethylene (slippery) sleeve, mechanically and environmentally protected by a layer of wires and plastic jacket. Minimum bend radius is 8 inches; maximum throw is 3 inches.

The Morse 33C Supreme Red-Jaket cable substitutes an extruded, nylon-covered multistrand wire cable for the solid stainless wire. The result is 45 percent less friction and a smaller 4-inch bend radius. The two cables are interchangeable.

Engine control levers translate lever motion into motion of the control cable core wire or cable within the jacket. The controls can be set up to make a pull on the lever correspond to either a pull or a push on the cable. The usual configuration is a pair of controls, as shown in the figure at right, but some models accept up to six separate control levers.

The desired action is a relative motion between the core and the outer jacket. Unless the ends of the control cable are firmly clamped at both the control-lever bracket (shown) and the clamping bracket on the opposite end, the relative motion will be reduced.

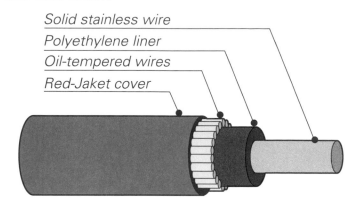

33C RED-JAKET

Solid stainless wire
Polyethylene liner
Oil-tempered wires
Red-Jaket cover

33C SUPREME RED-JAKET

Stranded wire cable
Extruded nylon sleeve

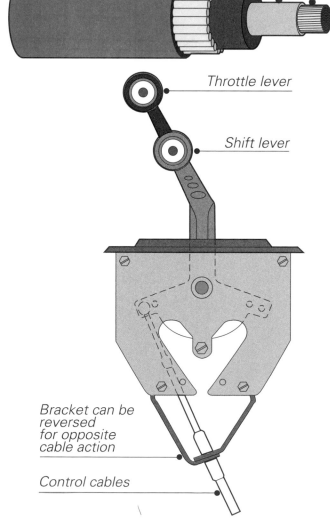

Throttle lever

Shift lever

Bracket can be reversed for opposite cable action

Control cables

Powerboat Controls

Outboard Mechanical Steering

Mechanical steering uses the same type of push-pull control cable as engine controls (page 58). In rotary steering (top figure), the cable wraps around a drum connected to the steering wheel. The drum may be directly connected for 1:1 steering or geared so that a turn on the drum corresponds to several turns of the wheel.

Rack-and-pinion steering also uses a push-pull control cable, but the rotary drum is replaced by a pinion gear on the steering shaft that drives a rack (linear gear). The number of turns of the wheel for the full stroke of the control cable depends on the diameter and number of teeth on the pinion gear.

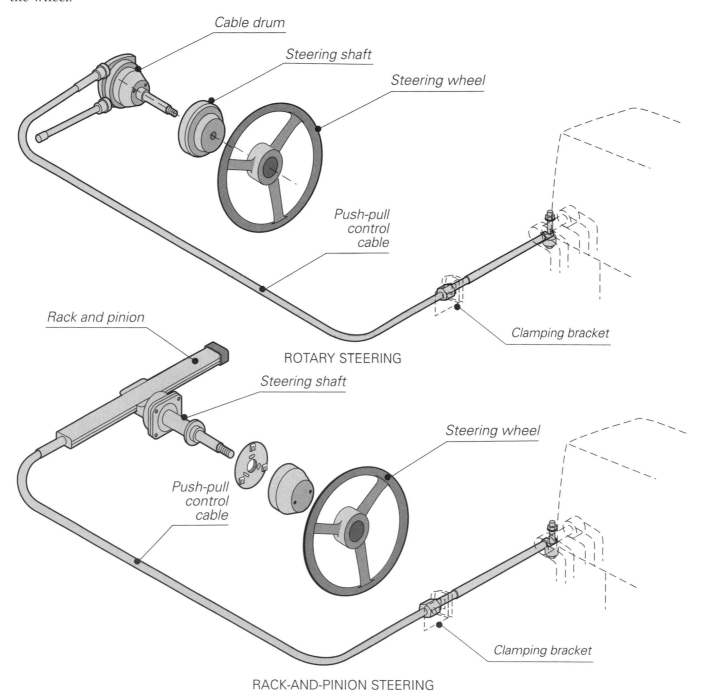

Cable drum

Steering shaft

Steering wheel

Push-pull control cable

Clamping bracket

ROTARY STEERING

Rack and pinion

Steering shaft

Steering wheel

Push-pull control cable

Clamping bracket

RACK-AND-PINION STEERING

Single-Station Hydraulic

The majority of large inboard powerboats have hydraulic steering. The helm (wheel) operates a dual-acting (port and starboard output) hydraulic pump that is connected to a double-acting (port and starboard input) hydraulic cylinder near the rudder. The helm pump usually has check valves (flow limited to one direction) so that the wheel controls the rudder but wave action on the rudder is not transmitted to the wheel.

The number of turns of the wheel, and thus the force available to turn the rudder, can be varied by the gear ratio in the pump and the bore of the cylinder. In very large vessels, the hydraulics may be power-assisted by electric hydraulic servo-pumps. Here the output of the manual pump is magnified by a more powerful electric hydraulic pump, as in the case of automotive power steering.

The pressure in the hydraulic lines is up to 1,000 psi. The elasticity of rubber hydraulic hose, small as it may be, tends to make the steering response spongy. For this reason rigid metal tubing (copper refrigeration line is recommended) is used for long runs. For short runs, and for terminations where the hydraulic cylinder pivots, hydraulic hose can be substituted.

When the hydraulic pump contains check valves, installation of bypass valves between the port and starboard lines is recommended so that an emergency tiller can be installed in case of hydraulic failure.

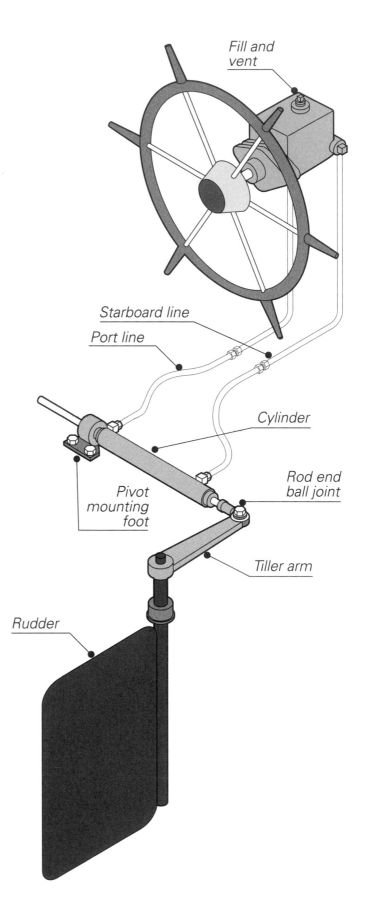

Dual-Station Hydraulic

Where there is a flying bridge, a second steering station with separate hydraulic pump can be fitted. In fact, there is no limit to the number of steering stations that can be connected in parallel. The only requirement is that each hydraulic pump be fitted with check valves in both lines. Otherwise, the wheels will turn each other in addition to, or instead of, the rudder.

A fill-and-vent line should also connect the two pump reservoirs. The line must slope continuously up toward the upper pump so no air bubbles can become trapped in the line.

If the hydraulic lines are long and of rubber, the hose will expand a little and the steering will seem spongy. If the hydraulic lines are instead copper refrigeration line (recommended), spongy steering indicates air in the system, and the system must be bled. For draining the system, special bleeder fittings are recommended on the hydraulic cylinder—the lowest point in the system. Air may be bled from the system at its highest point—the fill-and-vent plug on the highest steering station pump.

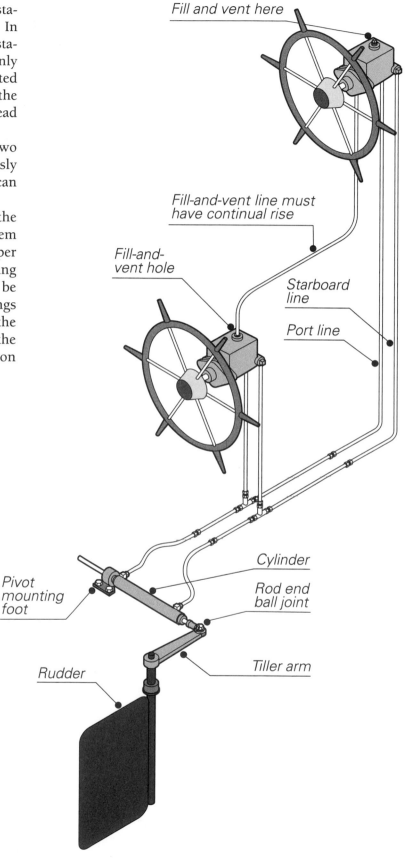

Fill and vent here

Fill-and-vent line must have continual rise

Fill-and-vent hole

Starboard line

Port line

Pivot mounting foot

Cylinder

Rod end ball joint

Tiller arm

Rudder

Outboard Hydraulic Steering

Hydraulic steering for outboard engines follows the same general principles as that for boats having inboard engines, except that the hydraulic lines tend to be a lot shorter and can thus be hose and that the hydraulic cylinder is specially designed for outboard engines. A range of adapters can fit nearly any outboard, no matter how old.

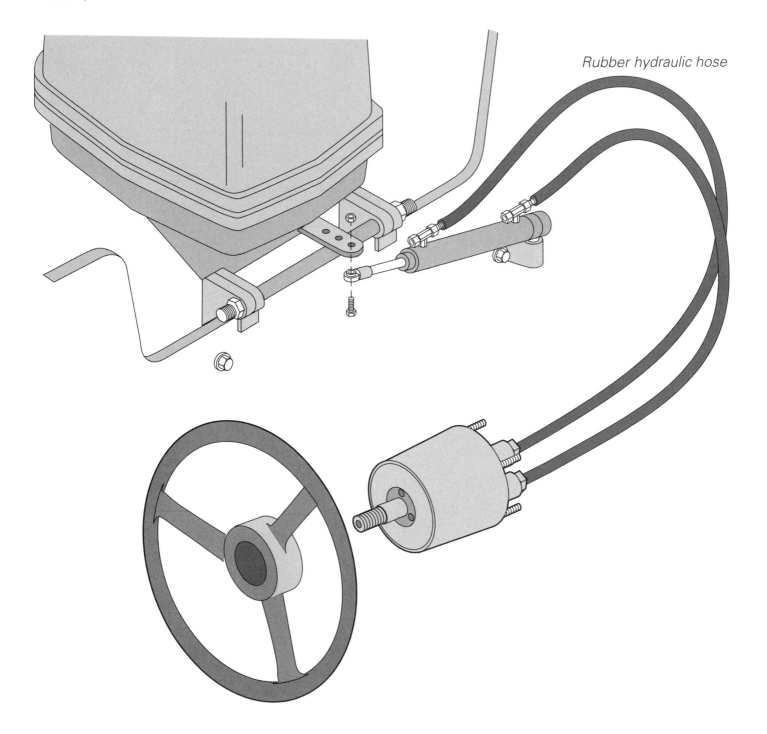

Rubber hydraulic hose

Sailboat Steering

Pedestals

Unless a sailing vessel has a tiller, it probably has some form of pedestal steering. There are two basic types of pedestals. The first (shown here) has a pinion gear on the wheel shaft, which drives a gear quadrant. The quadrant turns a vertical tube inside the pedestal, to the bottom of which is attached an output lever. The lever is then directly connected by way of a rod to the steering arm of the rudder.

The second type of pedestal appears the same on the outside, but the linkage is totally different. Here a bicycle sprocket replaces the pinion gear. As shown on page 66, bicycle chain looped over the sprocket converts rotation of the wheel into a pull on one side or the other of the chain, depending on how the ends connect to wire cables; the cables then run through sheaves to the rudderstock. The cables run around either a radial drive wheel or a quadrant (quarter of a circle, see page 67), turning the pull of the cable back into rotation of the rudderstock.

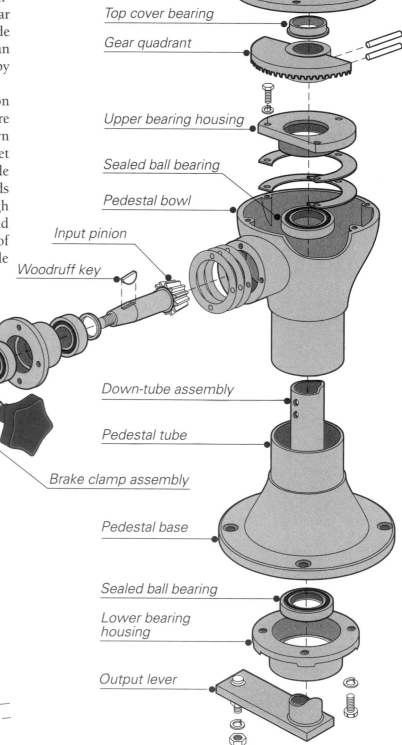

Top cover

Top cover bearing

Gear quadrant

Upper bearing housing

Sealed ball bearing

Pedestal bowl

Input pinion

Woodruff key

Down-tube assembly

Pedestal tube

Brake clamp assembly

Pedestal base

Sealed ball bearing

Lower bearing housing

Output lever

Rack-and-Pinion Pedestal Linkage

The illustration shows how the output lever of an Edson rack-and-pinion pedestal is connected to the steering arm of a single rudder. Turning the wheel to the right (clockwise) pulls on the rod and steering arm, turning the rudder and boat to starboard.

Reversing either output lever or steering arm would reverse the steering relationship. Reversing both levers would preserve the clockwise/starboard relationship, but could also place the connecting rod in a more convenient location.

Edson also offers conversion kits by which outboard rudders and rudders on tillers can be converted to rack-and-pinion pedestal steering. The possibilities are limited only by one's imagination.

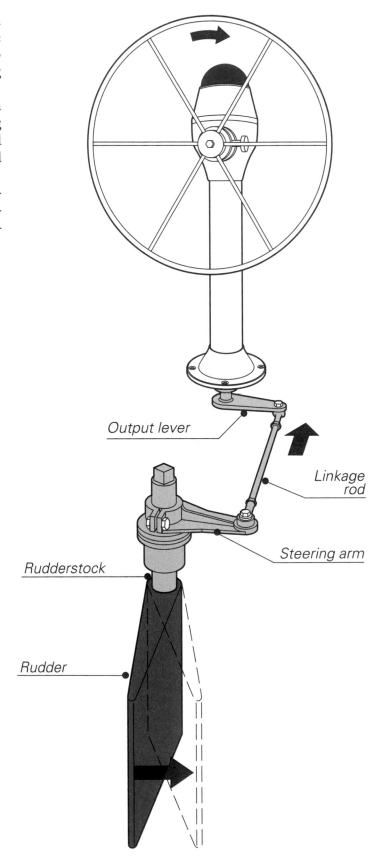

Output lever

Linkage rod

Steering arm

Rudderstock

Rudder

Twin-Rudder Rack-and-Pinion Pedestal Linkage

Reversing the steering arm on the port rudder and connecting it to the port side of a balanced output lever allows two rudders to turn in the same direction. An alternative, though not as strong or redundant, would be to control one rudder from the pedestal and link the two rudders by a separate connecting rod so that the starboard rudder controls the port rudder.

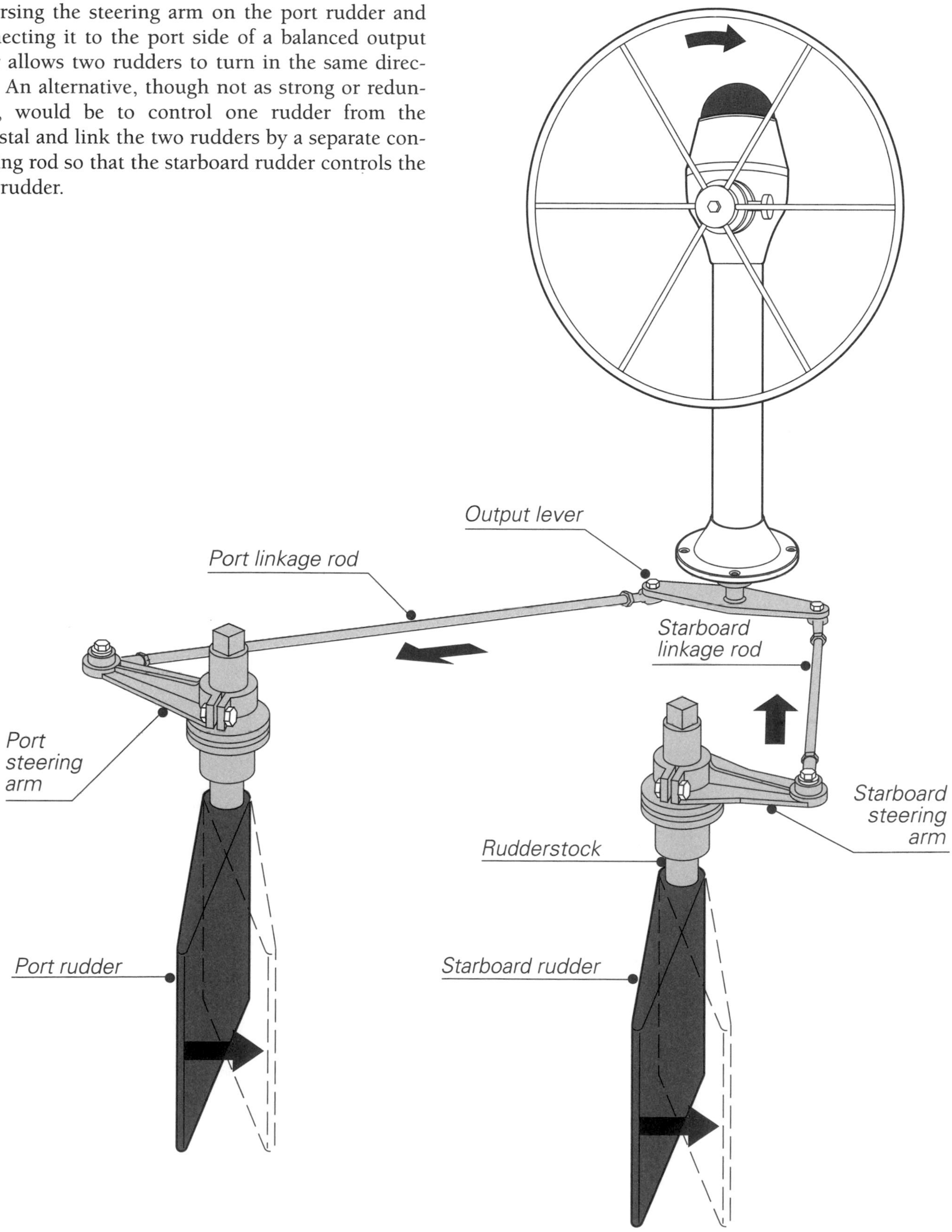

Output lever

Port linkage rod

Starboard linkage rod

Port steering arm

Starboard steering arm

Rudderstock

Port rudder

Starboard rudder

Chain-and-Wire Drives

Chain-and-wire drive systems offer greater flexibility than rack-and-pinion systems because the flexible wire can be routed by sheaves through unused spaces.

The direction of pull—and therefore steering—can be switched either by crisscrossing the wires and sheaves between the pedestal and rudder or by swapping the sheaves at the bottom of the steering pedestal (illustration below).

Switching would not be required in the case of a radial drive (see facing page), but might for rudders having steering arms.

The illustrations also show that the sheaves should be mounted so one is slightly forward of the other so the wire doesn't chafe.

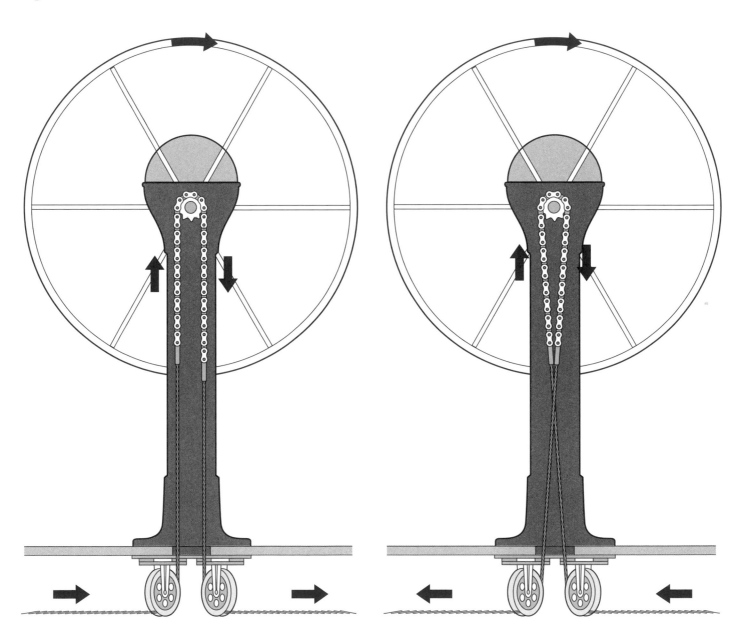

Radial and Quadrant Drives

Edson offers two types of radial drives: full radial drive wheels in radii from 6.5 to 15 inches and quadrants with radii of 8 to 36 inches.

With the radial drive wheels, the cables are led aft around the wheel, then forward to eyebolts, which makes tensioning the cable simple.

The large wheels are split for easier installation in cramped spaces. Each wheel is custom-bored to the diameter of the rudderstock and can be secured with throughbolts, a key, or setscrews.

Drive wheels are supplied with substantial rudder stops on either the top or the bottom of the wheel to prevent the rudder from turning back into the propeller or hull.

Drive wheels can be driven directly from the pedestal sheaves, provided there is a clear path for the cables. Where there isn't a clear path, where there isn't room for a full wheel, or where the angle of the rudderpost is not vertical, the wheel can be replaced with a quadrant—essentially a quarter or less of a wheel. With a quadrant, the two cables operate over the same section of circumference, so must approach in opposite directions. Edson offers a wide range of sheaves to facilitate cable routing.

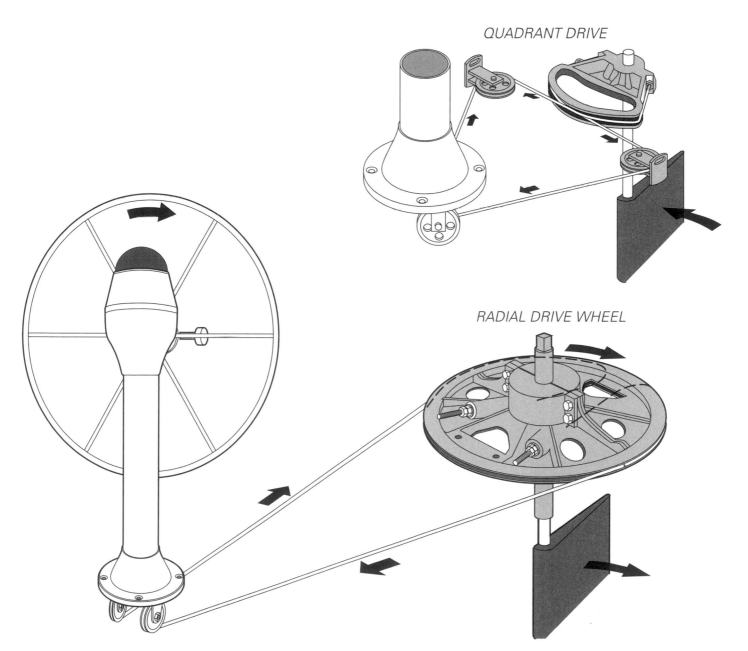

QUADRANT DRIVE

RADIAL DRIVE WHEEL

Forward-Mounted Rack-and-Pinion Steering

Rack-and-pinion steering without pedestal-mounted wheels is common in traditional-design sailing vessels. Typically the shaft of the steering wheel leads aft, under the helmsman's seat. Just aft of the helmsman, the rack and pinion converts the wheel rotation to rudder rotation at right angles. Typically the gearing is such that one full turn of the wheel produces 30 to 40 degrees of rudder.

When the steering wheel shaft and rudderstock fail to conform to a right angle, a universal joint can be inserted between the wheel shaft and the direct drive.

In case of failure, the helmsman's seat is easily removed and an emergency tiller fitted to the rudderstock.

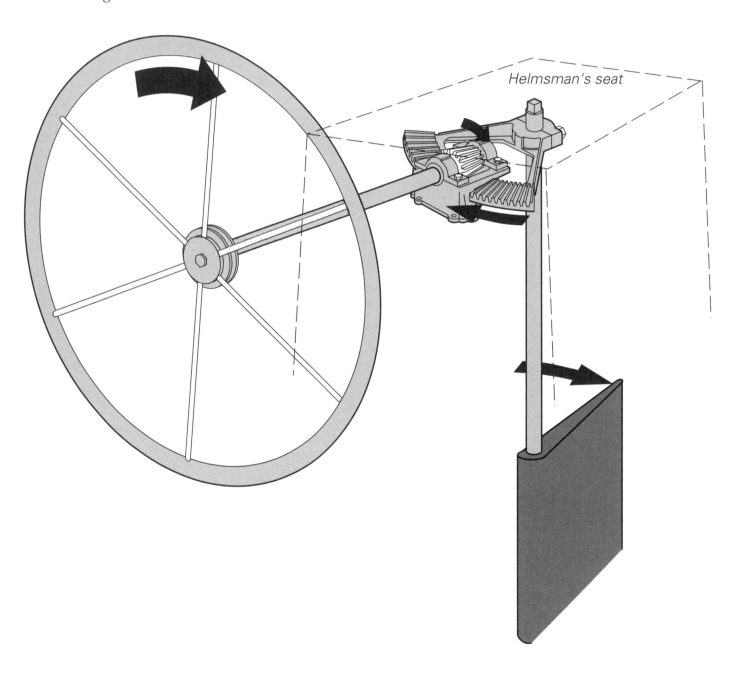

Helmsman's seat

Autopilots

Like a helmsman, a mechanical autopilot actuates a vessel's rudder to maintain a fixed magnetic compass course. At the start of operation, the autopilot is powered up in "standby" mode, allowing it to determine the vessel's magnetic heading. The vessel is then manually steered to a desired compass course, and the autopilot is switched to "auto"(matic) mode. From that point the autopilot uses error signals from its built-in compass to keep the vessel on the selected heading.

Modern autopilots use electronic fluxgate compasses, in which a magnetic field is induced in a ferrite rod by a current-carrying coil. The amount of current required to saturate the core in one direction is compared to the current required in the opposite direction, the difference in currents being attributed to the earth's magnetic field. When the currents are the same, the rod is perpendicular to the earth's field, i.e., the ferrite rod is aligned along magnetic east-west.

Instead of physically rotating the rod, though, the system uses two perpendicular rods and coils, and a computer chip calculates north from the two signals. Like a compass card, however, the fluxgate sensor must be maintained parallel to the earth's surface, so it too is mounted in a miniature gimbal. Additionally, the computer can automatically calculate the amount of rudder trim required to offset the vessel's helm, as well as the optimum amount of deadband (the range of heading variation ignored by the servo) for efficient steering. The servo gain (speed of response) is set manually by the operator.

The computer powers a small but powerful DC motor. The motor can drive a belt, which drives a lead screw assembly, which drives a push rod, which engages the tiller of a sailboat (shown here), or it can power a pulley, which drives a belt, which drives a second pulley attached to the vessel's steering wheel. It can also power a hydraulic pump that actuates a push-pull hydraulic cylinder that engages a lever arm on the rudderstock.

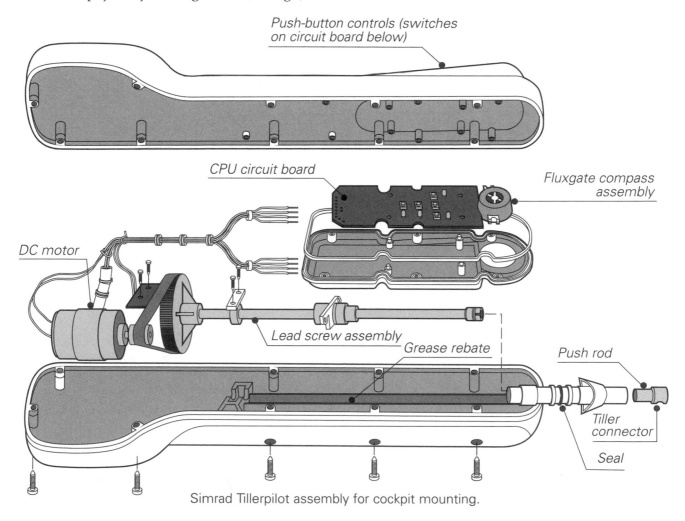

Push-button controls (switches on circuit board below)

CPU circuit board

Fluxgate compass assembly

DC motor

Lead screw assembly

Grease rebate

Push rod

Tiller connector

Seal

Simrad Tillerpilot assembly for cockpit mounting.

Servopendulum Windvane

A good windvane automatically, and without electrical power, holds a boat on a fixed course relative to wind direction. Here is how it works, with reference to the Aries windvane:

1. The boat is manually steered to the desired course.

2. The snaffle lines are used to position the plywood vane's leading edge directly into the wind.

3. If the boat strays off course, wind pressure on the vane pivots it fore or aft, lifting or dropping the lifting strut.

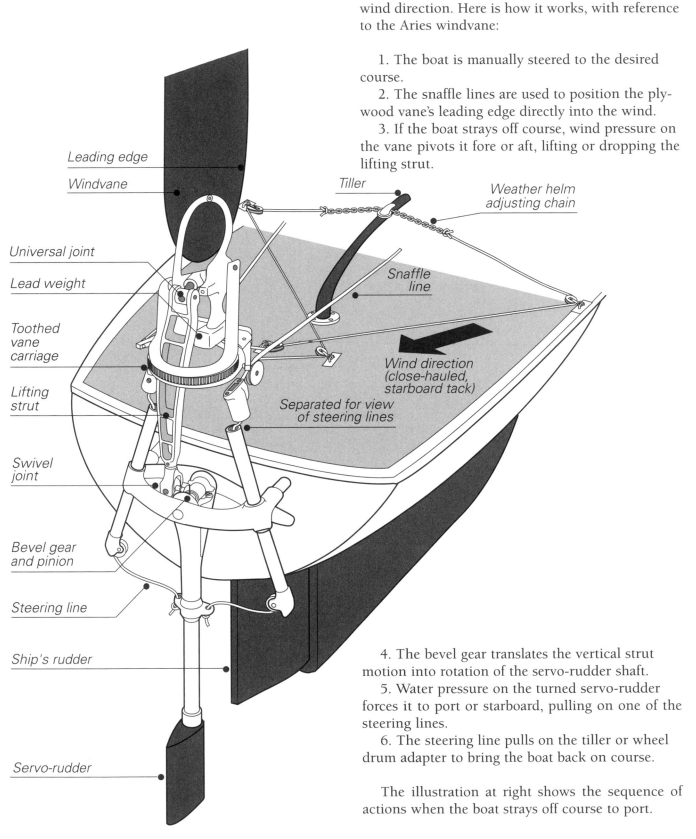

Leading edge

Windvane

Universal joint

Lead weight

Toothed vane carriage

Lifting strut

Swivel joint

Bevel gear and pinion

Steering line

Ship's rudder

Servo-rudder

Tiller

Weather helm adjusting chain

Snaffle line

Wind direction (close-hauled, starboard tack)

Separated for view of steering lines

4. The bevel gear translates the vertical strut motion into rotation of the servo-rudder shaft.

5. Water pressure on the turned servo-rudder forces it to port or starboard, pulling on one of the steering lines.

6. The steering line pulls on the tiller or wheel drum adapter to bring the boat back on course.

The illustration at right shows the sequence of actions when the boat strays off course to port.

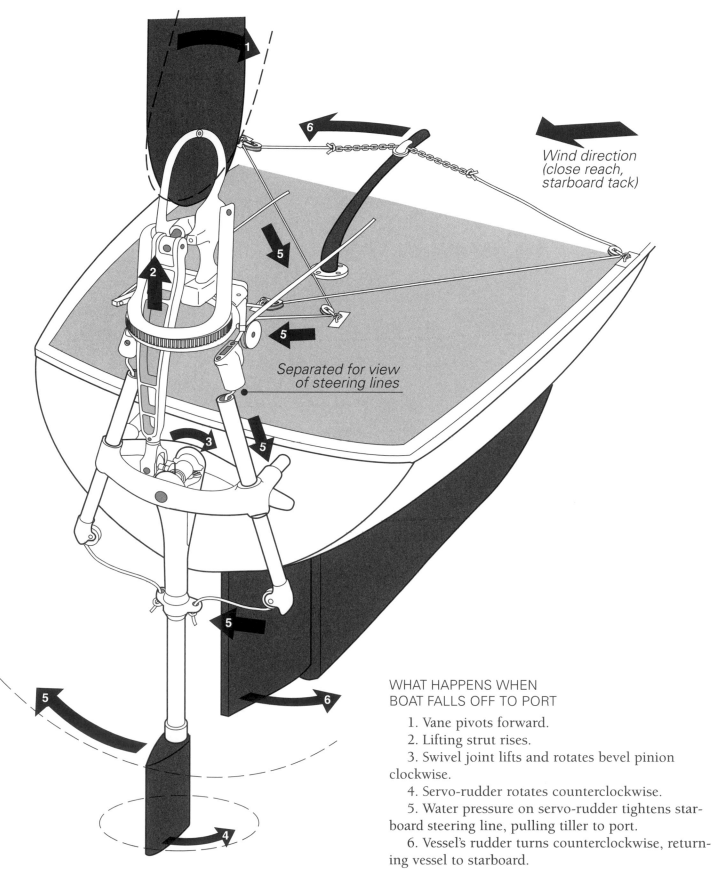

Wind direction
(close reach,
starboard tack)

Separated for view
of steering lines

WHAT HAPPENS WHEN
BOAT FALLS OFF TO PORT

1. Vane pivots forward.

2. Lifting strut rises.

3. Swivel joint lifts and rotates bevel pinion clockwise.

4. Servo-rudder rotates counterclockwise.

5. Water pressure on servo-rudder tightens starboard steering line, pulling tiller to port.

6. Vessel's rudder turns counterclockwise, returning vessel to starboard.

Magnetic Compass

As many sailors have discovered, when electrical power is lost at sea, the old standby magnetic compass suddenly becomes the most important navigational tool.

As early as the twelfth century, sailors recognized that an iron needle, magnetized by rubbing on iron ferrite, or lodestone, and floated on a piece of straw or cork, would point to magnetic north.

The modern magnetic compass, after compensation for local magnetic disturbances due to a vessel's own magnetism and magnetic fields produced by electric currents, can indicate magnetic north within a fraction of a degree. Obtaining this precision in spite of a ship's pitching, rolling, and yawing requires a number of elements:

1. A nearly neutrally buoyant compass card pivoting on a hardened-steel post in a cupped jewel.

2. A pair of strong directive magnets attached to the card.

3. A pair of gimbals and counterbalance weights to maintain the card in a horizontal axis.

4. A fluid-filled body dome to dampen the card's motion.

5. A diaphragm to allow thermal expansion and contraction of the fluid without bubble formation.

6. A pair of adjustable compensating magnets to cancel out any permanent local magnetic disturbances.

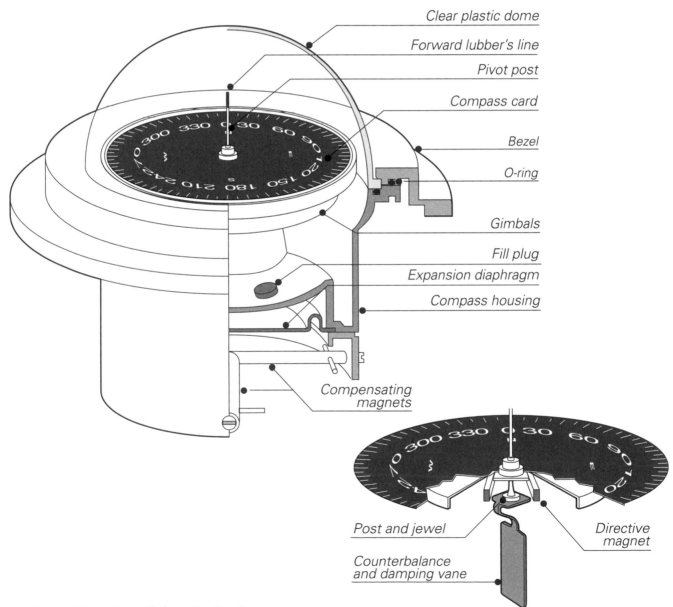

Clear plastic dome
Forward lubber's line
Pivot post
Compass card
Bezel
O-ring
Gimbals
Fill plug
Expansion diaphragm
Compass housing
Compensating magnets

Post and jewel
Directive magnet
Counterbalance and damping vane

3 *Standing Rigging*

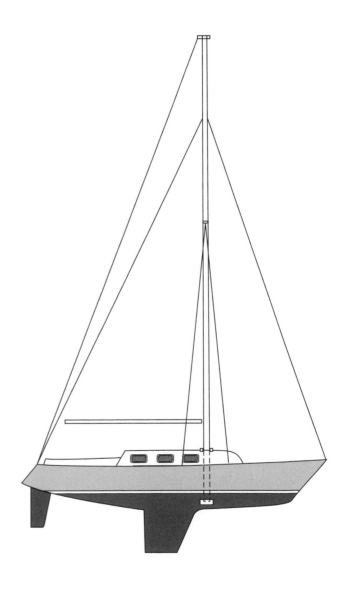

Wire and Fittings

igging is the collection of ropes that support and operate a vessel's spars and sails. *Standing rigging* consists of ropes and lines that do not move. *Running rigging* are lines that do move, the name deriving from their running through blocks. This chapter deals with the former; the next chapter with the latter.

Wire Rope

Standing rigging requires two qualities: great strength in tension and minimal stretch. Most standing rigging consists of wire rope with end fittings.

Wire rope is specified by four descriptors:

- maximum diameter, in inches
- lay: number of strands x wires per strand, i.e., 6 x 12
- wire material: improved plow steel (IPS), galvanized improved plow steel (GIPS), stainless steel (SS)
- the core: fiber core (FC) or wire strand core (WSC)

Wire ropes fall into one of two major categories: those having fiber cores and those with wire cores. The purpose of a fiber core is to retain oil, which lubricates the wire strands, allowing them to slide over each other as the wire rope bends. The oil also helps prevent rusting of the wire. The oil in a fiber core is periodically replaced by "slushing" the rope (dipping it in oil).

The primary marine applications for fiber core wire rope are in tug towing and the lifting of cargo.

The marine applications of wire core wire rope include standing rigging (shrouds and stays) and sometimes running rigging (halyards and outhauls).

Generally, the greater the number and the smaller the wires, the more flexible the wire rope. Halyards and outhauls, which must turn around small sheaves, are generally of 7 x 19 stainless wire.

Larger and fewer wires make a wire rope stiff. Traditional sailing vessels often have 7 x 7 galvanized wire rope as shrouds and stays.

The fewer the voids between wires, the less the stretch under load. Cruising sailboats usually employ 1 x 19 stainless wire rope for standing rigging. Racers desiring the absolute minimum stretch use either solid rod rigging or die-formed wire (see the

Dyform 1 x 7). Passing the wire rope through a die eliminates most of the voids by compressing and distorting the wires.

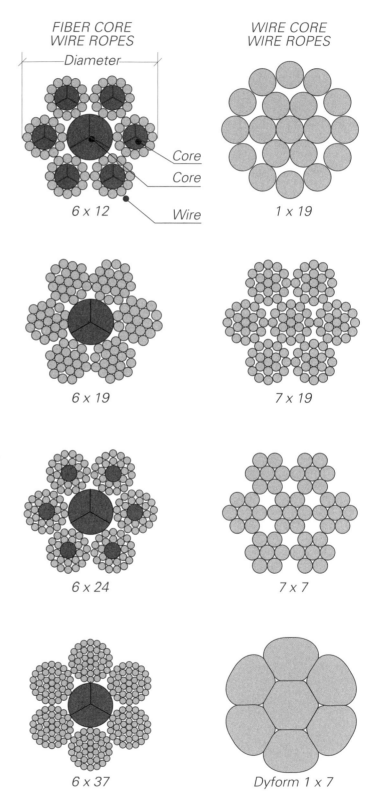

FIBER CORE WIRE ROPES

WIRE CORE WIRE ROPES

Diameter

Core

Core

Wire

6 x 12

1 x 19

6 x 19

7 x 19

6 x 24

7 x 7

6 x 37

Dyform 1 x 7

Swaged Fittings

A swaged fitting is a metal sleeve whose inside diameter closely matches the outside diameter of the wire rope to which it is swaged. Swaging consists of passing the fitting through a set of rollers that exert enough pressure to compress the shank of the fitting around the wire. Two advantages of swaged fittings are low parts cost and a diameter just larger than that of the wire. Disadvantages include the expense of swaging equipment, the inability to inspect for internal corrosion, and the impossibility of repair in the field using common tools.

ASSEMBLING SWAGED FITTINGS

STEP 1: Cut the cable to length, allowing for socket depth.

Swaged terminal   Cable

STEP 2: Insert the cable into a terminal specific to the cable.

STEPS 3–6: Choose and mount the proper dies for the terminal. Attach the terminal to the collet. Adjust the length of the pull arm to position the terminal shank at the end of the socket. Apply hydraulic pressure to pull the terminal through the rotating dies and compress the terminal shank.

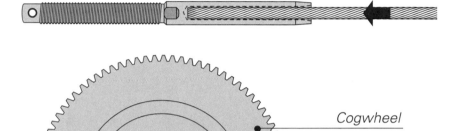

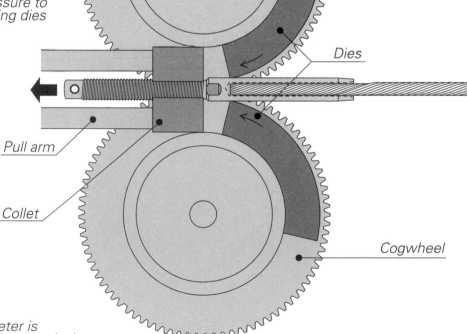

Cogwheel

Dies

Pull arm

Collet

Cogwheel

RESULT: The terminal shank diameter is reduced by approximately 20 percent, producing a strong and enduring grip on the cable.

Swageless Fittings

Swageless, or compression, fittings are relatively expensive and bulky, but require no special fabrication equipment. They are also simple to disassemble and reassemble in the field, although the wedge should be replaced each time.

The two principal brands of swageless fittings are Sta-Lok and Norseman. Both involve a hollow, split wedge inserted between the core and outer strands of a wire rope (see page 77). A threaded sleeve with a tapered opening is drawn down tight over the wedge and outer wires. The outer wires are compressed between wedge and sleeve, while the core wires are compressed by the inside of the wedge. The resulting connection is as strong as the wire itself. Some riggers fill the sleeve with a marine-grade sealant before drawing it up to seal against moisture.

The illustration opposite shows the step-by-step procedures for assembling Sta-Lok fittings.

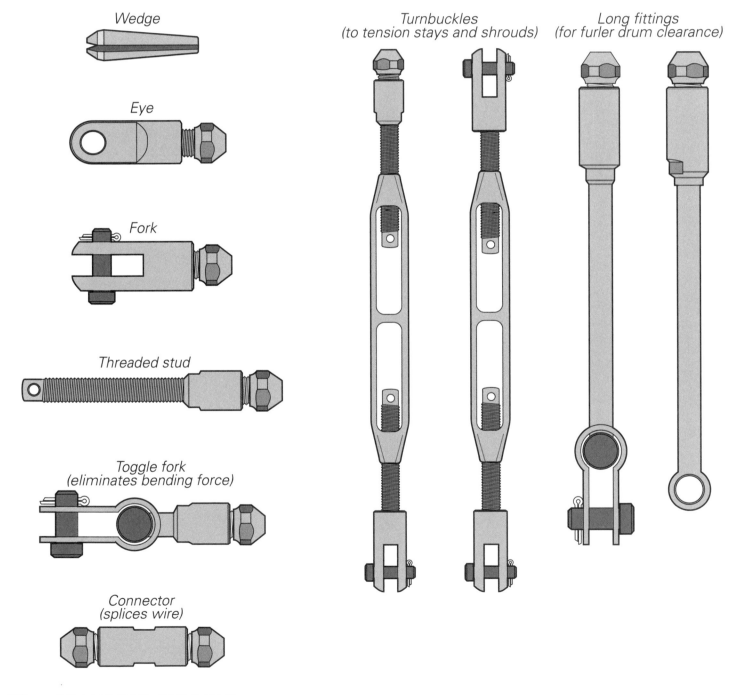

Wedge

Eye

Fork

Threaded stud

Toggle fork
(eliminates bending force)

Connector
(splices wire)

Turnbuckles
(to tension stays and shrouds)

Long fittings
(for furler drum clearance)

ASSEMBLING SWAGELESS FITTINGS

STEP 1: Cut wire rope.
TIP: If using a hacksaw, tape around the wire and saw through the tape to preserve the lay of the strands.

STEP 2: Slide the socket component over the wire.
TIP: Wind PVC tape around the wire about 12 inches from the end.

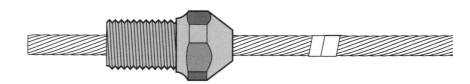

STEP 3: Unlay the outer strands 2 to 3 inches to expose the central core.
TIP: Use a penknife to prise the initial strands out of position.

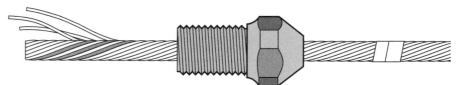

STEP 4: Slide the wedge component over the central core of the wire rope.

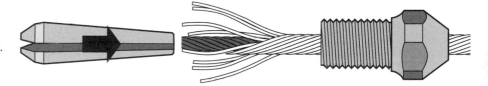

STEP5: Re-lay the outer strands in the original direction of twist around the wedge component. Ensure that approximately $\frac{1}{8}$ inch of the central core protrudes from the end of the wedge. The outer strands should be evenly situated around the wedge. Care should be taken that a strand does not slip into the slit of the wedge.

TIP: Push the socket toward the end of the wire while repositioning the outer strands. When the wire strands are in position, push the socket firmly to hold the wires in position.

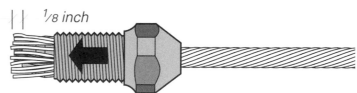

1/8 inch

STEP 6: Ensure the former component sits in the bottom of the end fitting. Screw the socket assembly and tighten with wrenches. The assembly is now complete.

Turn end fitting   Clamp socket assembly

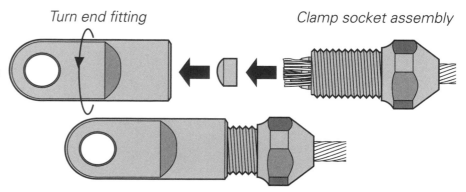

Rigging Terminology

Masthead Rig

While there exist unstayed rigs (rigs where the mast is strong enough to be supported only at the keel and deck), the majority of production sailboats today employ the stayed Bermuda rig, where the luff of a triangular mainsail slides up and down the mast in or on a continuous groove or track. Two subgroups of the Bermuda rig are the masthead rig (below) and the fractional rig (facing page).

In both rigs the mast is stabilized athwartships by shrouds. *Cap shrouds* run from the masthead all the way to the deck. Horizontal *spreaders* stiffen the mast by introducing larger angles between mast and shroud. Most often forward and aft *lower shrouds* prevent athwartship bending of the mast and a degree of fore-and-aft stability as well. A few modern

rigs, however, have only single lowers. Rigs with more than a single pair of spreaders employ *intermediate shrouds*.

Fore and aft the mast is stabilized by a *backstay* and a *forestay*, both running from masthead to the deck. A *baby stay* (sometimes missing or removable) runs from the base of the spreaders to the foredeck.

Both the advantage and the disadvantage of the masthead rig lie in its symmetry of support. With both its base and head supported in all four directions, the masthead rig is less likely than the fractional rig to collapse. However, the ability to bend a mast fore and aft is an advantage in shaping the mainsail, accounting for the popularity of the fractional rig among racers.

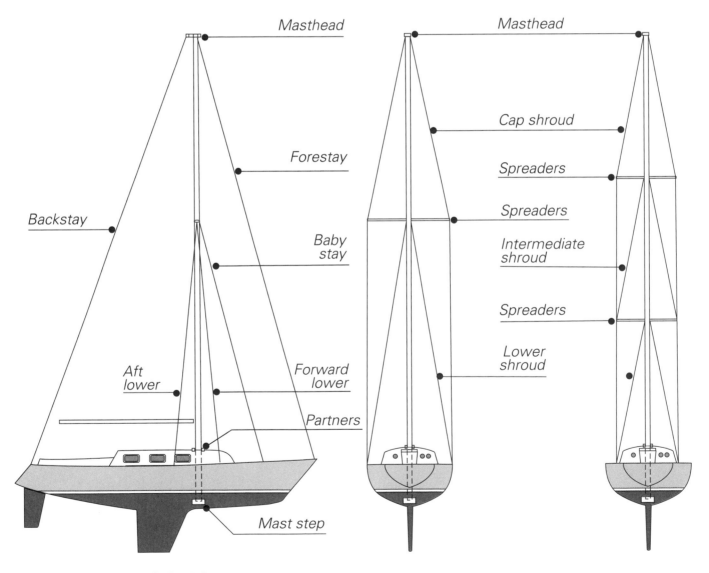

Masthead

Forestay

Backstay

Baby stay

Aft lower

Forward lower

Partners

Mast step

Masthead

Cap shroud

Spreaders

Spreaders

Intermediate shroud

Spreaders

Lower shroud

Fractional Rig

In the fractional rig, the arrangement of athwartship shrouds is essentially identical to that of the mast-head rig.

The fore and aft stay arrangement differs, however. Here the forestay is attached to a point between two thirds and seven eighths of the way up the mast, and there is less commonly a baby stay. The backstay still runs to the top of the mast, but the point of attachment of the forestay is stabilized by *running backstays*, both port and starboard. The windward one is tensioned by means of its tackle, while the leeward one is slacked off and moved closer to the mainsail. Cruising sailboats with heavy masts sometimes dispense with running backstays, but lightweight racing masts require them to prevent mast pumping or, worse, failure.

If the mast is stepped on deck, it fits into a *mast step* fixed to the deck. When the mast is stepped on the keel, its base fits into a mast step fixed to the keel, and the mast is stabilized at deck level by wedges or chocking driven between the mast and the deck-level mast *partners*.

The advantage of the fractional rig is that its mast—particularly the upper portion—is easily bent in the fore-and-aft direction by adjusting forestay and backstay tensions. The rig is often set up with a degree of prebend, then the amount of bend under sail is controlled by adjusting the backstay tension. Racers change the bend of the mast to control the shape of the mainsail.

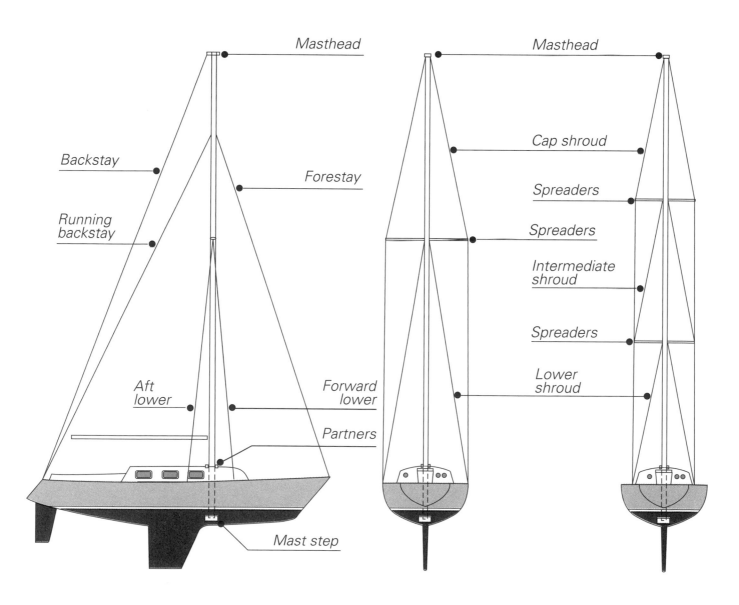

Rig Tuning

A rig will usually be pretuned at the dock by the crew stepping the mast. The intent of the preliminary adjustment is to make sure the mast is vertical athwartships and straight. Final tuning, particularly by racers, is often performed under sail with enough wind to heel the boat 15 to 20 degrees.

Note that rig tension involves a compromise between perfect rigidity and the structural limitations of the hull. Before performing final tuning, consult the boat's builder or designer or a professional rigger. *A word of warning:* prop shaft alignment should be checked after tensioning of the backstay, as the shape of the hull may be affected.

Stays: The fore-and-aft tilt of the mast (the *rake*) is controlled primarily by the length of the forestay. Starting with a fairly loose backstay, a crew member watches the sag of the forestay as the backstay is tightened. The backstay is deemed tight enough when further tightening ceases to produce a significant effect (some sag is inevitable).

Shrouds: While at the dock with no sails, release all tension on the lower shrouds. With the cap shrouds only hand tight, use the main halyard to compare distances from masthead to rail on both sides. Adjust the cap shrouds until the distances are equal (the mast is vertical). Then tighten the cap

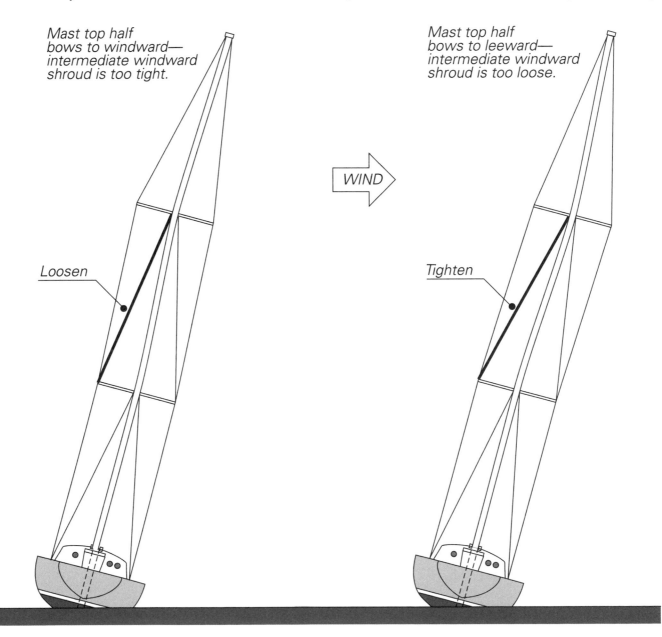

Mast top half bows to windward— intermediate windward shroud is too tight.

Loosen

WIND

Mast top half bows to leeward— intermediate windward shroud is too loose.

Tighten

shrouds with equal turns on port and starboard turnbuckles until intuitively tight. Hand-tighten all intermediate and lower shrouds to remove slack. If there is any athwartship bend in the mast, remove it at the dock by adjusting intermediates and lowers, as shown in the underway illustrations below.

Final Tuning: Final tuning may be performed underway in smooth waters with the boat heeling 15 to 20 degrees. First tighten port and starboard cap shrouds, using equal turns, until any slack in the leeward cap shroud disappears. Repeat on the opposite tack.

The illustrations on pages 80–82 describe how to eliminate athwartship mast bend by adjusting the appropriate shrouds. Note that each adjustment is accompanied by an equal and opposite adjustment of the opposing shroud.

Due to their light construction, it is a good idea to reduce the backstay tension on racing hulls when not under way. Otherwise, the hull may creep. While this will have little effect on sailing performance, it may throw the shaft out of alignment and cause wear on the transmission and Cutless bearing.

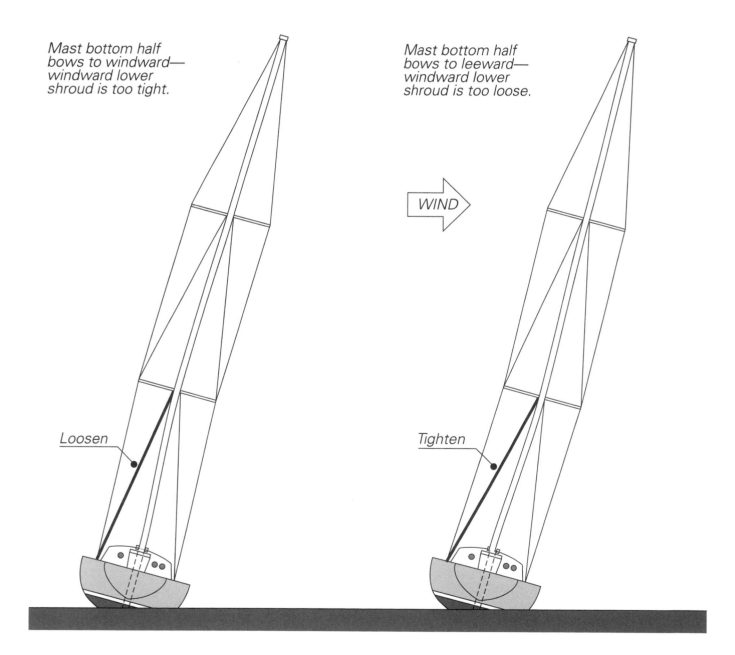

Mast bottom half bows to windward—windward lower shroud is too tight.

Loosen

WIND

Mast bottom half bows to leeward—windward lower shroud is too loose.

Tighten

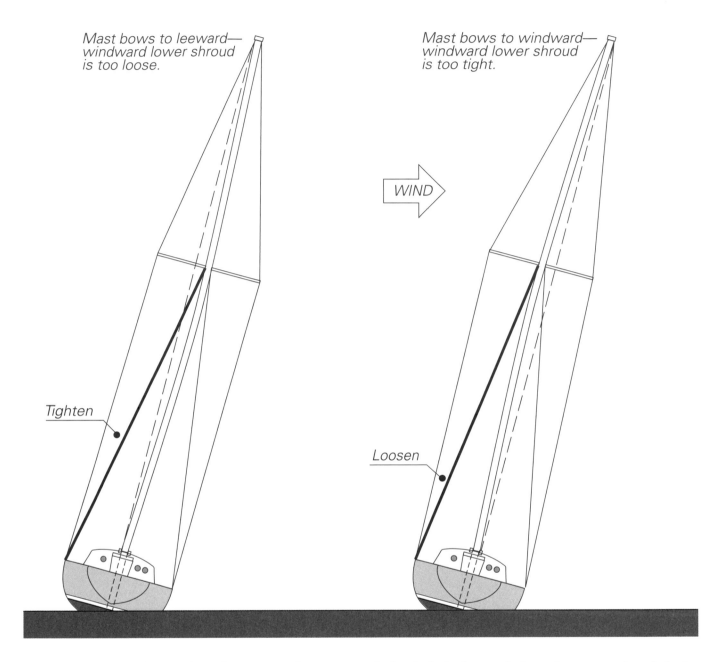

Mast bows to leeward—
windward lower shroud
is too loose.

Mast bows to windward—
windward lower shroud
is too tight.

WIND

Tighten

Loosen

Do not try to tighten a shroud or stay under great tension—damage to turnbuckle threads could result. In practice this means that when a shroud must be tensioned underway, you should change tacks to put it to leeward first. If you must tension the headstay underway, head off the wind first. Bear in mind that a little slack in leeward shrouds is normal and desirable. Finally, when correcting a bowed mast, remember that each tightening probably needs a corresponding loosening on the opposite side to avoid excessive tension buildup.

4

Line Handling

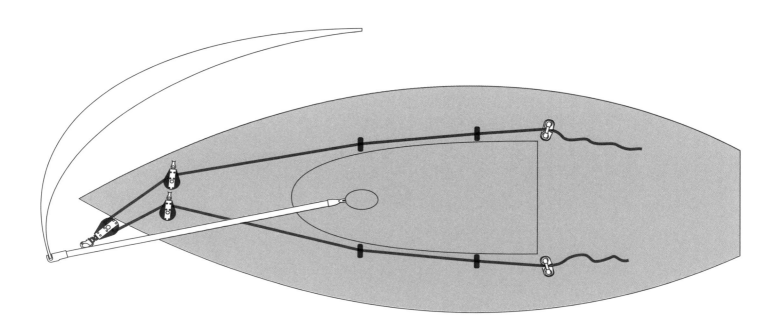

Rope

The term *rope* applies to a great number of twisted and braided products, each made from a wide variety of materials. The method of fabrication determines texture and flexibility, while the basic material controls strength and stretch.

The three most common materials are nylon, polyester (Dacron), and polypropylene. Each has a distinctive useful property:

- Nylon stretches up to 20 percent without damage.
- Dacron stretches very little.
- Polypropylene floats.

Three basic fabrications are:

Twisted: Long individual fibers are twisted into yarn, yarns into strands, and strands into rope. For hawsers in docking ships, ropes are further twisted into cable. Conventionally, the first twist (fibers into yarn) is counterclockwise, resulting in a "right-handed yarn." The direction of the twist reverses with each step, so a rope with right-handed yarn is also a right-handed rope. Twisted rope is also commonly referred to as "three-strand."

Single-braid: Fibers are twisted into yarn and yarns into strands, but pairs of strands are then woven or braided into the rope. The resulting rope doesn't have an unbalanced twist, so it has no tendency to twist under load or when coiled. The rope is hollow, however, so it tends to flatten under tension.

Double-braid: A core of single-braid rope is sheathed in a second single-braid. The combination is stronger, has less stretch, and allows combining of materials for different properties.

Once cut, all ropes tend to fray. Ropes made of synthetic (plastic) materials are often cut with a heated knife, which fuses the cut fibers in a solid mass and prevents fraying. The classic—and more long-lasting—method of finishing the end of a rope is whipping, shown at right.

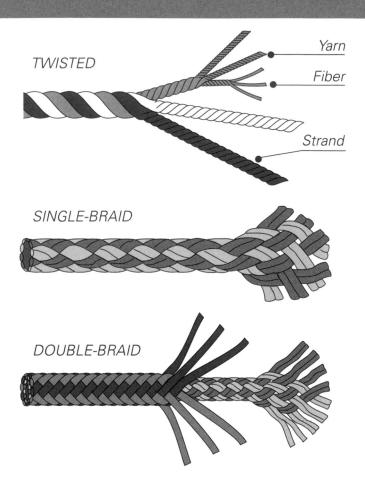

TWISTED

Yarn

Fiber

Strand

SINGLE-BRAID

DOUBLE-BRAID

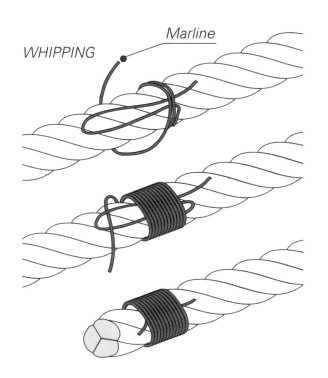

WHIPPING

Marline

Splices

Long Splice

The long splice is used for permanently joining two twisted ropes of the same diameter. The advantage of the long splice is that it retains the original diameter of the rope, allowing it to run freely through blocks and fairleads. The only drawback is a reduction in strength of 10 to 15 percent.

To keep the strands from unlaying on their own, tie an overhand knot in two strands (light blue in illustration) and immediately seize the knot. Then unlay one strand at a time and carefully replace it with a single strand from the other rope. All strands must be uniformly tensioned so that each carries the same load. The standard number of tucks is three, but many riggers feel the slipperiness of nylon requires more.

For maximum strength run full-size strands out to the last tuck. If you wish to make the splice less apparent, after the first full tuck, remove half of the yarn of each strand with each succeeding tuck. After completing all of the tucks, place the splice on a clean, smooth surface and roll it underfoot to settle the strands into place and smooth the splice.

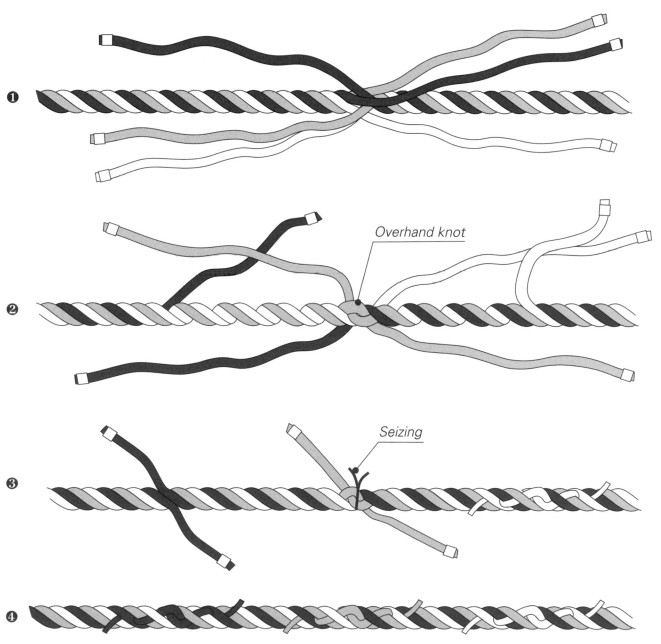

❶

❷ *Overhand knot*

❸ *Seizing*

❹

Short Splice

The short splice is also used for permanently joining two twisted ropes of the same diameter. While it may not appear so, the short splice is as strong as uncut rope. Its only drawback is a 40 percent increase in diameter, which may prevent its running freely through blocks.

It is important to tape or otherwise bind (plastic wire ties work well) each rope before the first tuck. Otherwise the strands will continue to unwind as you tuck, resulting in a very loose splice.

As with the long splice, three tucks are the old standard, but conservative riggers employ more when working with nylon, which is quite slippery.

Perform all of the tucks in one direction before any of the tucks in the opposite direction. This allows you to bind half the strands to prevent them from unlaying as you work.

At the cost of a slight decrease in strength, the splice can be made more finished by removing half the yarns from each strand before the final tucks.

After finishing all of the tucks, roll the splice underfoot to settle the strands and produce a more finished look.

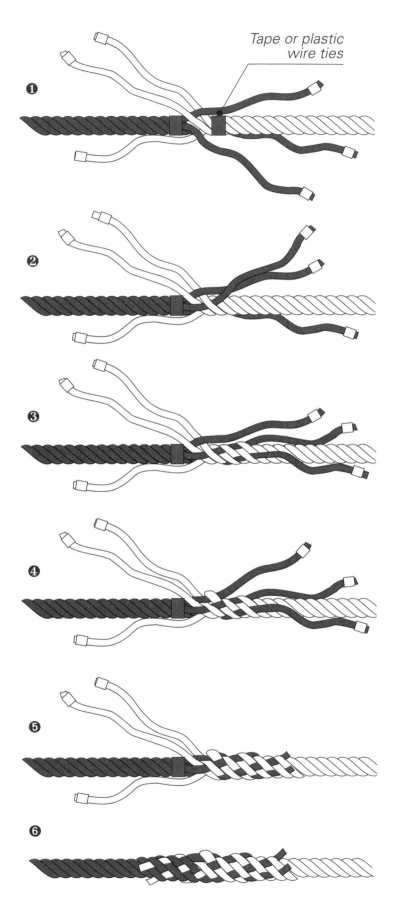

Tape or plastic wire ties

End Splice

The end, or back, splice is similar to a short splice turned back on itself. The key to success is the first set of tucks, which form a crown knot. If you don't get it right, the end will become loose. After forming the crown, take three tucks with each strand.

Of course a rope end may also be whipped (page 84), but the backsplice is even more nautical and gives the end of the line increased heft, which makes it easier to handle.

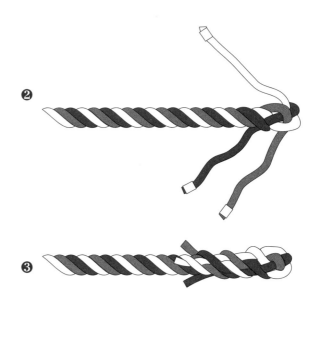

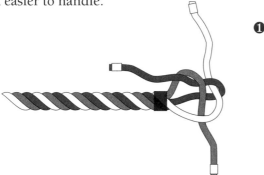

Eye Splice

The eye splice is the most useful and common of the splices because it replaces many knots. While most knots reduce the rope's strength by half, the three-strand eye splice retains about 90 percent of its strength.

Some splicers find it useful to seize (bind with marline) the rope at the point of unlaying. Otherwise there is a tendency to pull on the strands when tucking, causing the rope to unlay beyond the desired point. The seizing is removed after completion of the splice.

After taking the three initial tucks, simply tuck each strand straight down the standing part, over and under, three to six times.

For a more finished appearance, remove half of each strand before taking the final tucks.

When the eye is formed around a thimble it is also common to whip the splice just beyond the thimble in order to tighten the eye and prevent the thimble from falling out.

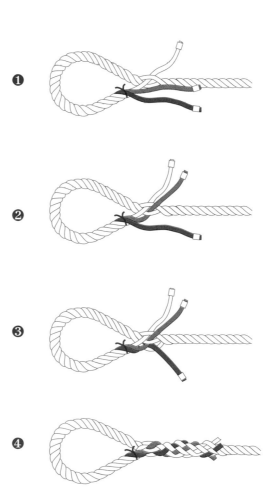

Wire Rope Eyes

Wire rope is extremely difficult to splice, so eyes are usually formed by other means. Swaging offers a tidy solution (see page 75), but it requires expensive specialized equipment to achieve the required pressure on the swage sleeve.

Crimping requires much less expensive crimping sleeves and tools. One version of a crimping tool resembles a large bolt cutter with dull, formed blades; the other a die that is squeezed by tightening bolts. A soft metal sleeve of the correct size is slipped onto the wire rope. The end of the rope is then turned back on itself (with or without the thimble) and inserted into the sleeve. The sleeve is then crimped at several places along its length.

The portability of crimping tools recommends their use as much as their low cost.

A temporary eye can easily be formed by substituting wire rope clamps for the soft metal crimp sleeve.

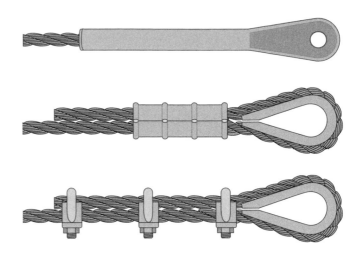

The eye is as strong as any other. It is considered temporary only because of its unfinished appearance. The exposed threaded ends of the U-bolts also tend to snag lines and clothing.

Eye Splice in Double-Braid

Double-braid rope is considerably more difficult to splice than three-strand rope. The prevalence of double-braid, however, makes mastery of at least the eye splice worthwhile.

Aside from the usual sharp knife, the only special tool required for this splice is a tubular fid, sized for the diameter of the rope. Splicing kits are available containing tubular fids for various sizes of rope, as well as splicing directions for different braids.

STEP 1: Tie a tight slip knot about eight fid lengths (FL) from the end of the rope. Using a felt-tip marker, mark Point A one FL from the end. Form the desired eye, and mark Point B next to Point A.

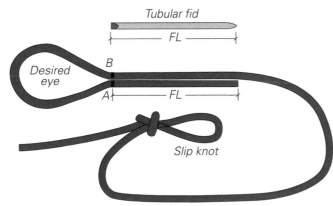

STEP 2: Carefully pry open the sheath at Point B and extract the core from the free end of the sheath. Mark Point C on the core where it exits.

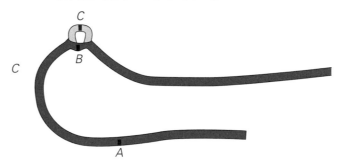

STEP 3: Pull the sheath back toward the knot and mark on the core Point D (1 FL from C) and Point E ($2/3$ FL from D).

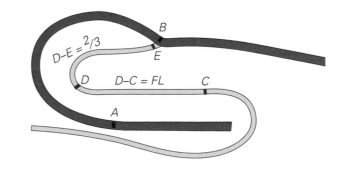

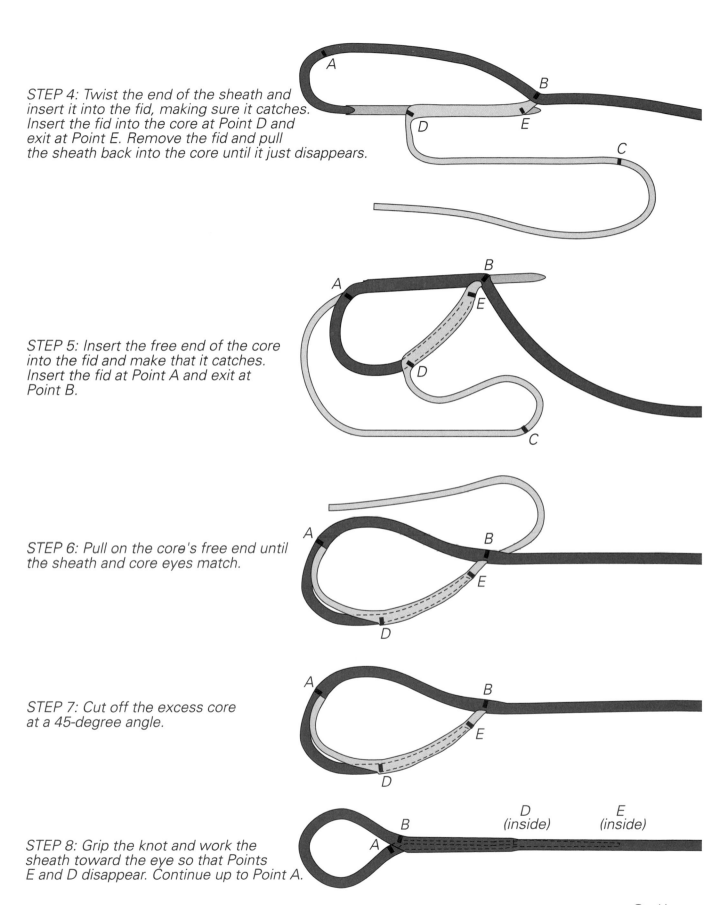

STEP 4: Twist the end of the sheath and insert it into the fid, making sure it catches. Insert the fid into the core at Point D and exit at Point E. Remove the fid and pull the sheath back into the core until it just disappears.

STEP 5: Insert the free end of the core into the fid and make that it catches. Insert the fid at Point A and exit at Point B.

STEP 6: Pull on the core's free end until the sheath and core eyes match.

STEP 7: Cut off the excess core at a 45-degree angle.

STEP 8: Grip the knot and work the sheath toward the eye so that Points E and D disappear. Continue up to Point A.

Coiling and Cleating

THE SEA GASKET COIL

THE HALYARD COIL

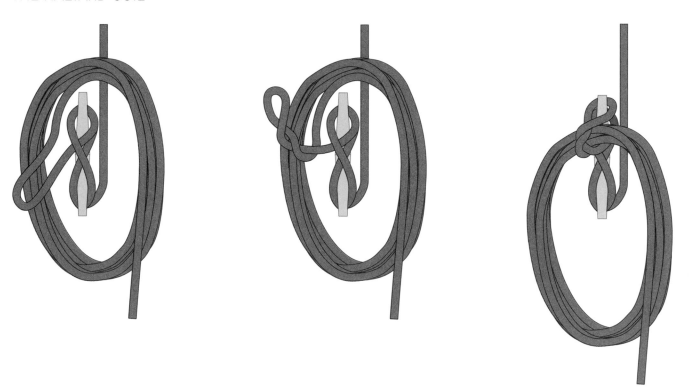

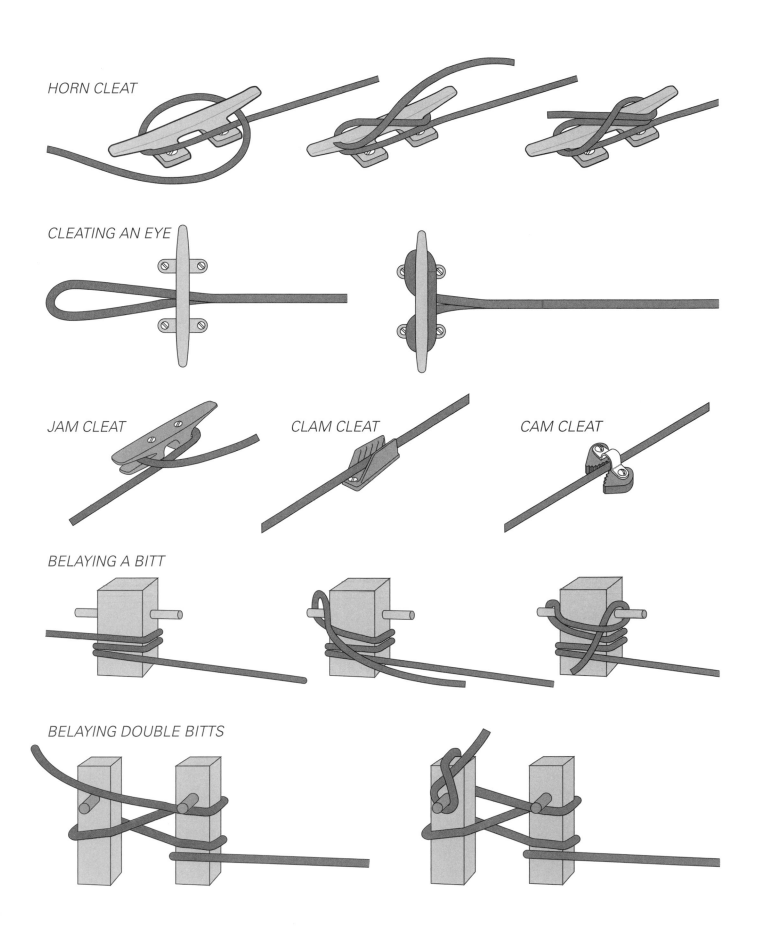

HORN CLEAT

CLEATING AN EYE

JAM CLEAT

CLAM CLEAT

CAM CLEAT

BELAYING A BITT

BELAYING DOUBLE BITTS

Knots

Reef (Square) Knot

The reef knot derives its name from being used to tie reefs in sails. Contrary to its reputation, it is not a great all-around knot. It can be used only when both ropes are identical in size and the knot won't be subject to great strain.

Its popularity is probably due to the fact that it is easy to learn. Holding a bitter end in each hand, it is: "Left over right; right over left." When finished, the knot has a symmetric appearance, thus its other common name, the square knot.

The reef knot jams under tension and can be virtually impossible to untie. To avoid this dilemma, tie the slipped reef knot, shown at right. A tug on the end of the loop quickly releases the knot.

If the slipped reef knot seems strangely familiar, it is because the knot we commonly use to tie our shoelaces is a double-slipped reef knot.

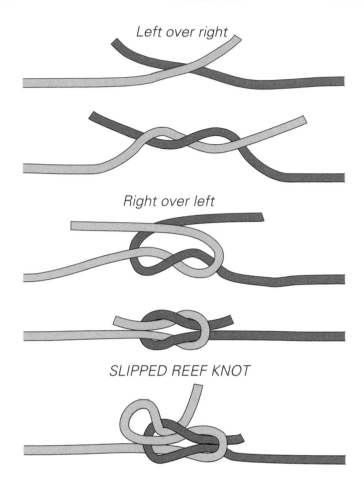

Left over right

Right over left

SLIPPED REEF KNOT

Sheet Bend

The sheet bend probably derives its name from its use in attaching (bending on) a sheet to the clew of a sail. The knot's principal use today, however, is in joining two ropes of differing size—attaching a large dockline to a dinghy painter for towing the dinghy, for example.

The knot can also be used to join ropes of the same size. In fact, it is superior to the reef knot for this purpose.

The security of the sheet bend depends on tension. The greater the tension, the tighter the knot. Once the tension is released, however, it loosens and is easy to untie. For greater security in towing and ease in untying, use two bowlines.

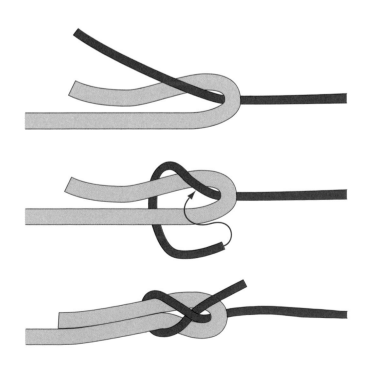

Bowline

Used to tie up the bow of a boat, the bowline (*bow* pronounced as in to tie a *bow*) is the most useful of all sailor's knots. It is fairly simple to tie ("The rabbit runs out of the hole, around the tree, and down the hole again"), yet it will not slip, jam, or untie itself. If you learn only one knot, this is the one to know.

Although it involves more knot tying, the most secure way to attach ropes of differing size is to tie a bowline in the end of each rope, with the loop of one passing through the loop of the second. Unlike the sheet bend, the bowline will never come loose, no matter how much or how little tension is applied.

This security feature is the reason the bowline is used to tie up boats left unattended for long periods.

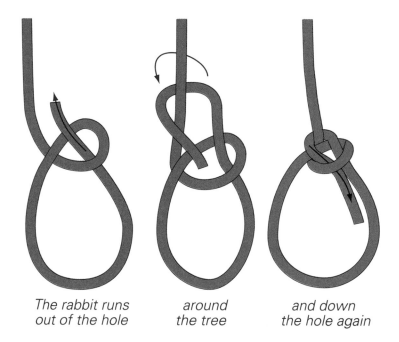

The rabbit runs out of the hole   *around the tree*   *and down the hole again*

Bowline on a Bight

The bowline on a bight produces two equal-size loops in the end of a doubled rope. Its first use is as a bowline with doubled strength. The second use is in rescue operations. A conscious victim can place a leg through each of the loops and hold onto the standing part while being hoisted. In the case of an unconscious victim, both legs go through one loop and both arms (up to the armpits) through the second loop.

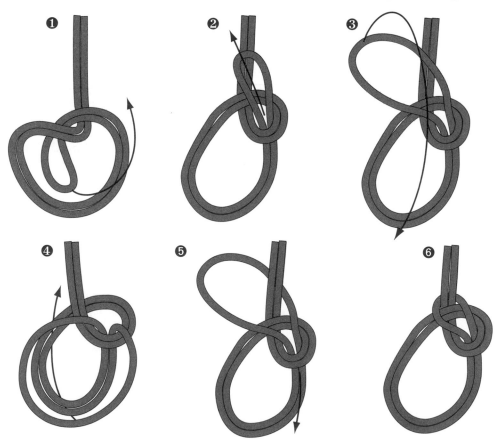

Clove Hitch

The clove hitch is a simple, temporary knot used for securing a line to a pole, either vertical or horizontal. The integrity of the knot depends entirely upon friction between the rope and the surface of the pole, so the pole must not be too smooth or greasy.

The simplest way to remember the knot is by its finished appearance: the lines entering and exiting the knot run parallel and opposite in direction.

When the end of the pole is open and within reach—a wharf pile, for example—the clove hitch is quickly tied by taking two loops, separating them, and slipping one behind the other. The two loops are then slipped over the pile and tightened.

Two Half Hitches

A hitch is generally any knot used to attach a rope to an object. Why two half hitches isn't called a full hitch is a mystery.

Half hitches (single loops taken around the standing part) are either temporary knots, such as one would use for tying a boat up at a fuel dock, or for finishing off another knot for added security.

The knot shown is actually two half hitches with a round turn. I show it because the marginal effort of the added turn is exceeded by the added security.

Don't be quick to laugh at novice sailors who are wont to pile half hitch upon half hitch. Although it is far better to tie a bowline, each half hitch does increase the security of the knot.

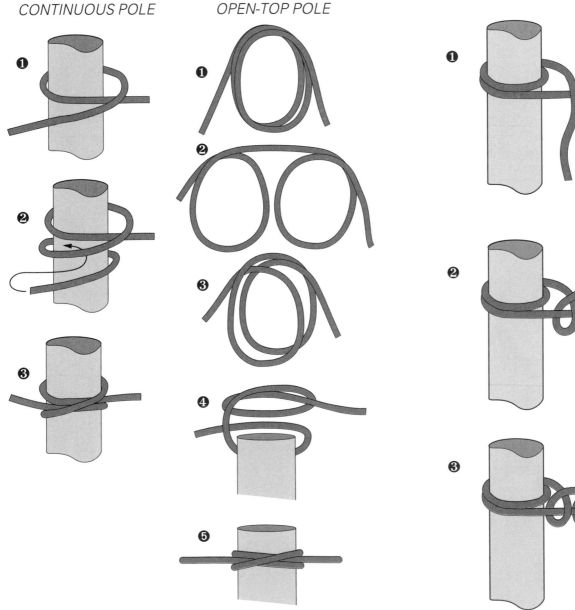

CONTINUOUS POLE   *OPEN-TOP POLE*

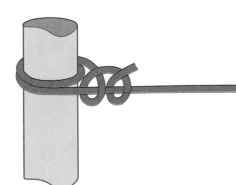

Tautline Hitch

The tautline hitch is a camper's favorite, being the knot that allows tightening of the guylines of a tent. It is not generally recognized as a boater's knot, but when adjusting an awning tied off to stays and shrouds, you will be glad to have it.

Here's how the knot works. With no tension in the turns, there is little friction between the turns and the standing part, so the turns may be slid along the rope to adjust the size of the loop. As soon as the loop is tightened, however, the tension on the middle turn makes it try to climb, or roll, over the inner turn. This results in enough friction between the inner turn and the standing part to prevent slippage.

If you cannot remember the tautline hitch, three half hitches makes a fair temporary substitute.

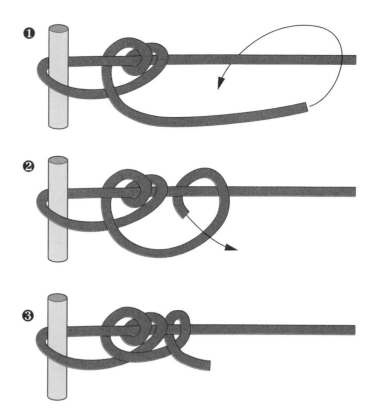

Rolling Hitch

The rolling hitch is used to bend a line to a round object, such as a spar, or to a larger-diameter line under tension (a taut line). With the standing part held at right angles to the taut line or spar, the hitch can be slid easily. As soon as tension is applied in the direction of the taut line, however, the hitch holds fast.

It is this property of holding only when under tension that makes the rolling hitch useful in holding an anchor rode while moving the rode from a windlass to a cleat. Though not a true stopper knot, when used to hold onto (stop) the anchor rode, the rolling hitch is sometimes incorrectly referred to as a stopper knot.

Caution is advised when using the rolling hitch. Its gripping power is quite dependent on the slipperiness of the line material (nylon is very slippery), the surface being gripped, and whether the line is wet.

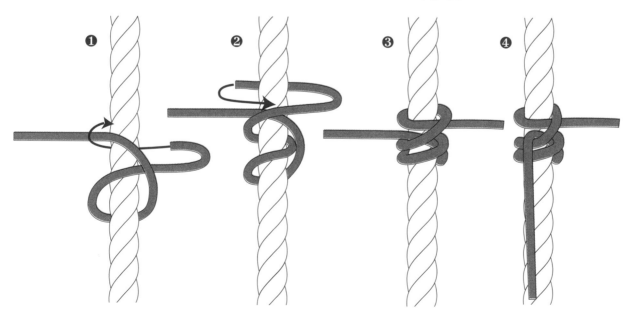

Trucker's Hitch

As its name implies, the trucker's hitch is used to bind loads tightly to a truck. Think of it as a pulley without a sheave. It can be used anywhere you need to tension a rope. A perfect use would be lash down loose cargo.

The beauty of the knot is that you can achieve a tension, ignoring friction, of twice the pull you exert on the free end of the line, yet the knot is always easy to untie.

To tie the knot, start with a bowline (page 93) in one line or end of a line, then follow the illustration to complete the knot in the other end of the line.

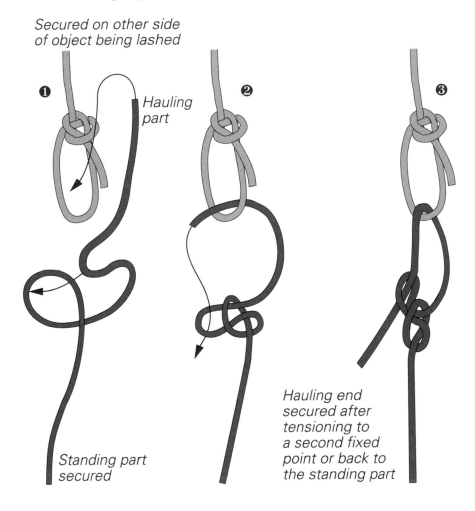

Becket Hitches

The single becket hitch (left illustration) is simply a sheet bend where the loop of the larger line is a fixed eye.

A second turn before tucking produces the double becket hitch (middle and right illustrations).

As with the sheet bend, becket hitches are most useful when the rope forming the eye is of larger diameter. Note, however, that the knot is not very secure. It should never be considered permanent.

Stopper Knot and Heaving Line Knot

The term *stopper* refers to several types of knots. The traditional term refers to a knot used to stop (hold fast) an anchor rode under tension while the rode is unwound from a windlass or capstan before being cleated. The rolling hitch (page 95) is an example of this type of stopper.

The second type of stopper—the type described here—is a knot tied in the end of a line to prevent its passing through a block or eye.

The heaving line knot can serve either as a stopper or to increase the weight of the end of a line being heaved. (Heaving lines are the light lines first thrown to the dock and used to haul the heavy hawsers ashore.)

The figure-eight knot is the stopper knot most commonly used on small boats for preventing the end of a sheet from escaping from its block.

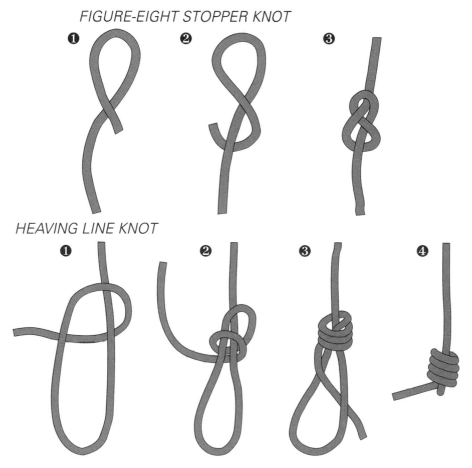

FIGURE-EIGHT STOPPER KNOT

❶ ❷ ❸

HEAVING LINE KNOT

❶ ❷ ❸ ❹

Anchor Bend

The anchor bend, also known as the fisherman's bend, is used for tying a line securely to a small-diameter object, such as the ring of an anchor. The knot is quite secure, as it would have to be to be used with an anchor.

As long as the line is flexible and of smaller diameter than the ring, the knot will cinch up tight and remain so, preventing chafe between the ring and the line. The multiple loops around the ring also help to prevent chafe. The bitter end can also be seized (see Step 3) for long-term use.

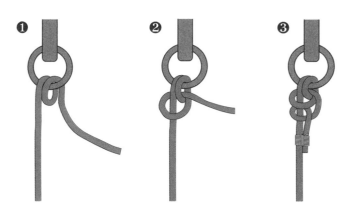

❶ ❷ ❸

Block and Tackle

Blocks consist of one or more sheaves turning inside a shell and serve two purposes aboard a boat:

1. Changing the direction of a line
2. Increasing the force applied to a line

Rules of thumb for sizing blocks to lines are:

- Traditional wood blocks with natural-fiber rope: Sheave diameter = 6 x rope diameter Block size (maximum dimension of shell) = 9 x rope diameter.
- Modern blocks with synthetic rope: Sheave diameter = 4 x rope diameter, minimum
- Blocks for wire rope: Sheave diameter = 20 x rope diameter, minimum

Shown are the three types of blocks:

Basic block, consisting of one or more sheaves within a close-fitting shell and points of attachment at one or both ends. The name of the block (single block, double block, etc.) is determined by the number of sheaves.

Snatch block, with one of the cheeks hinged, making it possible to open the block and snatch a line already fixed at both ends.

Turning block, any block used to turn a line, but usually one fixed in position, such as the double cheek block shown.

The fairlead, technically not a block because it has no sheave; used when the change in direction is slight.

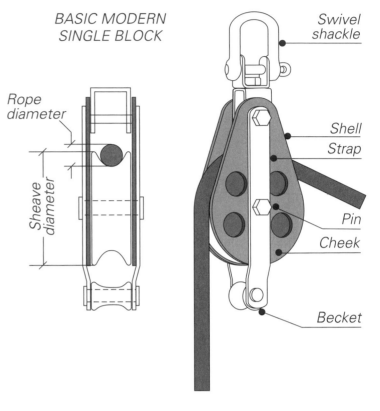

BASIC MODERN SINGLE BLOCK

Rope diameter

Sheave diameter

Swivel shackle

Shell

Strap

Pin

Cheek

Becket

FAIRLEAD

DOUBLE CHEEK BLOCK

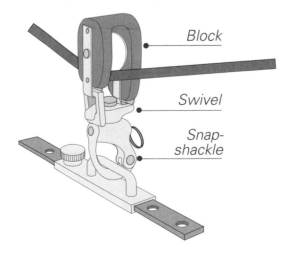

SNATCH BLOCK

Block

Swivel

Snap-shackle

Tackles consist of blocks and falls (ropes) and have the primary purpose of multiplying force in lifting or pulling.

Feeding rope around the sheaves is *reeving*. The *standing part* of a tackle is the block that doesn't move. The *hauling part* is the block that moves. Separating the blocks is *overhauling*, while pulling them together is *rounding in*. When pulled all the way together they are *two-blocked* or *chockablock*.

The names of the various tackles unfortunately derive from a mixture of logic and historical use. For interest they are shown in the illustration below, along with the nominal mechanical advantages achieved by each. More commonly, as in the illustrations of sail tackles on the following pages, they are referred to by their nominal (frictionless) mechanical advantages rather than their names.

Mechanical advantage is the ratio of force exerted by the moving block (the hauling part) to the pull on the end of the rope (the fall). The simplest way to calculate the nominal advantage is to count the number of lines supporting the weight. This is shown in the illustration below, with the advantage shown as the number on the weight. (If no weight is involved, just imagine the object being moved as a weight.) Mechanical advantage is expressed as a ratio, i.e., 4:1.

Note that two tackles having the same number of sheaves and lines may have different advantages. When the pull on the fall is in the direction of the lift, the tackle is *rove to advantage*. A fall pulling in the direction opposite the motion of the hauling part does nothing but change the direction of pull. The actual mechanical advantage of a tackle depends, in addition, on the friction of the sheaves and the stiffness of the rope. It is calculated as:

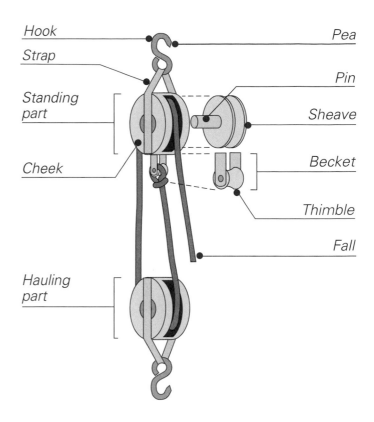

Hook — Pea
Strap — Pin
Standing part — Sheave
Cheek — Becket
Thimble
Fall
Hauling part

$$MA = \frac{\text{Nominal Advantage (NA)}}{(1 + [CF \times \text{Sheaves}])}$$

where CF is coefficient of friction, 0.00 to 1.00, and Sheaves is total number of sheaves.

For the classic wood and manila rope tackle, CF is usually assumed to be 0.10, while for a modern, ball-bearing block it is 0.02.

Example: for a wood luff tackle with manila rope,

MA = 4 ÷ (1 + [0.10 x 3])
   = 4 ÷ 1.30
   = 3.08

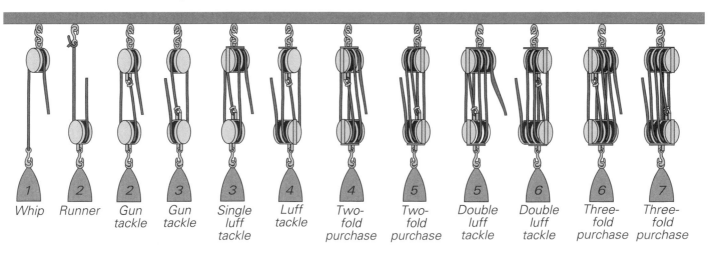

Whip	Runner	Gun tackle	Gun tackle	Single luff tackle	Luff tackle	Two-fold purchase	Two-fold purchase	Double luff tackle	Double luff tackle	Three-fold purchase	Three-fold purchase
1	2	2	3	3	4	4	5	5	6	6	7

Sail Control Systems

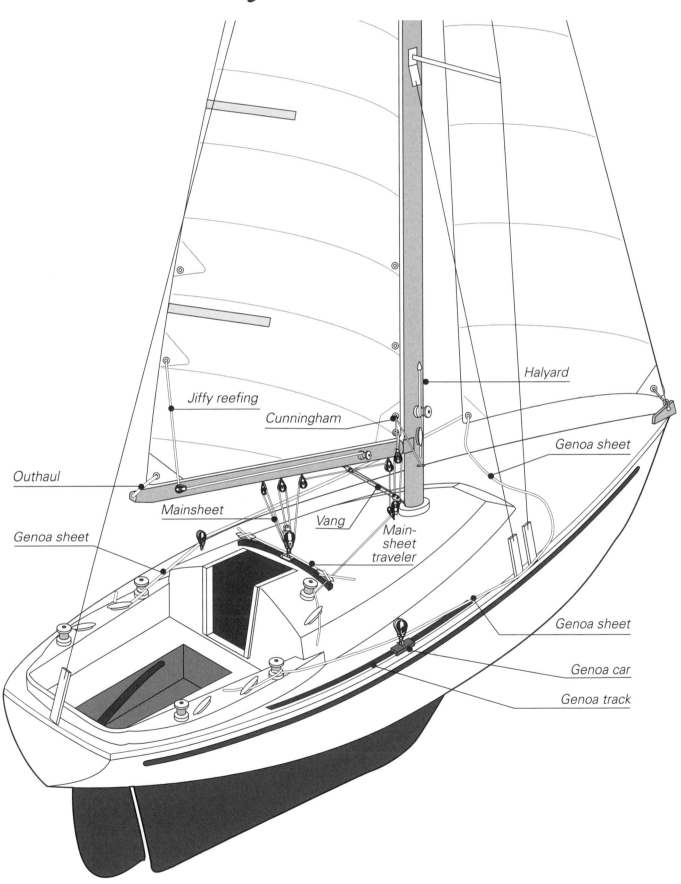

Halyard

Jiffy reefing

Cunningham

Genoa sheet

Outhaul

Genoa sheet

Mainsheet

Vang

Main-
sheet
traveler

Genoa sheet

Genoa sheet

Genoa car

Genoa track

Systems involving blocks and cleats of various sorts are used extensively for sail control. The principal systems are:

cunninghams
jibsheets
mainsheets
outhauls
jiffy reefing
spinnaker controls
travelers
boom vangs

Pages 101–13 contain numerous examples from each category, adapted with permission from literature published by Harken, a leading manufacturer of yacht hardware.

Where a mechanical advantage is shown (for example, 4:1 in the illustrations below) it is the nominal advantage, not accounting for friction. Friction in modern yachting blocks, however, is usually quite small, on the order of 5 percent per sheave.

Cunninghams

A cunningham is a tackle for pulling down on a cringle in the mainsail or genoa just above the tack. Pulling down on the cunningham stretches the sail just aft of the luff, pulling the draft (point of maximum belly) forward. It is more effective at mov-

ing the draft than tightening the halyard, because the halyard is fastened to the less giving luff bolt rope.

On a racing boat the cunningham is adjusted frequently, so the lead(s) need to be led to the crew station.

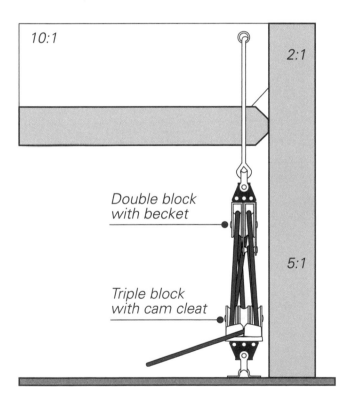

1. The most basic cunningham is a self-cleating tackle positioned at the mast base. Many cruisers like to use an S-hook to engage the cunningham in the grommet of the sail, but running a line through the grommet and down to an eyestrap on the opposite side of the mast doubles the purchase.

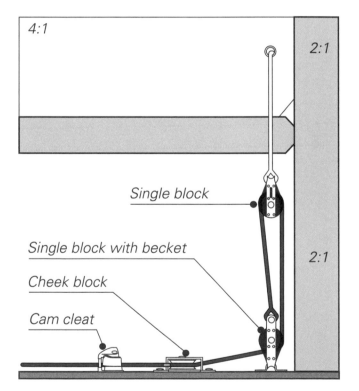

2. This simple system is led aft to the cockpit. The purchase can easily be increased to 6:1 by using a double block at the base of the mast and a single block with becket in place of the single block shown.

Self-Tacking Jibs and Staysails

Self-tacking jibs and staysails are popular on boats of all sizes because they simplify boat handling—tacking is nearly automatic, with no need to grind in a jibsheet.

The simple jibsheet, however, alters both the jib's angle of attack and its belly at the same time, i.e., you can't control the amount of belly (fullness) and angle of attack (angle relative to the boat's centerline) independently.

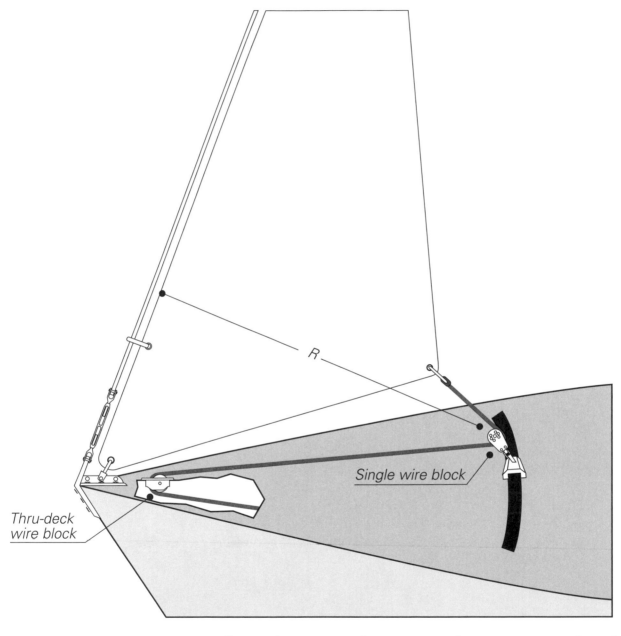

Single wire block

Thru-deck wire block

1. This simple system is occasionally used on course-racing keelboats. The traveler track is bent in a radius, R, equal to the perpendicular distance from the headstay to the sheeting point. The sheet is typically wire and passes through a wire block and forward to a thru-deck wire block mounted near the headstay. The thru-deck block must be very far forward to prevent sheet tensioning when the car moves along the track. A tackle may be placed under deck and led to cam cleats in the cockpit. Larger offshore boats use a variation that leads the sheet forward to a footblock near the headstay, then above deck aft to a winch.

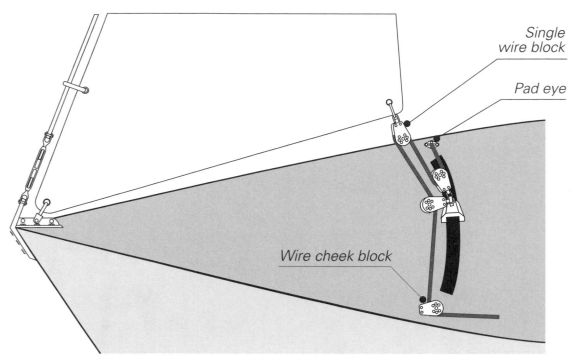

Single wire block

Pad eye

Wire cheek block

2. The above system is popular because it keeps the foredeck clear. The track is bent as in system 1 or is bent in a horizontal plane to follow the radius of the sail. The sheet starts on a pad eye or eyestrap and leads through wire blocks on the traveler car and clew and to a wire cheek block before heading aft to a winch.

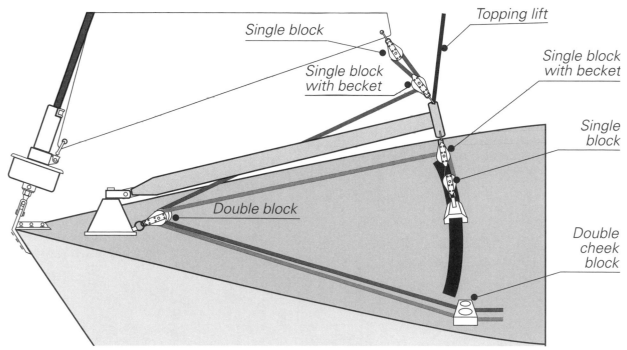

Single block

Single block with becket

Topping lift

Single block with becket

Single block

Double block

Double cheek block

3. Self-tacking jibs and staysails work well with furling systems and with jib booms. In this system there are two "sheets." One controls the movement of the sail in and out much like an outhaul. The other sheet controls the boom. Typically, each sheet is rigged using a block with becket on the boom and a single block on the clew and the car, respectively. A double block is mounted under the jib pedestal. The sheets lead aft through a double cheek block.

Mainsheets

Mainsheets are simple hardware systems but are among the most important, as they are in almost constant use.

There is no one mainsheet for every boat. The best choice depends on the size of the boat, the configuration of the deck and cabinhouse, and the number and strength of the crew.

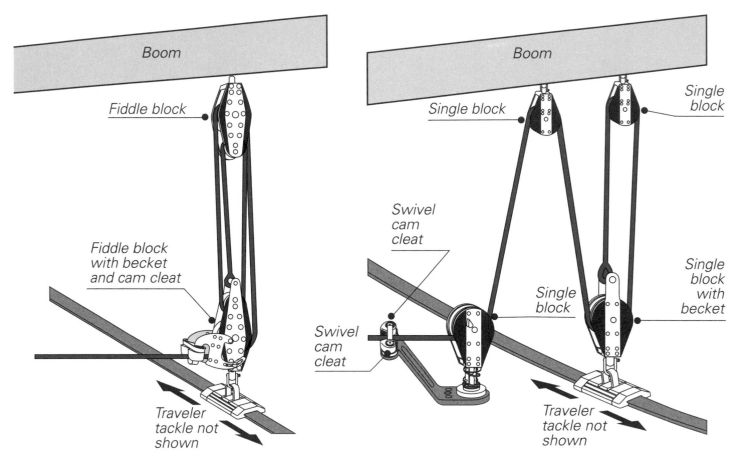

1. The most common mainsheet on boats under 28 feet (8.5 m) is a four-part tackle featuring ratchets and adjustable cam cleats.

2. Placing the mainsheet off the traveler car allows adjustment of the main without dragging the car to windward. It tends to tighten the leech, but this can be overcome by curving the track ends up.

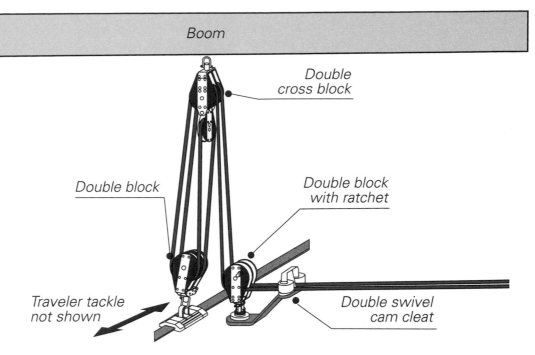

Boom

Double cross block

Double block

Double block with ratchet

Traveler tackle not shown

Double swivel cam cleat

3. This system features two mechanical advantages. Both lines lead back to the cockpit. Pulling on both lines allows rapid adjustment with a mechanical advantage of 3:1. Pulling on one with the other fixed in the cam cleat gives a mechanical advantage of 6:1 for fine-tuning.

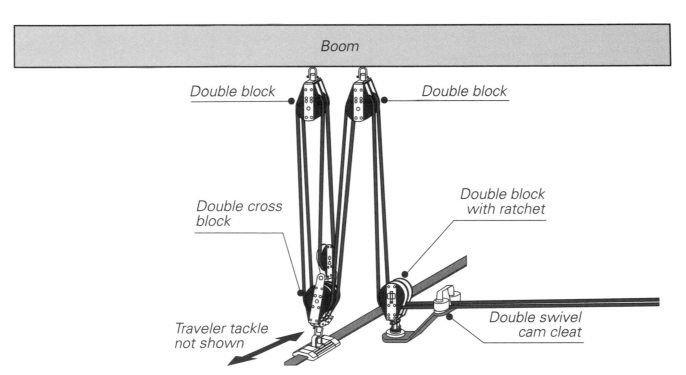

Boom

Double block

Double block

Double cross block

Double block with ratchet

Traveler tackle not shown

Double swivel cam cleat

4. This system operates in the same way as the system above, but adding another the double block on the boom increases the mechanical advantages to 4:1 and 8:1.

Outhauls

Adjustable outhauls are important in shaping the mainsail. A tight outhaul flattens the lower part of the main for upwind sailing. Loosening the outhaul increases the draft of the main, especially in the lower third, and is especially effective in light air or off the wind. Because outhauls must release freely when there is little load on the sail, use oversized blocks for very low friction.

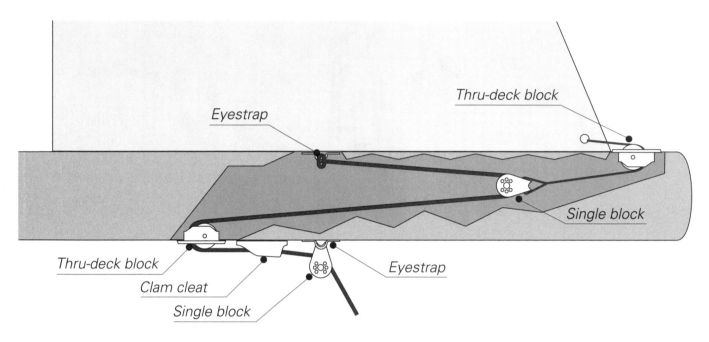

1. In the 4:1 outhaul shown here, a flexible wire rope shackles to the sail and enters the boom through a thru-deck wire block. Placing a single block aft of the clam cleat allows the crew to pull from a variety of positions in the boat.

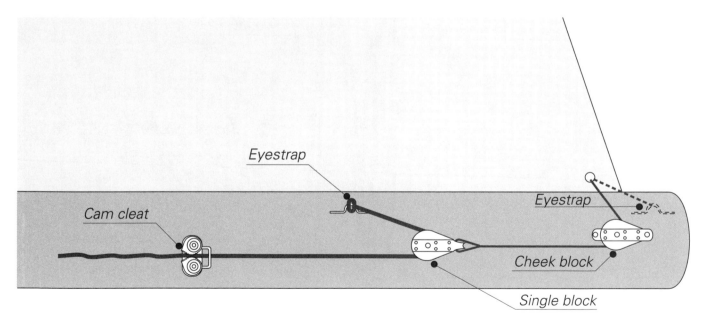

2. A simple, totally external outhaul system is formed by a cascade of two 2:1 tackles to produce a 4:1 advantage.

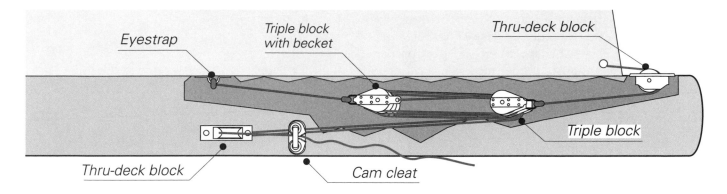

3. This 6:1 internal outhaul system is popular on small- to medium-sized offshore boats. The outhaul wire rope passes into the boom through a thru-deck wire block and is attached to one of a pair of triple blocks.

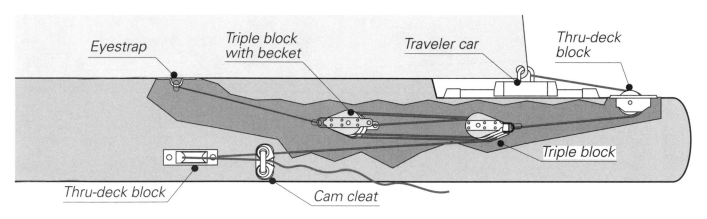

4. This variation of system 3 uses a traveler car to carry the clew of the mainsail. A short length of track is attached to the top of the boom and the clew is shackled to the car. Choose a car the same size as would be required for use on the main-sheet traveler.

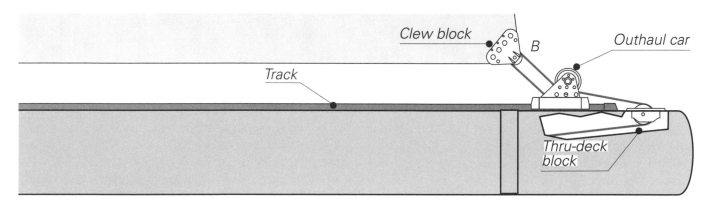

5. Mainsails that furl into the mast are loose-footed and usually have an outhaul car that rides the whole length of the boom. The outhaul starts at the car and leads through the clew block on the sail (B), back to the sheave on the car, and into the boom, where it or-dinarily leads to a winch.

Mainsail Jiffy Reefing

The reefing system for a mainsail must be designed to operate efficiently under adverse conditions and to provide proper sail shape when reefed. A proper reefing system is a must for both racers and cruisers.

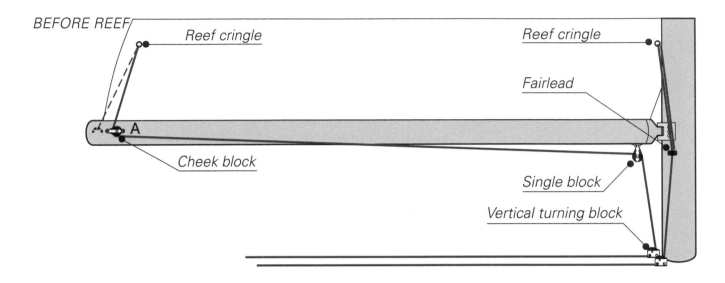

BEFORE REEF

Reef cringle

Reef cringle

Fairlead

Cheek block

Single block

Vertical turning block

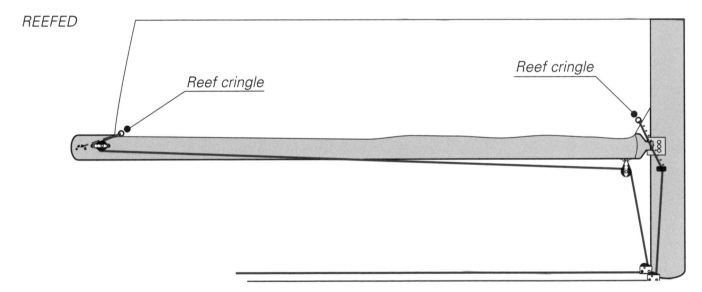

REEFED

Reef cringle

Reef cringle

1. A cheek block is mounted on one side of the boom (A) for the aft reef point. A line starts at an eyestrap or pad eye on the opposite side of the boom and passes up through the reef cringle, down to the cheek block, and forward, where it can lead to a cleat on the boom or be routed to the cockpit. If both reef lines are led to the cockpit, the forward line originates at an eyestrap or pad eye on one side of the mast, passes up and through the reef grommet, and leads down to a fairlead on the mast before being routed to the cockpit. Position of the blocks and eyestraps is important—they must be positioned to pull both down and out to keep the sail flat and to prevent lateral loads being placed on the luff rope or luff slides.

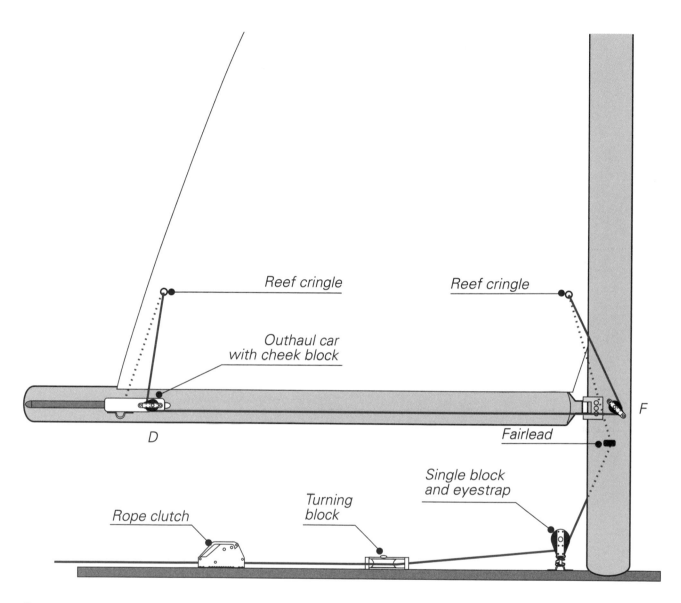

Reef cringle

Reef cringle

Outhaul car
with cheek block

D

F

Fairlead

Single block
and eyestrap

Rope clutch

Turning
block

2. Reefing systems are available as kits that depend on the size of the boat. With these systems, reefing is easy—just ease the halyard to a predetermined mark and pull the single reef line taut. The better kits in-clude blocks mounted on a track (D) for the aft reef point so that positioning is simple. The forward reef blocks (F) are positioned to keep the pull on the for-ward reef point both down and forward.

Spinnaker Controls

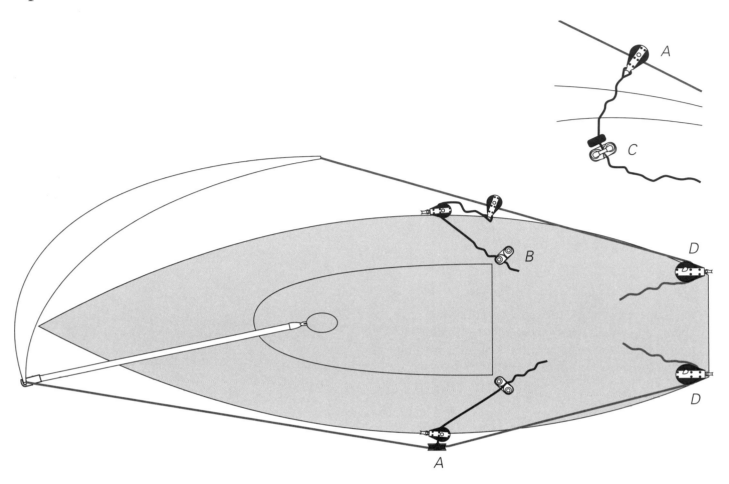

1. To fly a spinnaker, boats up to about 30 feet can use a simple arrangement with one pair of sheets. The windward sheet becomes the guy. During jibes the pole is disconnected from the mast and passed end-for-end through the foretriangle. Tweakers can be used to bring the guy to the deck near the point of maximum beam to increase control over the pole. A tweaker on the sheet can be used to adjust lead angle, allowing the lead position to be moved for-ward to choke down the spinnaker during heavy air runs. The tweaker consists of a block riding on the sheet (A) and a cleat that can be mounted at the cockpit (B) or at the rail (C). Ratchet blocks (D) allow the sheet to be handheld for good control without the need for a winch. Because sheet blocks also carry the load of the guy and because the force required to winch a pole off the headstay can be extremely high, the sheet blocks (D) must be large.

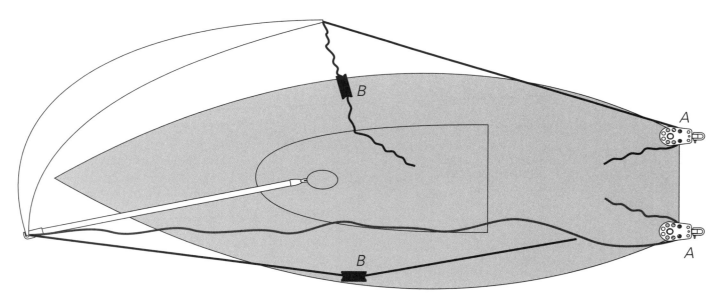

2. Offshore boats over 30 feet generally use separate sheets and guys. The sheets lead to turning blocks near the transom (A), while the guys lead to blocks at the point of maximum beam (B). While the windward guy is in use, the sheet on that side of the boat is "lazy." Jibing is accomplished by leaving the inboard end of the pole attached to the mast and dip- ping the outboard end through the foretriangle. An adjustable car on a track mounted on the mast raises the inboard end and facilitates dip-pole jibing, allowing more room for the pole to swing inside the headstay. Again, loads on the sheet blocks can be extreme, so the size must be carefully considered.

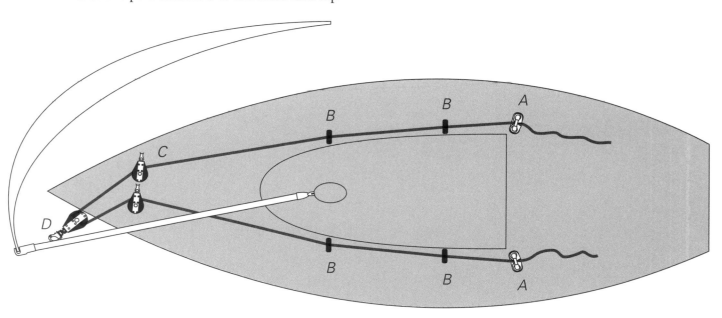

3. A double-ended foreguy facilitates adjustment from either side of the boat. A cam cleat (A) is mounted on each side of the cabinhouse. Fairleads (B) hold the foreguy near the cabinhouse. The foredeck blocks (C) should be two single blocks rather than a double block. The block on the pole (D) is a single block and is fitted with a snapshackle for easy removal from the pole.

Travelers

Traveler controls should be powerful enough to move the car easily under load and should lead to a position where the crew can operate them conveniently.

Smaller boats usually position the controls so the helmsman can make the adjustment. Larger boats position the controls for the mainsheet trimmer.

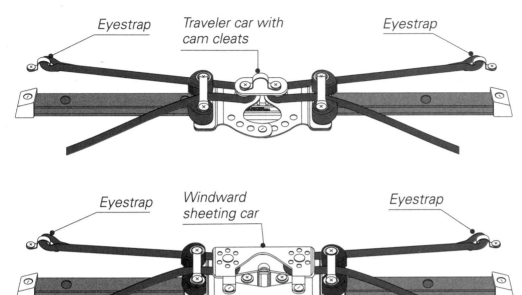

1. This simple system only requires bolting the track to the deck and providing an eyestrap for dead-ending the control lines. The cam cleats shown are on adjustable arms so they can be angled to best suit the layout of the boat.

2. This more sophisticated system similarly requires only bolting the track to the deck and providing an eyestrap for dead-ending the control lines. The difference is the slider mechanism that allows the car to be pulled to windward without releasing the leeward control line. When the boat is tacked, the car stays in place and can be pulled to the new windward side without releasing the leeward control line.

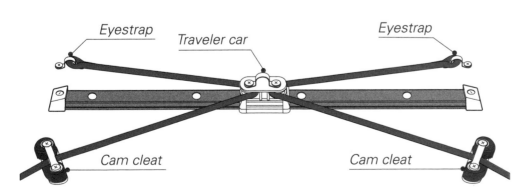

3. When the traveler is mounted ahead of a companionway, it is convenient to place the cam cleats at the after edge of the cabinhouse so the crew does not have to reach forward to move the traveler car. A swiveling cam cleat will allow the crew to control the car from various positions in the cockpit.

4. Popular on small, flush deck boats, where the crew sits outboard of the traveler, this system is easily operated from the rail. The cam cleats should be oriented to the anticipated position of the crew.

5. On boats where the crew sits on the coaming above the traveler, the control lines lead up the cockpit sides to a cam cleat; adjustment is an easy vertical pull. Mount the upright blocks to the cockpit sides.

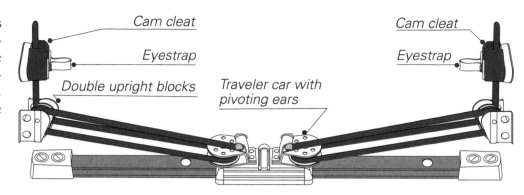

6. Larger boats generally require winches to adjust the traveler under load. Any of the previous traveler systems can be adapted to include winches. With the higher loads, rope clutches work better than cam cleats.

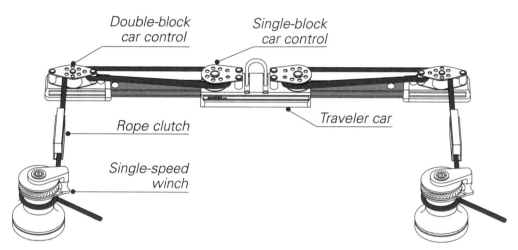

Boom Vangs

Boom vangs allow vertical adjustment of the boom. Tensioning the vang tightens the leech of the sail. Cruising sailors use the vang to keep the boom from rising downwind. Racing sailors use the vang primarily for shaping the mainsail.

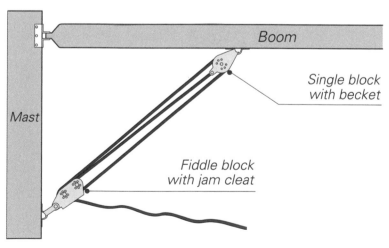

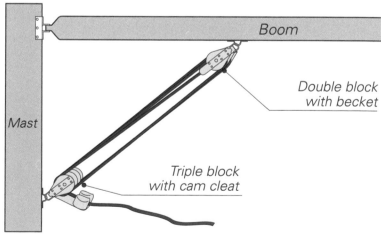

1. This simple self-cleating vang with a mechanical advantage of 3:1 is appropriate for sail areas up to 60 square feet.

2. The combination of double and triple blocks increases the mechanical advantage to 5:1, appropriate for sail areas up to 100 square feet.

Winches

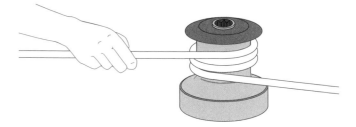

Two properties of a winch make it useful: increasing the pull on a line (mechanical advantage) and holding fast when the handle is released. Mechanical advantage derives from two factors:

1. The ratio of the length of the handle to the radius of the drum. If the length of the handle is 12 inches and the diameter of the drum is 4 inches, the drum radius is 2 inches and the advantage is $12 \div 2 = 6$.

2. In a geared winch, the ratio of teeth in the base of the drum to teeth in the driving ratchet gear. If the drum has twice as many teeth as the ratchet gear, the drum advances half as fast and the mechanical advantage is doubled.

Multispeed winches shift gear ratio and hold fast against reverse rotation through a system of ratchets and pawls.

When the handle turns the spindle in the high-speed (clockwise) direction, the pawls in the top of the drum engage the ratchet at the top of the spindle and the drum turns with the spindle, while the bottom (ratchet) gear spins freely. When the handle is released, both ratchets engage, locking the spindle against reverse rotation. If the load is light, the line tail can be hauled manually, spinning the drum and both ratchets freely.

When the handle turns the spindle in the low-speed (counterclockwise) direction, the bottom pawls engage the ratchet gear, driving the drum through the idler gear while the top pawls spin free. The pawls lock against reverse rotation but allow forward rotation as above.

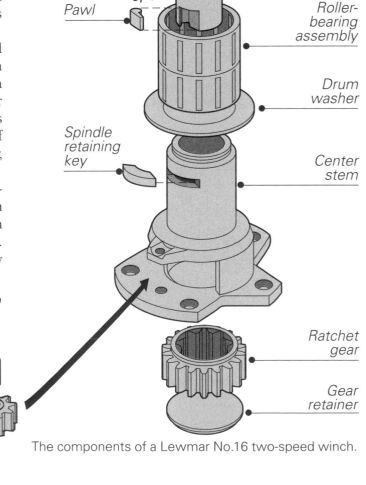

The components of a Lewmar No.16 two-speed winch.

To take in line with a winch, the line is given three wraps clockwise around the drum. To maintain friction against the drum, tension must be maintained on the free end of the line or the line will slip. This is called tailing the line.

Self-tailing winches eliminate the need for tailing. After the three wraps, the line is fed over the feeder arm into the ribbed groove between the upper and lower crowns. Since the diameter of this groove is slightly larger than that of the drum, the line around the drum is kept in constant tension. A stripper ring peels the line out of the groove as it accumulates.

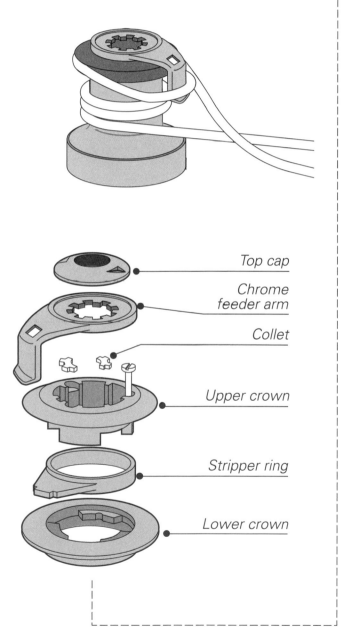

Top cap

Chrome feeder arm

Collet

Upper crown

Stripper ring

Lower crown

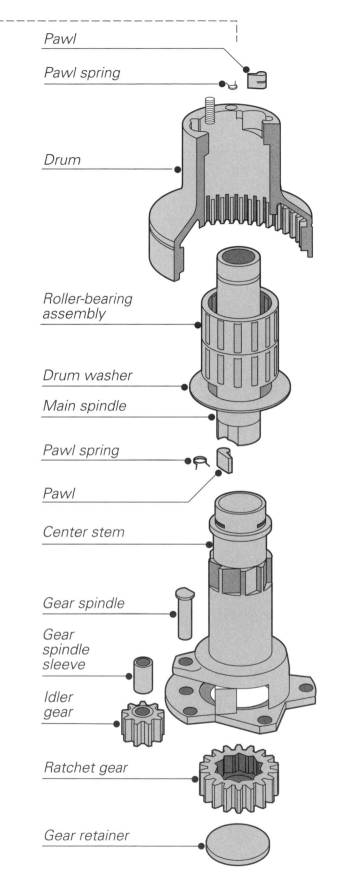

Pawl

Pawl spring

Drum

Roller-bearing assembly

Drum washer

Main spindle

Pawl spring

Pawl

Center stem

Gear spindle

Gear spindle sleeve

Idler gear

Ratchet gear

Gear retainer

The single-speed Lewmar No. 16ST winch shown here has a self-tailing mechanism for convenience.

Roller Furling

Headsail roller furlers (roller reefers) are assembled over the headstay. Most consist of, from bottom:

- lower stud with toggle for attaching assembly to boat
- line guard assembly (fixed to the lower stud)
- furling drum for imparting twist to the foil
- tack swivel, compensating for extra twist in middle of sail
- torque tube, marrying drum to bottom of foil
- hollow extruded foils with luff grooves for rolling up sail
- foil connectors containing plastic bearing sleeves
- halyard swivel, sliding over extrusions, at-

tached to head of sail and jib halyard, allowing sail to furl without halyard twist
- upper swaged eye with toggle at top of headstay

With the headsail unfurled, the furling drum contains several dozen turns of the furling line. Pulling on the line turns the drum, twisting the foil and furling the sail. The sail is unfurled by releasing the furling line and pulling on its sheets.

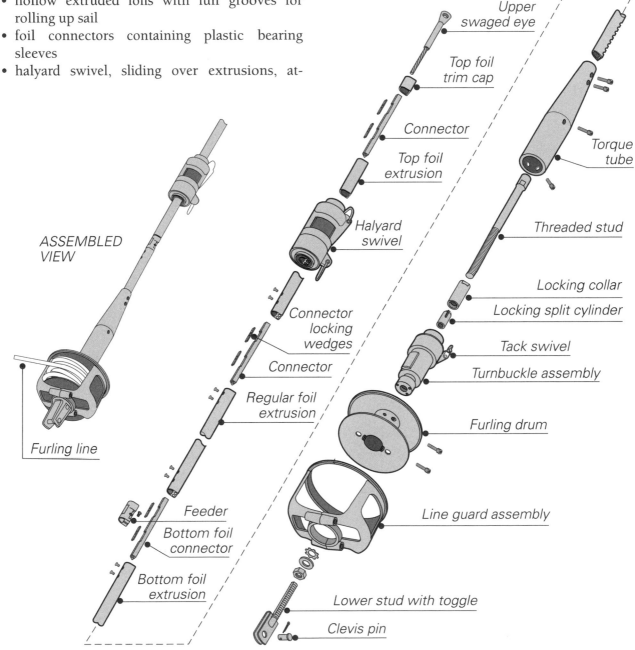

ASSEMBLED VIEW

Furling line

Upper swaged eye

Top foil trim cap

Connector

Top foil extrusion

Halyard swivel

Connector locking wedges

Connector

Regular foil extrusion

Feeder

Bottom foil connector

Bottom foil extrusion

Torque tube

Threaded stud

Locking collar

Locking split cylinder

Tack swivel

Turnbuckle assembly

Furling drum

Line guard assembly

Lower stud with toggle

Clevis pin

The working parts of a typical roller furling unit, in this case a Harken Mark III.

5 Ground Tackle

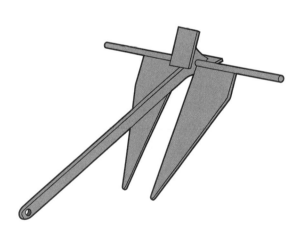

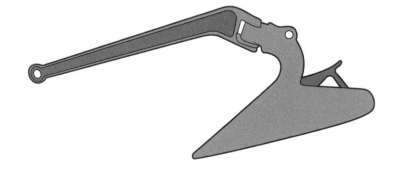

Moorings

A proper permanent mooring consists of the following components:

1. At the business end, a mushroom anchor weighing 5 to 10 pounds x the boat's length in feet.

2. A length of 1-inch chain equal to twice the depth of the water at high tide, fastened to the mushroom with a shackle.

3. A second length of $^1/_2$-inch chain equal to the depth of the water at high tide, shackled to the heavy chain.

4. A swivel, shackled to the $^1/_2$-inch chain. The swivel is critical in any anchorage where either the tide or a combination of wind and tide swings boats in a circle. The extra length of chain acts as a shock absorber when the boat heaves. Without a swivel the chain will twist and shorten, reducing the cushioning effect.

5. A mooring buoy attached directly to the swivel with a shackle.

6. A 20-foot pendant of three-strand nylon with a minimum diameter of 1 inch. Boats under 25 feet may not have large enough bow cleats, and $^3/_4$-inch nylon may be substituted. Boats over 40 feet should have $1^1/_2$-inch pendants. The pendant should be attached to the swivel with an eye splice, thimble, and shackle. At the free end should be an eye splice just large enough to fit over the bow cleat and a pick-up buoy on $^1/_4$-inch line.

All shackle pins should be seized with stainless or galvanized wire.

In areas subject to winter ice, the mooring ball and $^1/_2$-inch chain should be taken up and replaced with a rope and log. In any case, all elements of the mooring should be thoroughly inspected for wear annually.

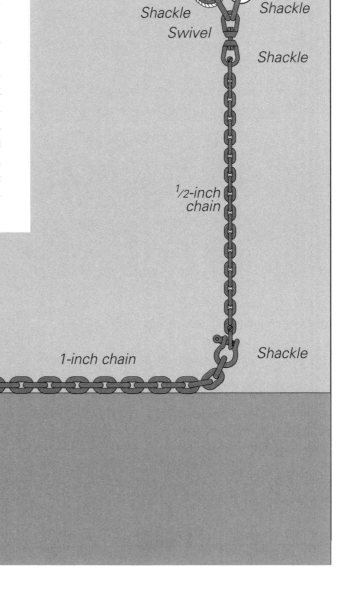

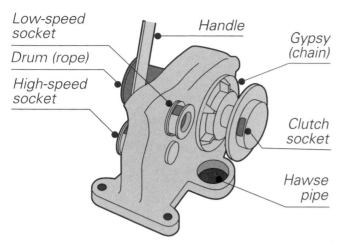

Low-speed socket

Handle

Gypsy (chain)

Drum (rope)

High-speed socket

Clutch socket

Hawse pipe

In the Simpson Lawrence Sea Tiger 555 two-speed windlass, the crank handle, a straight bar, fits into external sockets, one connected by shafts to a large-diameter, high-speed crank gear and the other to a smaller-diameter, low-speed crank gear. Upper and lower spur gears with elongated bores are pulled into engagement with the high-speed crank gear by a strong connecting spring.

When the crank handle is pushed forward (top figure), the upper spur engages both crank gear and idler gear. The idler gear then drives the drive gear and drum clockwise. At the same time, with both the crank gear and drive gear teeth pushing in the same direction, the lower spur is kicked out of the way.

When the handle is pulled in the opposite direction, the upper spur is kicked out, while the lower spur is pulled into the crank gear and the drive gear. As a result the drive gear and drum are again driven clockwise. Thus, whether the crank handle is pushed or pulled, the drum always rotates to bring the anchor in.

With the crank handle placed in the low-speed crank socket, the low-speed crank gear drives the high-speed crank gear with the same results, except the ratio of gear teeth increases the mechanical advantage.

When the handle is neither pulled nor pushed, the spur-gear spring pulls both spurs into contact with the crank, idler, and drive gears so the system locks up.

In high-speed mode the mechanical advantage is simply the length of the crank handle divided by the radius of the drum or gypsy (chain sprocket)—with the supplied handle, 17:1. In low-speed mode the 17:1 mechanical advantage is multiplied by the 2:1 ratio of teeth on the high-speed and low-speed crank gears, increasing it to 34:1.

Since no combination of cranking allows the gypsy and drum to turn in the opposite direction (to let out the rode), the gypsy is connected to the drive gear by a clutch. Loosening the clutch wheel allows the gypsy to freewheel. To veer rope, simply ease the tail tension.

Fore ← → Aft

HIGH-SPEED PUSH

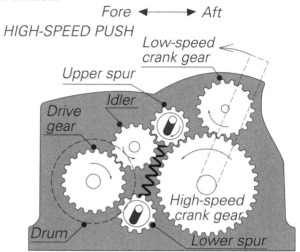

Low-speed crank gear

Upper spur

Idler

Drive gear

High-speed crank gear

Drum

Lower spur

HIGH-SPEED PULL

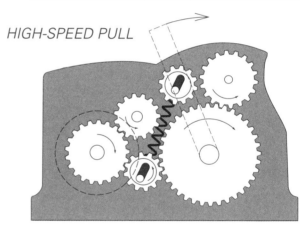

IDLE: LOCKED

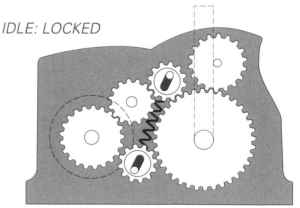

The drawings above indicate how the Simpson Lawrence Sea Tiger 555 two-speed windlass works. In these drawings, the handle is ghosted into the high-speed socket.

Anchors

Lightweight

Commonly known as the Danforth, the brand name of its best-known version, the lightweight steel anchor has a very high holding power to weight ratio. This feature, and its relatively low cost, make it the most popular anchor among recreational boaters.

In a favorable bottom (mud, sand, soft clay), the anchor digs in within a few boat lengths and buries itself totally. However, on a hard or weedy bottom it may never dig in.

Its worst feature, though, is that when the direction of the pull is reversed, it may flip out. Of course, it may reset itself. But then again, it may not!

The anchor is also available in aluminum, theoretically increasing its holding power to weight ratio by a factor of three. However, in any current, the aluminum anchor tends to sail and is more difficult to set.

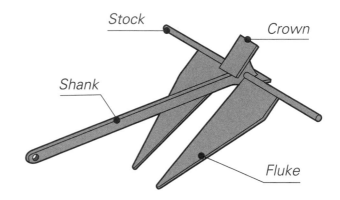

Plow

Commonly known as the CQR, again for its best-known trademarked version, the plow gets its name from its shape. Plows are heavy, with 1 pound per foot of boat length recommended. However, experienced boaters who regularly anchor out tend to favor the plow over all others. It is relatively difficult to set—often requiring several boat lengths to dig in—but once set, it usually stays put. The unique swiveled stock allows the plow to turn, following the direction of the pull without breaking free.

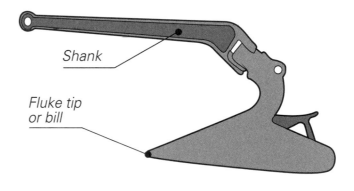

Bruce

The Bruce anchor, a relative newcomer, has some of the advantages of both the lightweight and the plow. Lighter than the plow, it also has some ability to follow the direction of pull without breaking out. It is also said to set more readily than the plow.

Its single weak point appears to be the tendency of the shovel-like flukes to dislodge and clog with solid chunks of clay, preventing it from resetting.

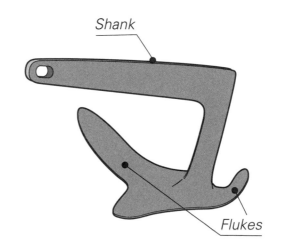

Kedge

Also known as the fisherman, this traditional-looking anchor is rarely used as the primary anchor on recreational boats. The name derives from the act of kedging off—rowing the anchor out and using the anchor to pull the vessel out of an awkward situation or off the bottom.

Unlike the anchors on the previous page, the kedge is not designed to bury itself in a soft bottom. It is intended that one of the sharp flukes will catch on coral or rock. The thin arms and narrow flukes are also better at penetrating grass.

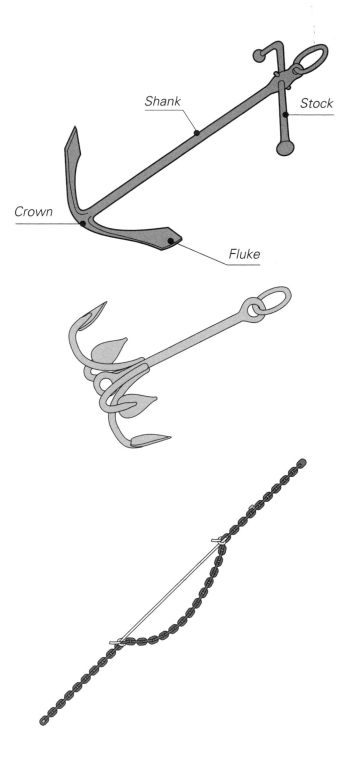

Grapnel

Although often used as a lunch hook for small vessels, the grapnel is not intended as an anchor. Its purpose is dragging across the bottom to grapple (fasten onto) a lost mooring chain or other accidentally dropped object.

Snubbers and Shock Absorbers

While chain is strong, it has no stretch. In heavy seas a chain rode can deliver damaging shock loads to windlasses and cleats. Nylon, on the other hand, has the unique ability to stretch elastically as much as one third under load. Experienced sailors use nylon snubbers—short lengths of line from the bow cleat to the anchor chain—to create an elastic shock absorber in the rode. The shock absorber can also be placed further down the chain, as shown.

For maximum cushioning effect, the nylon must be of fairly small diameter. For boats up to 40 feet, except in extreme conditions, 3/8-inch, three-strand nylon is recommended.

Anchoring

Single Anchor

This method is used when there is plenty of room to swing. Pick your spot and calculate the length of rode (L). Approach into the wind (or current, if stronger) and stop upwind at the distance, L, from where you want your boat to ride. Put the engine into reverse, lower the anchor, and pay out rode for a 6:1 scope. Snub the rode on a cleat (if chain, tighten windlass brake). Power back until the rode goes taut. When the anchor sets, the bow will dip suddenly and the boat will spring forward. Finally, pay out rode to match the conditions: calm, 6:1; average wind, 7:1; heavy wind, up to 10:1.

Two Anchors off the Bow

Two anchors are used to limit swing. Set the first anchor, as above, to port of the position you would place a single anchor. After setting the first anchor, power to starboard to a point equidistant on the other side and drop the second anchor. Carefully drop back, paying out a scope of 6:1, then set the anchor. Finally, pay out rode until the two rodes are of equal length.

Bahamian Moor

This technique is used when the current is strong and reverses direction. Prepare two anchors on the bow and calculate the final lengths of rode, L. Power upwind or upcurrent. Drop the first anchor at the distance, L, upwind of your desired spot. Feed out rode until you have let out 2L. Drop the second anchor and power forward to set it. Retrieve L of the first rode, placing the boat halfway between the two anchors.

Retrieving the Anchor

Power slowly toward the anchor while the crew takes in the rode. Since the helmsman cannot see the rode, the crew should point in its direction for guidance.

As soon as the rode is vertical, snub the rode around a cleat. The inertia and buoyancy of the boat will exert a great force straight up, breaking the anchor out of the bottom. When the anchor breaks free the bow will dip, then spring back. Then retrieve the anchor with the boat in neutral or slow ahead.

With a chain rode, have a snubber line with a chain hook already cleated. As the rode goes vertical, snub the chain with the hook. This will prevent the chain from running out if it jumps out of the gypsy.

Mediterranean Moor

This anchoring methcod is common in Mediterranean ports. Calculate the length of rode, L. Drop the anchor a distance of L plus one boat length out from fastening point on shore. Back down toward the shore, setting the anchor, as in the single-anchor mothod. Adjust dock lines and rode for final position. If your boat backs poorly, run the anchor out in a dinghy.

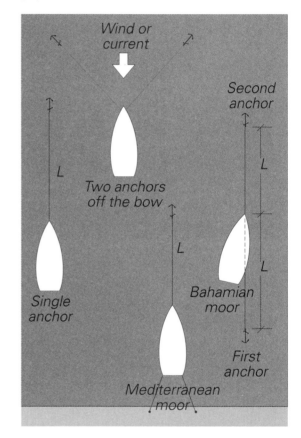

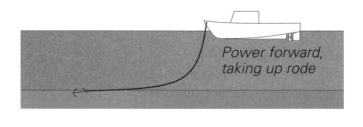

Power forward, taking up rode

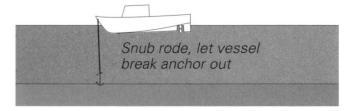

Snub rode, let vessel break anchor out

6

Electrical

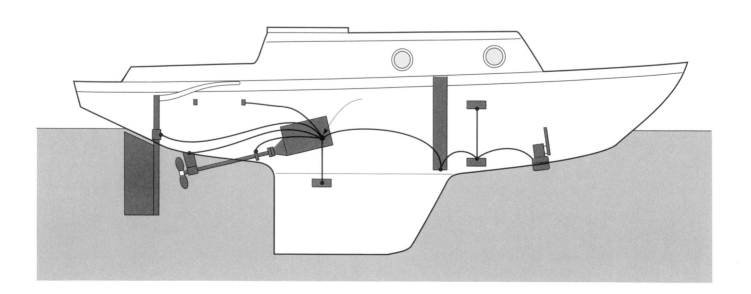

DC Circuits

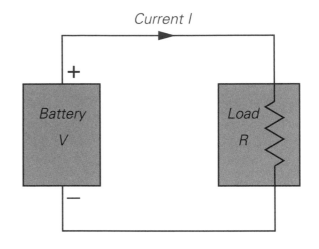

Direct current (DC) is a continuous flow of electricity in one direction through a conductive material. This flow requires an unbroken conductive loop through which the electricity can flow.

We call this continuous loop a circuit. If a circuit is unbroken, we call it a closed circuit. If it is broken, preventing the flow of electricity, we say the circuit is open.

At room temperature, all materials resist the flow of electricity to some degree, but the variation is so great that we call some materials conductors and others insulators.

Electrical current is the rate of flow of electrons. In a circuit, two factors control this current (I): the electromotive force (E) and the resistance (R) to flow. Aboard a boat, the source of the driving force, E, is usually the 12-volt ship's battery, while the resistance, R, is primarily that of a load, such as a lamp, a piece of electronic gear, or the starter motor for the engine.

The relationship between I, E, and R is very simple and is expressed by Ohm's law:

$$I = E \div R$$
where I is in amperes
E is in volts
R is in ohms

The law can be rearranged for calculating E and R:

$$E = I \times R$$
$$R = E \div I$$

Some people find the graphic at right useful. Simply cover the value you wish to compute, and what remains visible is the required formula.

As an example, calculate the current, I, flowing in the circuit illustrated at far right, where the voltage is supplied by a 12-volt battery and the load has a resistance of 6 ohms.

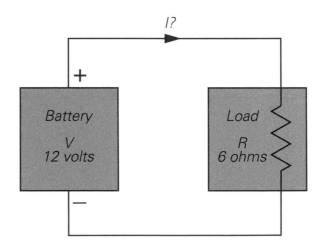

$$I = E \div R$$
$$= 12 \div 6$$
$$= 2 \text{ amperes}$$

A Common DC Circuit

The illustration below shows a simple cabin light circuit in pictorial form.

The source of power for the circuit is the ship's 12-volt battery. Point (1), the battery's positive terminal, is at 12 volts relative to (14), the battery's negative terminal.

A wire connects the battery's positive terminal to the battery-disconnect switch. This switch has two input terminals (not shown) for two batteries, and a single output terminal. With the switch handle in either position "1" or "Both," the input terminal (2) and the output terminal (3) are connected so electricity can flow. With the handle in the "Off" position, the terminals are disconnected.

A wire connects the switch output (3) to the positive bus bar (a copper strip) in the distribution panel at (4).

Inside the distribution panel, a circuit breaker labeled "Cabin lights" is wired to one of the bus bar terminals at (5). With the circuit breaker "On," voltage is present at terminal (7). If too much current flows through the circuit breaker due to an overload or a short circuit (positive wire accidentally touching ground), the breaker opens, stopping current flow.

From (7) a wire leads around the cabin to the various light fixtures. This wire, and any other at 12 volts, is said to be "hot," and is color-coded red by convention. Inside the first fixture the red lead is connected at (8) to the switch controlling the fixture.

With the switch "On," current flows from the switch output (9) to the center contact of the lamp (10). The lamp filament is the purposeful resistance, or load, in the circuit. One end of the filament is soldered to the lamp's center contact (10), the other to the lamp's shell (11). For current to flow through the filament, the electricity has to have a path back to the battery. This is the black wire to the negative bus bar in the distribution box, which is connected to the battery's negative terminal (14). By convention, all wires at the same voltage as the battery's negative terminal are considered to be at "ground," or 0 volts, and are color-coded black.

If the lamp filament is intact, current flow through the resistive filament causes it to glow and give off light. If the filament is burned out, the circuit is broken, and no current flows.

Additional light fixtures are added to the circuit simply by connecting their red wires to point (8) and black wires to point (11). Since points (8) and (11) are at 12 volts and 0 volts regardless of the status of any other cabin light switch or filament, each light fixture is independent.

We should note that, while the color conventions for general DC wiring are red for positive and black for negative, the American Boat and Yacht Council (ABYC) promotes an additional set of colors for engine wiring.

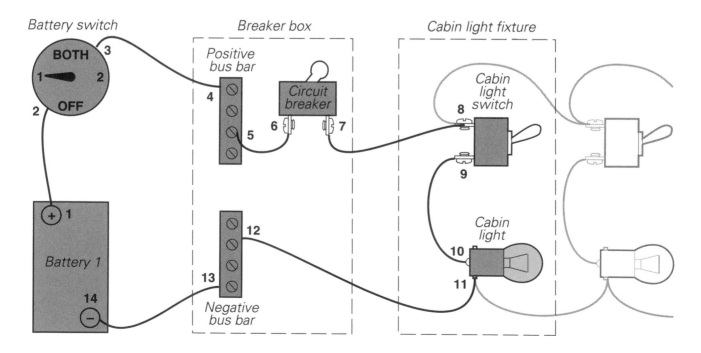

DC Grounding

The purpose of grounding is threefold:

1. If a positive (+12-volt) wire inside a piece of electrical equipment were to short by accidentally contacting the metal case, the case would be at 12 volts, creating a danger of spark ignition. A grounding wire to the case holds the case at ground potential by providing a low-resistance return path for the accidental current.

2. By providing a low-resistance return path for electrical current, the grounding wire prevents stray currents. As we'll see, these can result in damaging corrosion.

3. Grounding a metal electrical case prevents emission from inside or absorption from outside of radio frequency noise (RFI).

Following are components of the DC grounding system, as defined by the ABYC (see illustration on facing page).

DC grounding conductors are normally non-current-carrying conductors. They are used to connect metallic non-current-carrying parts of direct current devices to the engine negative terminal or its bus to minimize stray-current corrosion.

DC grounded conductors are the black current-carrying conductors seen on the previous page that are intentionally maintained at boat ground potential.

Ground is established by a conducting connection with the earth, including conductive parts of the wetted surface of a hull. Such parts might be the propeller and shaft (unless isolated, as by a Drivesaver), shaft strut, rudder, bronze thru-hulls, or grounding plate.

An **engine negative terminal** is the point on the engine to which the battery's negative terminal is connected.

A **panel board** is an assembly of devices for controlling and/or distributing power on a boat. It may include devices such as circuit breakers, fuses, switches, instruments, and indicators.

DC grounding conductors are physically similar to the bonding conductors defined on page 135. Why the difference in terms? *Bonding* is an all-inclusive term serving safety, lightning protection, and corrosion protection. *Grounding*, although sharing the same conductors, refers specifically to electrical grounding for safety and prevention of stray currents. Grounding conductors may be routed as separate conductors or together with the positive (hot) and negative (grounded) conductors as a third wire. They are also connected to the engine negative terminal, to the DC main-negative bus, or to a DC grounding bus, which is then connected to either the engine negative terminal or DC main-negative bus.

In the illustration at right, note that all DC electrical equipment is served by a DC positive conductor (usually a red wire) and a DC grounded conductor (usually black). In addition, equipment having an exposed metal case (the winch) is tied back to the DC main-negative bus and engine ground through DC grounding conductors (green).

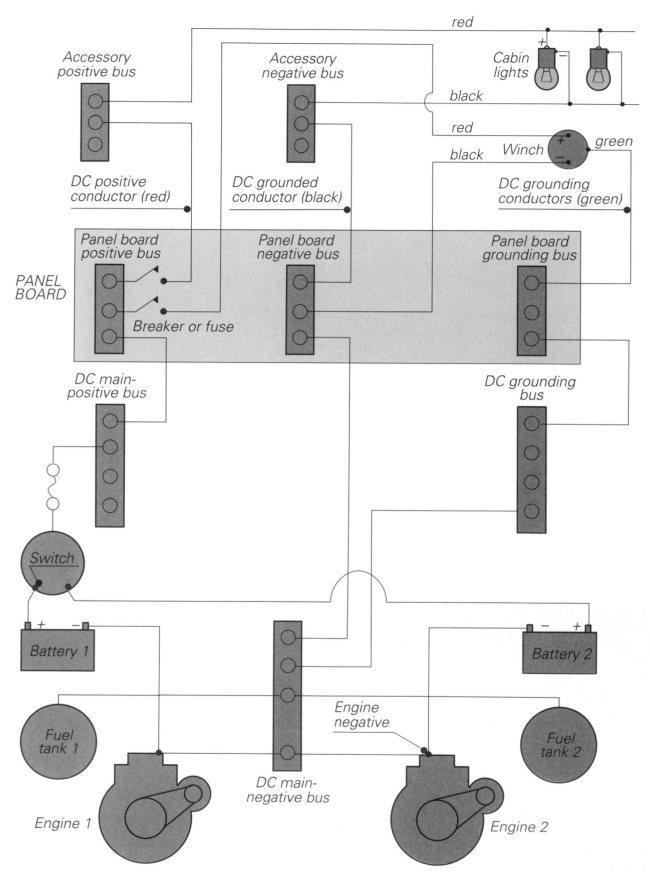

A typical inboard DC system with DC grounding. All DC electrical equipment shown is served by a DC positive conductor (red) and a DC grounded conductor (black).

Batteries

The lead-acid storage battery, whether automotive, marine, deep-cycle, or gel-cell, is essentially just a reversible chemical reaction between very simple components: lead and sulfuric acid:

$$\begin{array}{c} \text{charging} \\ + \Leftarrow - \\ PbO_2 + Pb + 2H_2SO_4 = 2PbSO_4 + 2H_2O \\ + \Rightarrow - \\ \text{discharging} \end{array}$$

The illustrations at right show the four phases of a lead-acid cell charge/discharge cycle:

1. **Fully Charged.** In the equation, application of an external charging voltage has driven the reaction all the way to the left. The negative electrode has become pure lead (Pb), the positive electrode is now pure lead peroxide (PbO_2), and the sulfuric acid electrolyte ($H_2SO_4 + H_2O$) is at its maximum concentration.

2. **Discharging.** By connecting a load (shown as a light bulb), we complete the electrical circuit, allowing the chemical reaction to proceed to the right in its natural direction. The H_2SO_4 breaks into H and SO_4 ions (molecules with either extra or missing electrons). The H is attracted to the positive electrode, where it steals the O_2 from the PbO_2 and forms water, H_2O. The now free Pb combines with the SO_4 ions to form $PbSO_4$ in place of the PbO_2. At the negative electrode, SO_4 ions also combine with the pure Pb to form more $PbSO_4$. Thus, both electrode materials are converted to lead sulfate ($PbSO_4$), while the electrolyte loses sulfuric acid (H_2SO_4), gains water (H_2O), and becomes more dilute.

3. **Fully Discharged.** The cell is fully discharged when it runs out of one of the necessary ingredients. Either the PbO_2 has been totally converted to $PbSO_4$ or all of the SO_4 ions in the electrolyte have been used up, reducing it to pure water. In either case, PbO_2 and electrolyte strength have been minimized and $PbSO_4$ maximized.

4. **Charging.** By connecting a charging voltage to the cell, we drive the chemical reaction in the reverse direction. Ideally, the negative electrode is restored to pure PbO_2, the positive terminal to pure Pb, and the acid electrolyte to its maximum strength.

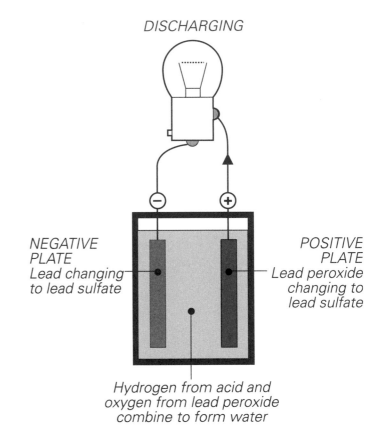

DISCHARGING

NEGATIVE PLATE
Lead changing to lead sulfate

POSITIVE PLATE
Lead peroxide changing to lead sulfate

Hydrogen from acid and oxygen from lead peroxide combine to form water

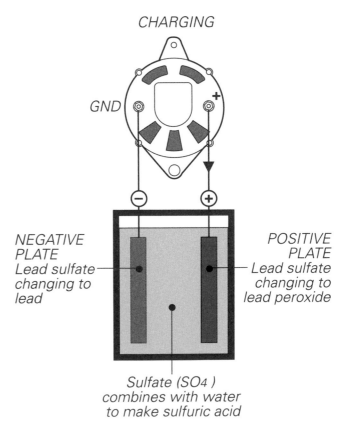

CHARGING

GND

NEGATIVE PLATE
Lead sulfate changing to lead

POSITIVE PLATE
Lead sulfate changing to lead peroxide

Sulfate (SO_4) combines with water to make sulfuric acid

Battery Construction

The chemistry of the lead-acid battery is simple, but the way in which it actually happens is a bit more complex

The illustration below shows a cross section of a wet-acid battery. Both positive and negative electrodes are immersed in electrolyte. The reactive materials, lead and lead peroxide, are suspended on lead grids that serve to support the materials and conduct electric current. So far, so simple. Now for the complications:

Batteries in automobiles and boats are bounced around. So that they do not touch each other, the many closely spaced plates (electrodes) are interleaved with porous fiberglass separators.

The lead that forms the grid is not very strong. For increased strength, it is alloyed with either antimony (conventional wet, deep-cycle batteries) or calcium (sealed, maintenance-free batteries).

During discharge, the lead sulfate forms first at the electrode surfaces. The sulfate then acts as a barrier between the electrolyte and the unreacted material beneath, slowing the reaction and limiting the current that can be drawn. The greater the surface area and the thinner the plates, the greater the possible current flow. Batteries whose primary purpose is engine starting have many very thin plates in order to provide large currents for short periods.

Lead, lead dioxide, and lead sulfate are not of the same density. Expansion and contraction cause stresses that dislodge the materials from the grids. If enough material is shed, the accumulation at the bottom may short out the plates. The more complete the reaction (the deeper the discharge), the greater the

loss. Batteries designed for deep-cycling have fewer but thicker plates.

If we overcharge the battery, the excess energy goes into hydrolysis—separation of the water of the electrolyte into gaseous H_2 and O_2. Various tricks are employed in sealed batteries to recombine the gases into water, but, if overcharging and gassing are too vigorous, all batteries will vent the gas and lose electrolyte. Lost water can be replaced in a conventional wet-acid battery. In a sealed or gel-cell battery, it cannot.

If a battery is left in a discharged state, with many of its electrodes in the form of $PbSO_4$, the fine and soft deposits grow into larger, harder crystals in a process termed *sulfation*. The crystals are difficult to reconvert, and so the battery is difficult to charge and displays reduced capacity. Vigorous overcharging and bubbling can break up and dislodge the crystals, resulting in recovery of much of the capacity. However, each time it is done, the plates shed more material and get closer to the end of their useful lives.

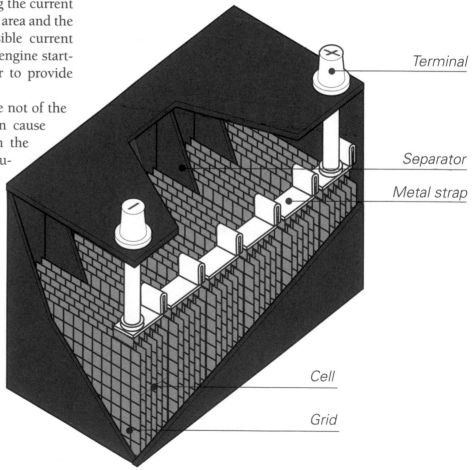

Terminal

Separator

Metal strap

Cell

Grid

Series and Parallel Connections

We think of a battery as a single entity, whereas it is actually a number of individual 2-volt cells internally connected in series to increase the voltage at the battery's terminals. (For some applications, 2-volt batteries can still be purchased.)

If the cells can be connected internally, why can't they be connected externally as well? The answer is, they can. In fact, the least expensive deep-cycle battery, in terms of watt-hours per dollar, is the 6-volt golf cart battery. Liveaboard boaters, for whom ship's batteries represent life itself, commonly connect golf cart batteries in series to achieve 12-volt power.

Batteries can be connected in three ways (below, right):

- *series*, where the negative terminal of one battery is connected to the positive terminal of another, resulting in the same ampacity (amps capacity) but the sum of voltages
- *parallel*, where negative is connected to negative and positive to positive, resulting in the same voltage but the sum of ampacities
- *series-parallel*, resulting in half the sum of ampacities and half the sum of voltages

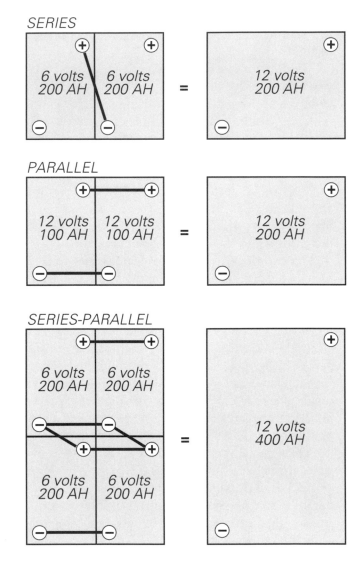

SERIES

6 volts 200 AH | 6 volts 200 AH = 12 volts 200 AH

PARALLEL

12 volts 100 AH | 12 volts 100 AH = 12 volts 200 AH

SERIES-PARALLEL

6 volts 200 AH | 6 volts 200 AH

6 volts 200 AH | 6 volts 200 AH = 12 volts 400 AH

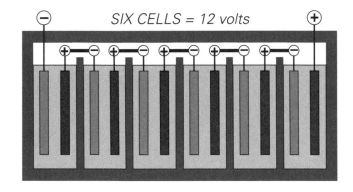

SIX CELLS = 12 volts

Measurement Units

The amounts of energy flowing and contained in a battery are described by three quantities:

- amperes (A)—the current, or rate of flow of electrons
- ampere-hours (AH)—current x time the current flows
- watt-hours (WH)—AH x the battery voltage (V)

AH allows you to calculate how many hours the battery will supply a certain number of amps.

WH is a measure of the total energy in the battery.

Optimal Fast Charging of Batteries

To fully charge a battery, we must convert 100 percent of the $PbSO_4$ back to Pb and PbO_2. The usual goal is to recharge the battery as quickly as possible without damaging the battery.

Optimal fast charging of a battery (as rapidly as possible without damage) involves three phases:

Bulk cycle. Wet-acid batteries discharged more than 75 percent will accept charge rates of 0.25 C (C = amp-hour capacity), until they are about 75 percent charged. Gelled-electrolyte batteries will typically accept charges of 0.5 C.

Absorption cycle. At 75 percent charge, voltage has increased to around 14.4 volts, and gassing begins. To avoid gassing, voltage is held constant at less than 14.4 volts, while the battery absorbs current at a decreasing rate. When current drops to 0.05 C, the battery is approximately 85 percent charged; at 0.02 C, about 90 percent charged; at 0.01 C, nearly 100 percent charged. How far the absorption cycle is carried depends on whether the engine is being run for the sole purpose of charging (0.05 C cutoff recommended) or whether the boat is underway or on shore power (0.01 to 0.02 C cutoff recommended).

Float cycle. The final stage, provided the battery is still on a charger, is designed to hold the battery in its fully charged condition. If the battery is removed from all loads, such as in winter storage, the ideal float voltage is about 0.1 volt above its rested, open-circuit voltage, or 13 volts. With periodic small loads, float voltage is 13.2 to 13.5 volts.

Equalization. In the wet-acid battery, electrolyte concentration may change through sulfation, gassing, or addition of water. After cycling many times, the charge states of the cells will get out of balance. Since the battery may only be discharged as low as its weakest cell, battery capacity is effectively reduced. Equalization is a controlled overcharge, during which all of the cells are brought back to their fully charged states. A constant current of 0.04 C is applied for four hours or until battery voltage rises to 16.2 volts, whichever occurs first.

The common voltage regulator, producing one constant voltage, is thus seen to be far from optimal. The liveaboard cruiser would be wise to invest in one of the computerized "smart" regulators that automate the optimal charging process.

WET-ACID BATTERIES

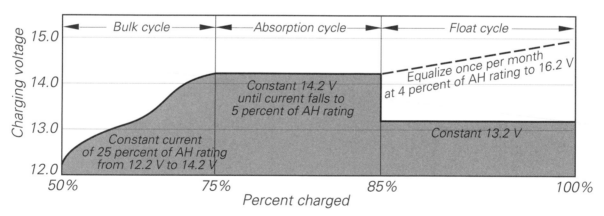

GELLED-ELECTROLYTE BATTERIES

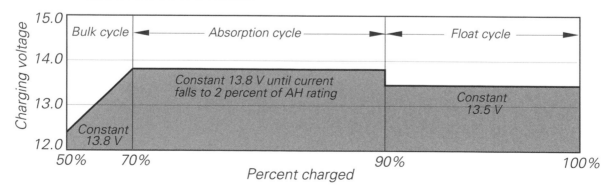

Galvanic Corrosion

Galvanic corrosion is the deterioration of the anode of a galvanic couple resulting from the flow of ions from the anode to the cathode through an electrolyte.

This sounds like something that happens only in a chemical laboratory. In fact, it is what happens inside the common carbon-zinc flashlight battery. If you slice such a battery in half (see top right), you will see a carbon rod in an electrically conductive paste, all inside a zinc-coated can. A voltmeter will show 1.5 volts between the carbon rod and the zinc can. Placing a 1.5-volt light bulb in series with the meter's positive lead, you will find that current flows from the positive terminal through the lamp to the negative terminal.

Now place an aluminum object and a stainless object in a glass of salt water (bottom right). Using a voltmeter, connect the negative lead to the aluminum and the positive lead to the stainless. Surprised? The meter will indicate over 0.5 volt.

Now switch the meter to amps. Depending on the sizes of the electrodes, you will measure a current of from 10 to 100 milliamps flowing from the stainless piece to the aluminum.

What's going on? When two dissimilar metals are placed together in an electrolyte (electrically conductive fluid, gel, or paste), one metal will assume a higher potential than the other. On page 125 we learned that current flows only in closed circuits. Two isolated electrodes, immersed in electrolyte, form an open circuit, and no current flows. But when we connect the two electrodes, we complete the circuit, and current flows between them.

In this case, the current flow through the voltmeter is from the stainless into the aluminum. Since electrons are negatively charged (sorry, not my decision!), electron flow is in the opposite direction, from aluminum to stainless. The aluminum atoms are breaking down by giving up electrons. The released electrons are flowing from the aluminum to the stainless through the wire, and the newly formed aluminum ions are departing the crystalline structure of the aluminum and moving into the electrolyte, i.e., the aluminum is corroding.

If you substitute other pairs of dissimilar metals, you will find that they always generate a potential difference. The potential difference can be predicted from a galvanic potential table. To form such a table, potential differences are measured between various metals and a reference electrode, such as silver-silver chloride. The table on the facing page lists values for metals and alloys in seawater flowing at 8 to 13 feet per second (4.7 to 7.7 knots) and at temperatures of 50°F to 80°F.

Example: What is the corrosion potential between silicon bronze and zinc? From the table we find the corrosion potentials of silicon bronze vs. the reference and zinc vs. the reference to be –0.26 to –0.29 volt (average, –0.28 volt) and –0.98 to –1.03 volt (average, –1.00 volt), so the potential between the two is 0.72 volt.

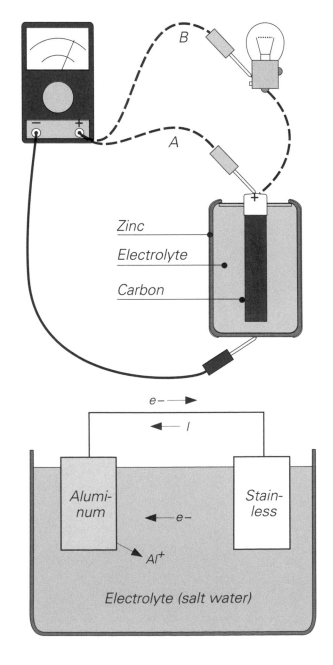

THE GALVANIC SERIES

ABYC STANDARD E-2, GALVANIC SERIES OF METALS IN SEAWATER

NOTE: Between any two metals, the one higher in the table (having more negative potential) is the one corroded.

Metals and Alloys	Corrosion Potential Range in Volts
Magnesium and Magnesium Alloys	−1.60 to −1.63
Zinc	−0.98 to −1.03
Aluminum Alloys	−0.76 to −1.00
Cadmium	−0.70 to −0.73
Mild Steel	−0.60 to −0.71
Wrought Iron	−0.60 to −0.71
Cast Iron	−0.60 to −0.71
13% Chromium Stainless Steel, Type 410 (active in still water)	−0.46 to −0.58
18-8 Stainless Steel, Type 304 (active in still water)	−0.46 to −0.58
Ni-Resist	−0.46 to −0.58
18-8, 3% Mo Stainless Steel, Type 316 (active in still water)	−0.43 to −0.54
78% Ni, 14.5% Cr, 6% Fe (Inconel) (active in still water)	−0.35 to −0.46
Aluminum Bronze (92% Cu, 8% Al)	−0.31 to −0.42
Naval Brass (60% Cu, 39% Zn)	−0.30 to −0.40
Yellow Brass (65% Cu, 35% Zn)	−0.30 to −0.40
Red Brass (85% Cu, 15% Zn)	−0.30 to −0.40
Muntz Metal (60% Cu, 40% Zn)	−0.30 to −0.40
Tin	−0.31 to −0.33
Copper	−0.30 to −0.57
50-50 Lead–Tin Solder	−0.28 to −0.37
Admiralty Brass (71% Cu, 28% Zn, 1% Sn)	−0.28 to −0.36
Aluminum Brass (76% Cu, 22% Zn, 2% Al)	−0.28 to −0.36
Manganese Bronze (58.5% Cu, 39% Zn, 1% Sn, 1% Fe, 0.3% Mn)	−0.27 to −0.34
Silicon Bronze (96% Cu max, 0.8% Fe, 1.5% Zn, 2% Si, 0.75% Mn, 1.6% Sn)	−0.26 to −0.29
Bronze, Composition G (88% Cu, 2% Zn, 10% Sn)	−0.24 to −0.31
Bronze, Composition M (88% Cu, 3% Zn, 6.5% Zn, 1.5% Pb)	−0.24 to −0.31
13% Chromium Stainless Steel, Type 401 (passive)	−0.26 to −0.35
90% Cu–10% Ni	−0.21 to −0.28
75% Cu–20% Ni–5% Zn	−0.19 to −0.25
Lead	−0.19 to −0.25
70% Cu–30% Ni	−0.18 to −0.23
78% Ni, 13.5% Cr, 6% Fe (Inconel) (passive)	−0.14 to −0.17
Nickel 200	−0.10 to −0.20
18-8 Stainless Steel, Type 304 (passive)	−0.05 to −0.10
70% Ni–30% Cu Monel 400, K-500	−0.04 to −0.14
18-8, 3% Mo Stainless Steel, Type 316 (passive)	−0.00 to −0.10
Titanium	−0.05 to +0.06
Hastelloy C	−0.03 to +0.08
Platinum	+0.19 to +0.25
Graphite	+0.20 to +0.30

anodic
least noble

cathodic
most noble

Cathodic Protection and Bonding

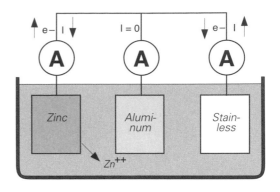

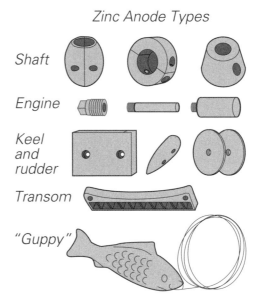

Zinc Anode Types

Shaft

Engine

Keel and rudder

Transom

"Guppy"

In the previous pages we established that any two dissimilar metals or alloys immersed in water generate a potential difference. We also found that if the two metals are isolated (neither physically touching nor electrically connected by wire), no current or corrosion occurs. But what happens if they cannot be separated, such as happens with a bronze prop on a stainless shaft?

To find out, set up the aluminum versus stainless experiment on page 132 again. This time, however, add a piece of zinc as a third electrode. Connect the aluminum, stainless, and zinc electrodes with wire leads, as shown in the figure at right. Now, one at a time, place the meter in each of the leads (circles containing "A") to detect current flow.

You will find that current is flowing out of the stainless electrode, but no current is flowing into or out of the aluminum electrode. Since metal is lost only by an electrode that receives current, it seems that the zinc is somehow protecting the aluminum by sacrificing itself. Positively charged zinc ions migrate through the electrolyte to balance the charges.

You can repeat this experiment with any three metals you wish, but the results will always be the same: When dissimilar metals in an electrolyte are mechanically or electrically bonded, the only metal to corrode will be the least noble (highest in the galvanic series) of the group. The metal most often used in boats for this purpose is zinc. The phenomenon is called *cathodic protection*, and the zinc masses are called zinc anodes, or "zincs" for short.

Stray-Current Corrosion

If you immerse two identical aluminum (or any other metal) electrodes, you will measure zero voltage and current through a wire between them. But if you connect a 1.5-volt battery between them, you will measure a large current, and one of the electrodes will soon disappear. Of course, we don't intentionally create voltage differences between the underwater metal parts of a boat, but they frequently occur without our knowing it.

A boat in a marina slip may be immersed in an electric field due to current leakages from other boats Assume the boat has a grounding plate for lightning protection, bronze thru-hulls, a stainless shaft, and a bronze propeller, and that all are properly bonded.

Since the electrical resistance of the path from ground plate to bonding wire to engine to shaft to prop is less than that of the water path, stray currents from surrounding boats can flow into the ground plate, through the bonding system, and out of the prop. And since the current is flowing into the prop from the bonding system, the prop will corrode. Strangely, this is a case where bonding actually increases corrosion.

As an example of a stray current originating in the boat rather than externally, the 12-volt lead to an immersed unbonded bilge pump may be poorly insulated and leaking current through the bilge water to a bronze thru-hull. When current flows through the bilge water, into the thru-hull, to the water outside the hull, and back through the prop, shaft, and engine path to ground, the thru-hull will corrode. If the thru-hull had been electrically bonded, the stray current would have found the bonding conductor the lowest-resistance path back to ground, thus preventing corrosion. In this case bonding prevents the corrosion.

Bonding

There are three reasons for electrically connecting (bonding) the large metal objects on a boat:

1. DC electrical system grounding
2. Lightning protection
3. Corrosion protection

Following are components of the DC bonding system as defined by the ABYC (see illustration on page 136).

Bonding is the electrical connection of the exposed, metallic, non-current-carrying parts to the ground side of the direct-current system.

Ground is a surface or mass at the potential of the earth's surface, established by a conducting connection with the earth, including any metal area that forms part of the wetted surface of the hull.

Bonding conductors are normally non-current-carrying conductors used to connect the non-current-carrying metal parts of a boat and the non-current-carrying parts of direct-current devices on the boat to the boat's bonding system.

The **common bonding conductor** is an electrical conductor, usually running fore and aft along the boat's centerline, to which all equipment bonding conductors are connected.

In practical terms, *ground* is the voltage of the water in which the boat is immersed. Voltage in the water may vary slightly due to stray currents, especially in marinas. The purpose of the bonding system is to force this voltage to be as uniform as possible through the use of low-resistance conductors and connections.

Bonding conductors are separate from, and in addition to, the DC (and AC) grounded conductors. They take as direct a route as possible to the common bonding conductor, which usually runs near the fore-and-aft centerline of the boat. The engine bonding conductor should be large enough to carry starter-motor cranking current. In multiengine installations with crossover starting systems (ability to parallel batteries), the engines should be bonded together with a conductor large enough to carry cranking current and separate from all current-carrying conductors. For identification, all bonding conductors are either bare or green.

The large common bonding conductor should be bare or green. It may consist of bare, stranded, tinned copper or insulated stranded wire of minimum size #8 AWG, or it may be an uninsulated copper or bronze strip or copper pipe. Although the only practical location for the common bonding conductor is often the bilge, care should be taken that it not be submerged due to likely corrosion of the connections.

Equipment to be connected to the boat's bonding system includes:

- Engines and transmissions
- Propellers and shafts
- Metal cases of motors, generators, and pumps
- Metal cabinets and control boxes
- Electronics cabinets
- Metal fuel and water tanks, fuel-fill fittings, and electrical fuel pumps and valves

Bonding or Grounding?

If you followed the discussion of DC grounding on pages 126–27, you may, by now, be scratching your head. If so, you are not alone. The difference between grounding and bonding is simply that of purpose. In fact, the same green or bare conductors accomplish both purposes. Call it bonding or call it grounding, just remember to connect all large metal parts and all metal electrical equipment cases to engine ground with green or bare wires.

By the above injunction, metal thru-hull fittings should be bonded, but there is much evidence that the practice in wood hulls is not a good idea. Current, flowing as a result of bonding the thru-hull to an underwater zinc, produces a chemical reaction that deteriorates the wood around the thru-hull. The answer is to either use plastic thru-hulls or unbond all underwater metal.

The latter option is discussed in the next section.

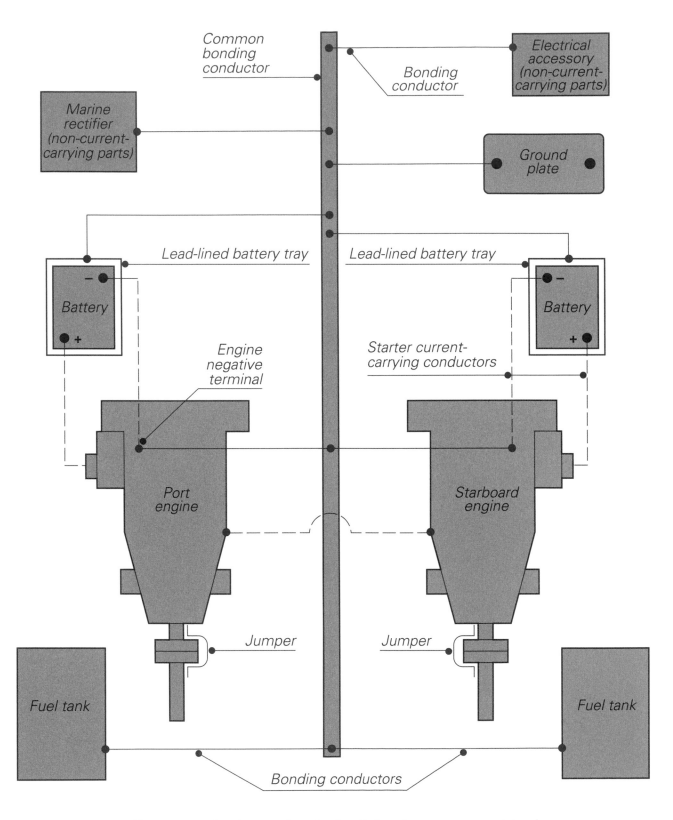

Common bonding conductor

Bonding conductor

Electrical accessory (non-current-carrying parts)

Marine rectifier (non-current-carrying parts)

Ground plate

Lead-lined battery tray

Lead-lined battery tray

Battery

Battery

Engine negative terminal

Starter current-carrying conductors

Port engine

Starboard engine

Jumper

Jumper

Fuel tank

Fuel tank

Bonding conductors

To prevent galvanic corrosion, the boat's bonding system consists of a common bonding conductor that connects via individual bonding conductors to the boat's major electronic and metal components.

To Bond or Not to Bond

We have just seen that bonding of immersed metal components prevents corrosion due to stray currents inside the hull. On the other hand, it causes corrosion due to stray currents outside the hull. There are two approaches to this dilemma:

1. Bond everything and protect with zincs.
2. Unbond everything and isolate.

Bond and protect. The top figure below shows the bond-and-protect principle. Every underwater mass is connected to the boat's bonding system. To protect against stray currents outside the hull, sacrificial anodes are connected to the bonding system and placed where they may best protect all underwater masses.

Unbond and isolate. The bottom figure below shows the alternative unbond-and-isolate principle. Underwater masses are isolated so neither galvanic nor outside stray current can flow between them. The only bonded underwater mass is the lightning and radio ground plate. Masses entirely within the hull (engine, transmission, metal tanks, and mast) are bonded to the boat's bonding system. The shaft is isolated by an insulating flexible coupling. The prop is protected by a shaft zinc, if necessary.

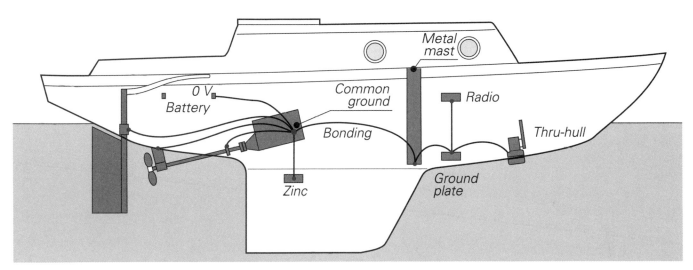

Every underwater part of this boat (rudder, propeller, etc.) is bonded together and connected to a sacrificial zinc.

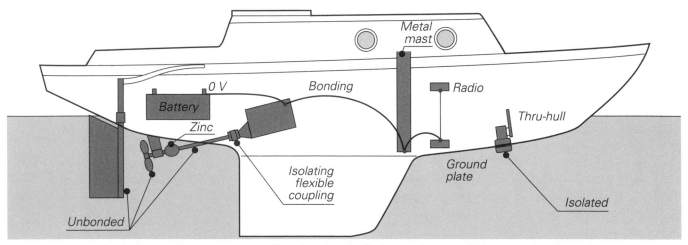

Isolating underwater parts, like the thru-hull shown here, will keep galvanic and stray currents from flowing between these parts.

AC Circuits

If you understand the relationships between voltage, current, and resistance in DC circuits (page 124), then you are ready for the similar relationships in alternating current (AC) circuits.

If we measured the voltage between the black or red (hot) wire and the white (neutral) wire in an AC circuit, we would see that the voltage and current swing in a sinusoidal waveform, as shown at right. One full oscillation of voltage is known as a cycle. The number of cycles completed in one second is the frequency. The unit of frequency (cycles per second) is the hertz (Hz). Utility electricity in the U.S. is precisely regulated at 60 Hz.

Read the labels on the undersides of your AC electric appliances. Which is correct: 110, 112, 115, 117, 120, or 125 volts? There is no universal agreement as to the "standard" AC voltage, but here we will use a nominal value of 120 volts.

Note that the peak voltage in a 120 VAC circuit is actually about 170 volts. The amount of power delivered by an AC voltage is equivalent to that of a steady (DC) voltage equal to the average AC voltage. This average is not halfway between zero and peak voltage, however. Rather, it is the root-mean-square (rms) of the peak voltage—70.7 percent of the peak.

Look at the three wires coming into your home. Two are covered with heavy rubber insulation and are hot. The third, forming a shield around the other two, is neutral and maintained at the potential of the earth or ground. If we plotted the voltages between the three wires, we would produce a graph like the one at right. Between wires A and C, we would have 120 volts AC. Between B and C, we would also have 120 volts AC, but the polarity would be opposite that of A and C. If we ignore the neutral wire, C, and look at the voltage between the two hot wires, A and B, we see the difference, or 240 volts AC. Thus from the three incoming supply conductors, we actually derive three different voltage sources: 120 volts AC, 120 volts AC, and 240 volts AC.

AC power can be brought aboard a vessel as shore power from a marina hookup, generated by an onboard generator, or synthesized from the vessel's DC supply by an inverter. Like DC systems, all of these methods and systems involve issues of grounding and bonding, as well as corrosion. They are too complex to discuss here (we have to draw a line somewhere), but are covered thoroughly by the ABYC Standards.

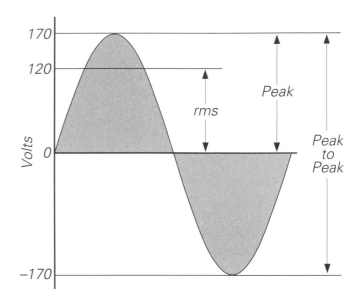

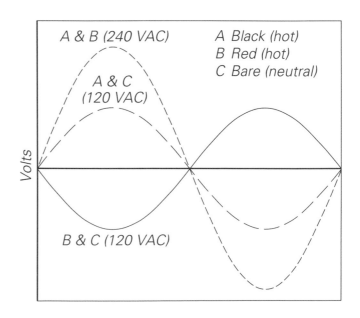

Grounding and Safety

Everyone knows that electricity can be dangerous. On the other hand, electricity is so useful that it has become indispensable. Methods for preventing accidental shock have, therefore, been developed.

The basic problem is that the human body is an electrochemical-mechanical system. At the center of this system is an advanced computer—the brain. External stimulations are converted to electrical signals by nerves, such as those in the eyes, ears, and skin. The electrical signals are conducted to the brain through nerve fibers that act much like conducting wires. The brain processes the incoming information and then sends out appropriate electrical signals in response. The effect of the outgoing signals is the stimulation and resulting contraction of muscles.

Unfortunately, the electrolytes in our body fluids make us conductors. When we bridge an electrical circuit, we become a part of that circuit, and electric current flows through us. Muscles in our bodies, including the heart, cannot distinguish between electrical signals from the brain and the electric current we call a shock. That is why a shock paralyzes muscles, including the heart.

As Ohm's law states, the greater the voltage, the greater the current, and it is the current that paralyzes. Fortunately, the threshold of danger is around 40 volts. A boat's 12 VDC system presents little danger of shock. A 120 VAC system, however, can be lethal. That is why the insulation is much thicker on AC cords than on DC wiring.

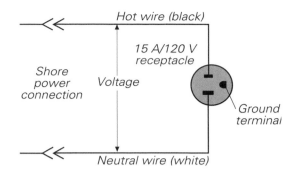

To avoid becoming part of an AC circuit, we must ground (connect by wire to the boat's ground) all of the exposed parts of an electrical device. This is done by providing a separate ground terminal in AC receptacles and electrical cords. The ground terminal is connected to a green wire that leads back to the boat's distribution panel. To prevent accidental reversal of the conductors in plug and socket connections, both sockets and plugs are designed so that they can be connected in only one way, and each terminal is assigned a color matching its conductor.

The illustration above shows the most familiar example: the 15 A/120 VAC polarized receptacle used in both residential and marine applications. Since the rectangular sockets are of different sizes, it is impossible to insert the mating polarized plug the wrong way and reverse the hot and neutral conductors. All screw terminals are color-coded to insure proper installation. The terminal for the hot (black) conductor is darkest; the neutral (white) terminal is silver; the grounding (green) terminal has a green tinge.

Ground Fault Circuit Interrupter (GFCI)

The green grounding conductor goes a long way toward providing safety, but what if the green wire is broken or missing? To protect against these situations, a clever form of circuit breaker is recommended for AC outlets located in head, galley, or machinery space or on deck.

In a normal AC circuit, all current flow is through the hot and neutral conductors. The green grounding conductor is connected to the neutral conductor at the distribution panel, but not at individual receptacles and devices. Thus, the green wire does not normally carry current. All current flowing in the hot conductor is intended to be returned in the neutral conductor. Any difference in current between the two conductors must therefore represent a stray (dangerous) current.

The GFCI is an electronic device that constantly compares the currents flowing in the hot and neutral conductors. A difference of as little as 5 milliamps (0.005 amp) causes the GFCI to break the circuit, rendering the circuit harmless. Although the sensitivity of these devices can sometimes be annoying, remember—it's better to be annoyed than dead.

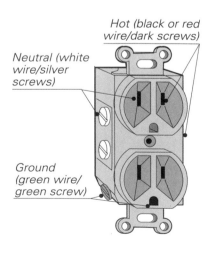

Alternators

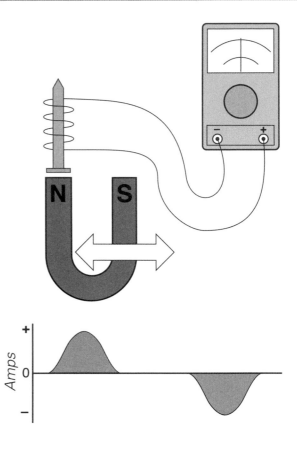

All you need to "get" the idea behind an alternator is a multimeter, a large steel nail or bolt, several feet of insulated copper wire, and a magnet.

Wrap half a dozen turns of the insulated wire around the nail and connect the bare ends of the wire to the meter. Hold the magnet as close to the head of the nail as possible without actually touching it. Now move the magnet rapidly back and forth, as shown in the illustration at right. The needle of the meter should jump back and forth across zero.

What's going on? An electric current is induced in a wire whenever the magnetic field around the wire changes. The moving magnet induces magnetism in the nail. As the permanent magnet moves back and forth, the magnetism in the nail alternates in direction, so the magnetic field through the coiled wire alternates as well. The alternating field produces pulses of current of alternating polarity, as shown in the graph. The current is proportional to the strength of the magnetic field, the speed of the magnet, and the number of turns in the coil.

A Rotary-Current Generator

Instead of passing the magnet back and forth across the head of the nail, we can make a rotating machine to do the same thing. The figure at right shows a straight bar magnet pivoted about its center between two coils connected in series. The coils are wound in opposite directions, so the opposite poles of the magnet produce current in the same direction. As the magnet turns, however, each coil sees alternating poles, so the current changes polarity, as shown in the graph.

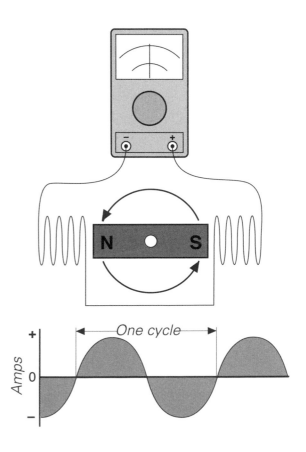

Increasing Current Output

We can make our rotary-current machine more efficient by placing more magnets on the rotating shaft and by adding a corresponding number of coils of wire. With three times as many magnets and coils, the result is three times as much generated power.

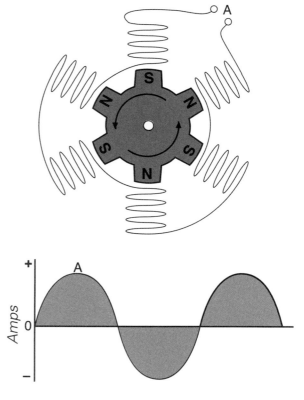

Three-Phase Output

We'll call the entire series-connected coil shown above coil A. Add coils B and C, identical in form to coil A but rotated one third and two thirds of the gap between the small coils of coil A, as shown at right.

The poles of the rotating magnet will pass each set of small coils in the order A, B, C, A, B, C, etc. The currents induced in coils A, B, and C will therefore be offset by one third and two thirds of a cycle, as shown. There are now three identical alternating currents, offset in phase by 120 degrees (one complete cycle equals 360 degrees).

Why would we want to complicate our rotary-current machine in this way?

1. We can triple power output without increasing the size of the wire in the coils.

2. It is easier to wind closely spaced coils than to increase the number of magnetic poles.

3. The three phases result in a more constant output.

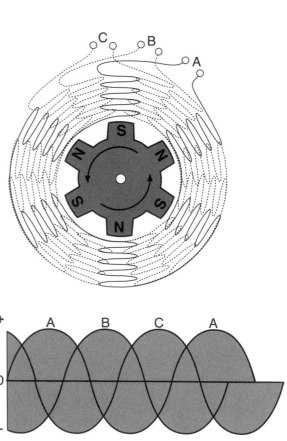

Converting AC to DC

As we saw on page 130, batteries produce direct current (DC), which is always of the same polarity or sign. To recharge a battery, we need DC. The rotary-current machine is of no use in charging batteries or powering DC electronics unless its three-phase AC output is converted to DC.

Enter the diode. A diode allows current to flow in only one direction—the direction of the arrow symbol. You can think of it as the equivalent of a check valve in a water-supply system, allowing water to flow in one direction but not the opposite.

Insert a diode into the circuit at the top of page 140. Now when you pass the magnet back and forth, the needle will deflect only in the positive direction. The magnet and wire coil still produce positive and negative pulses, but the negative pulses are blocked by the diode.

The illustration at right (top) shows how a diode would similarly block negative current in our rotary-current machine. The process of passing current of one polarity but blocking current of the opposite polarity is called rectification. Passing only the positive halves of an AC wave is called half-wave rectification.

Rectification would be twice as efficient if we could somehow pass both halves of the AC wave. In fact, this can be done by arranging four diodes in a particular geometry. As shown at right, regardless of polarity of current and voltage through the wire coil, two of four diodes always see a reverse voltage and act as if they were open circuits, while the other two see a positive voltage and pass the current. The diode arrangement is called a full-wave rectifier, for obvious reasons.

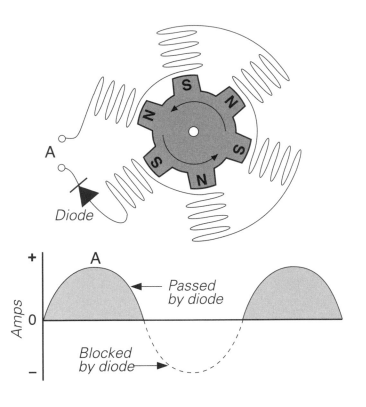

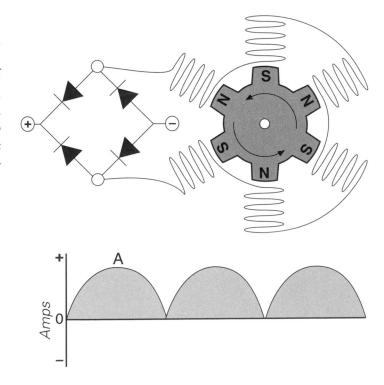

Controlling the Alternator

So far we can vary the output of the alternator only by changing engine rpm, which is obviously inconvenient.

The problem of control is solved by varying the strength of the magnet. Instead of the permanent magnet we have used so far, let's use an electromagnet. The iron core concentrates the magnetic field, which is generated by the current in the coil. The strength of the field generated is proportional to the current flowing in the field coil. Thus, alternator output can be controlled by varying current through the field coil. This current is supplied by the voltage regulator—a simple circuit either within the alternator or attached to it. The purpose of the voltage regulator is to produce the optimum voltage for battery charging. As discussed on page 131, there are sophisticated multistage regulators designed for optimal charging.

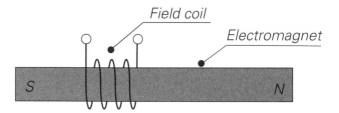

The Rotor

A magnet will induce magnetism of opposite polarity in any piece of iron in its close proximity, a phenomenon you can verify with any magnet and two or more nails.

In the figure at right, two additional iron bars placed at the ends of the core also become magnets. The added bars are actually iron disks with fingers that have been bent around and interleaved. In this way, current through a single field coil wrapped around the shaft results in alternating magnetic fingers around the circumference. It also shows how we get current to the rotating field coil through carbon brushes riding on copper slip rings fixed to the shaft.

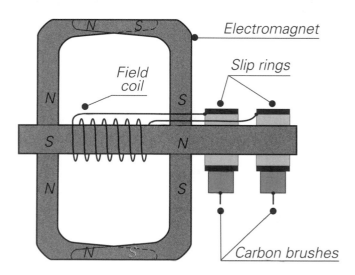

A Real Rotor

The illustration at right shows a typical real alternator rotor with interleaving magnetic poles, slip rings, and field coil wrapped around the inside shaft. The rotor rotates inside a collection of stationary coils—the stator—as seen in the exploded view of a real alternator on page 144.

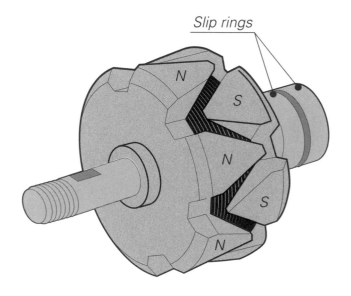

Volvo MD31A Alternator

In this exploded view of the Volvo MD31A alternator, you can recognize the rotor assembly with interleaving fingers, interior windings and slip rings, the stationary stator windings, the diode bridge for rectifying output voltage, the brushes for transmitting the field current, and the solid-state regulator.

The brushes, the regulator module, and the diode bridge are easily replaced in the field.

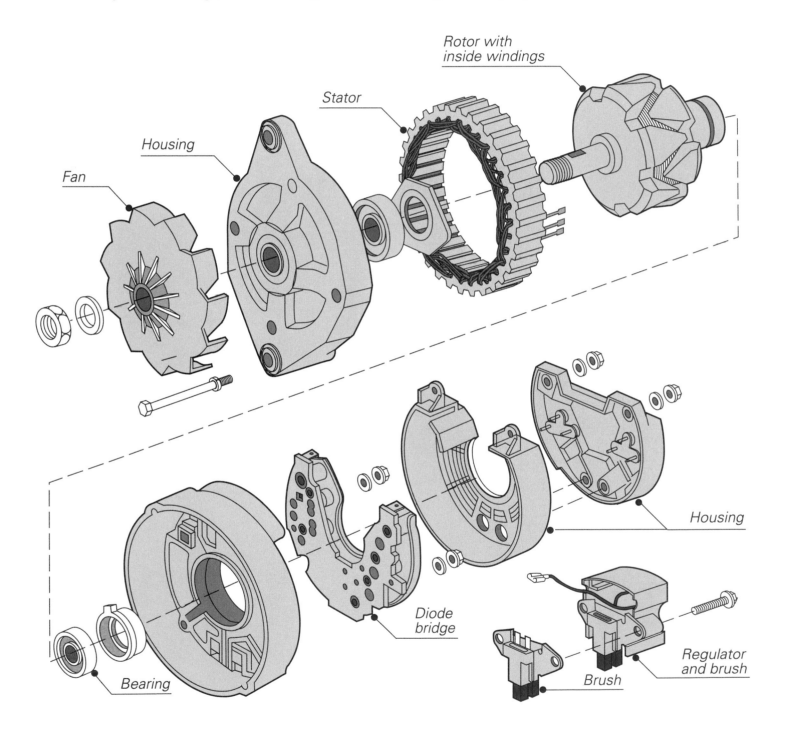

Fan

Housing

Stator

Rotor with
inside windings

Bearing

Diode
bridge

Housing

Brush

Regulator
and brush

7
Plumbing

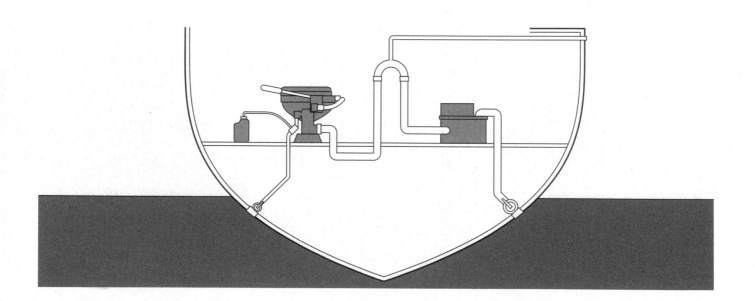

Pumps

Centrifugal Pump

The Groco CP-20 is an example of a centrifugal pump. Liquid enters axially at the center of the pump. The impeller blades impart rotation to the in-flowing fluid, which is then thrown outward by centrifugal force. The fluid's energy of motion (kinetic energy) translates into a pressure head.

Centrifugal pumps must be either primed or below the level of the fluid being pumped. And the flow rate depends strongly on the pressure or height to which the fluid is being pumped. On the other hand, there are no parts to wear except bearings and end seals, so the pumps are virtually maintenance free.

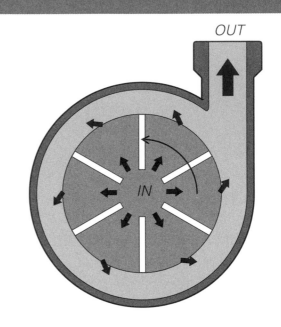

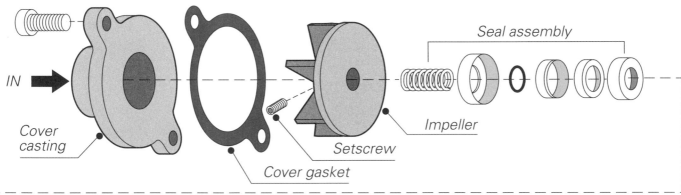

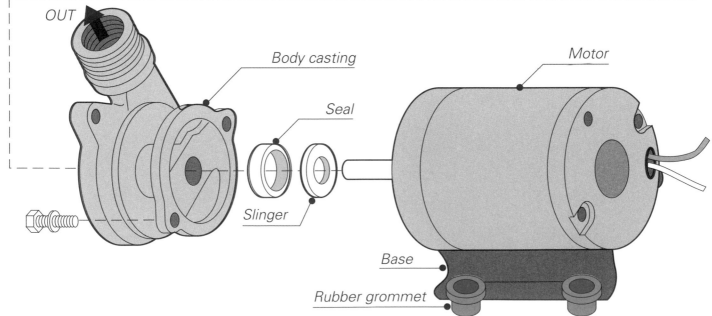

Flexible Impeller Pump

Used in most diesel raw-water cooling systems, the flexible impeller pump (here the Jabsco P35) gets its name from the flexible rubber-vaned impeller. As the impeller rotates, fluid is trapped in the spaces between adjacent vanes. In the forward direction the spaces are large, but in the reverse direction the vanes are squeezed by a cam, reducing the sizes of the spaces. As a result, more fluid is moved in the forward direction than the reverse, producing a net fluid flow. The tips of the vanes are fattened to give a larger wear surface.

Since the impeller forms a near-perfect seal with the pump casing, or body, the pump is self-priming (10 feet dry, 25 feet wet). On the negative side, the impeller will be damaged if operated dry for more than 30 seconds, as friction between the unlubricated rubber and the bronze pump body will build up intense heat.

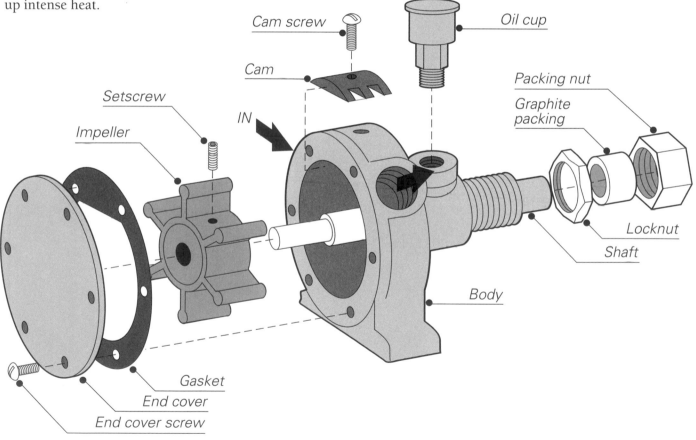

Vane Pumps

In the vane pump (Groco SPO Series shown), a circular rotor with blades (vanes) rotates inside a circular pump casing. However, the two circles are not concentric. As the rotor rotates, the blades slide in and out to maintain contact with the casing. As with the flexible impeller pump, the volume of fluid trapped by the blades is greater in the forward direction than the reverse, so a net fluid flow is produced.

The seal between the blades and pump casing is not quite as good as with the flexible impeller, but sufficient to provide self-priming to about three feet.

Maintenance consists only of replacing the blades and, occasionally, the shaft seal.

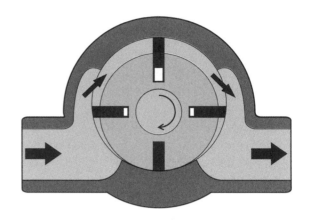

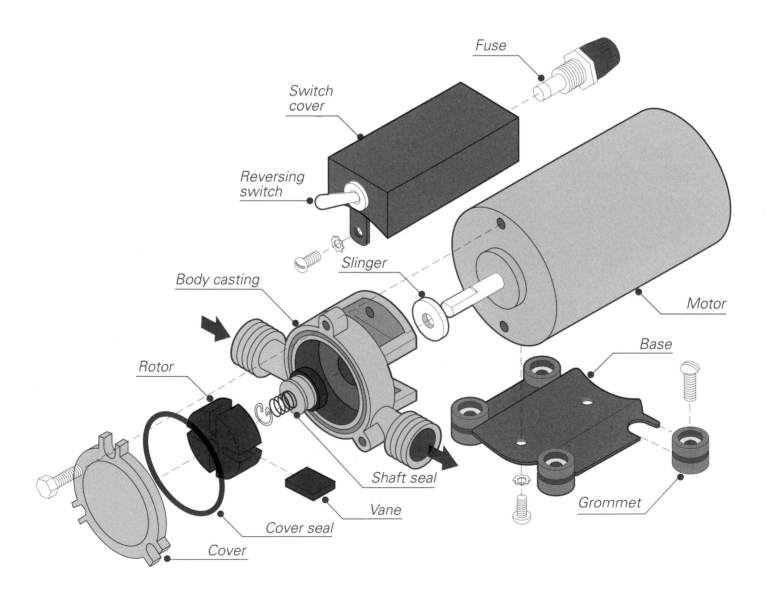

Diaphragm Pumps

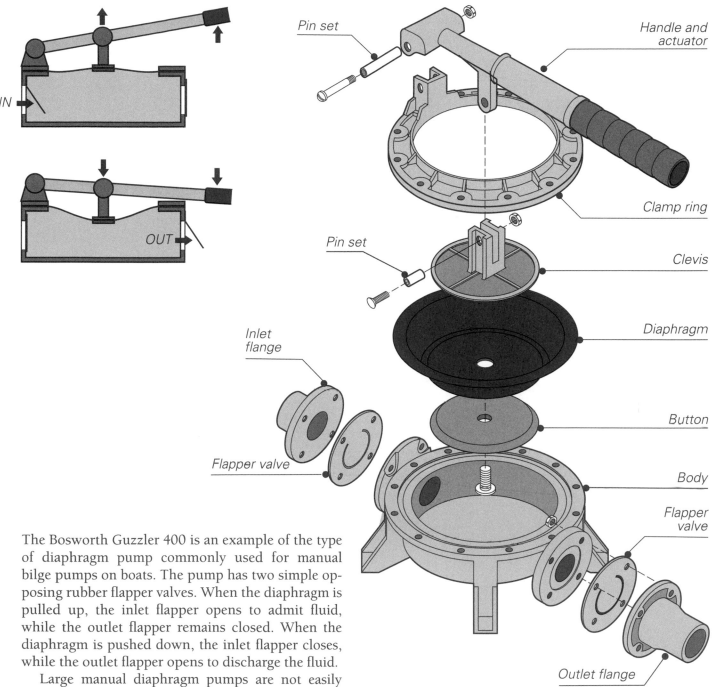

The Bosworth Guzzler 400 is an example of the type of diaphragm pump commonly used for manual bilge pumps on boats. The pump has two simple opposing rubber flapper valves. When the diaphragm is pulled up, the inlet flapper opens to admit fluid, while the outlet flapper remains closed. When the diaphragm is pushed down, the inlet flapper closes, while the outlet flapper opens to discharge the fluid.

Large manual diaphragm pumps are not easily clogged by debris so are excellent emergency bilge pumps. And their pumping rate is limited only by the strength and endurance of the operator.

On the other hand, when the flappers are dry, the pump has very limited self-priming ability, and the pump is difficult to prime. The flappers also distort over time and should be replaced periodically.

Whale Flipper Pump Mk. 4

This popular galley item is a manual piston pump. A linkage translates rotary motion of the handle to lift on a "bucket" (piston) inside a cylinder. When the bucket rises, it both lifts water above it and suctions water behind it through the bottom check valve. When the bucket drops back, the check valve closes and prevents backflow, while the ball valve opens to allow water up to the top of the bucket.

Whale V Pump Mk. 6

Where small space combines with small water demand, this simple pump is perfect. It also has two valves: a check valve at the bottom and a cup washer at the top. When the plunger rises, the cup washer lifts water above it and suctions water in through the check valve. When the plunger falls, the check valve closes to prevent backflow, while the cup washer forms an imperfect seal and allows water into the top of the barrel.

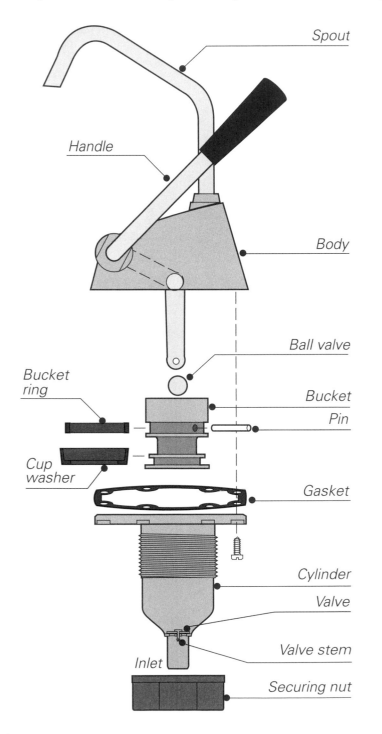

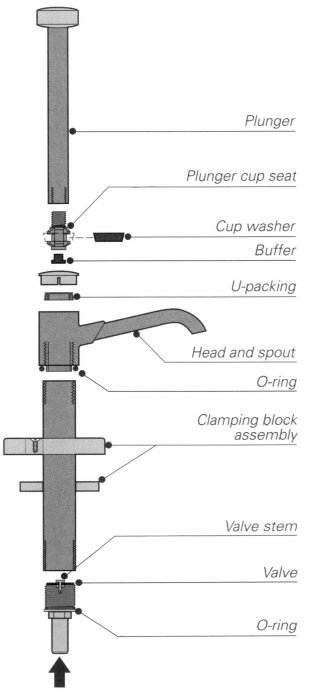

Whale Babyfoot Pump Mk. 2

Another popular galley pump, the Babyfoot is a simple foot-operated diaphragm pump. The rubber diaphragm is held up by a strong interior spring. In the base of the pump are two rubber disks (valve flaps) held in the inlet and outlet ports by rubber stems. The stems are installed in different directions so that when one flap opens, the other flap closes.

Stepping on the diaphragm depresses the spring, closes the inlet flap, and opens the outlet flap, so that water is ejected. Removing your foot allows the spring to raise the diaphragm. The resulting suction closes the outlet flap and draws water in past the inlet flap to refill the pump.

Small springs inside the inlet and outlet ports keep the valve flaps normally closed to prevent loss of prime.

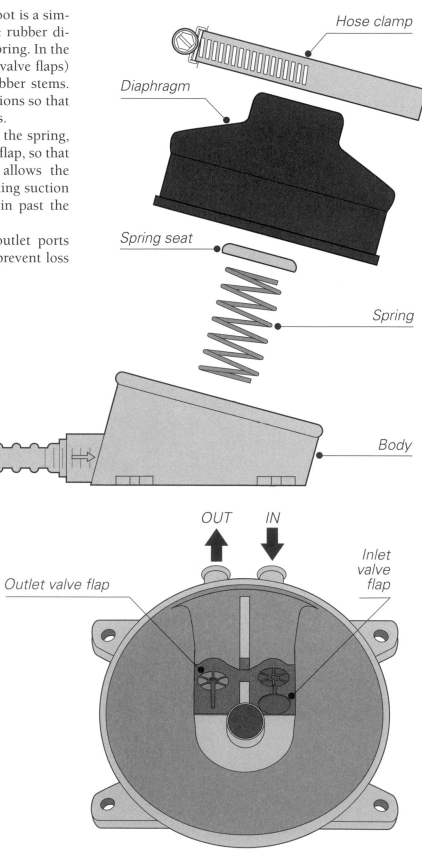

Whale Gusher Galley Mk. 3

The Gusher is a foot-operated, double-acting pump, employing two diaphragms, two inlet valves, and two outlet valves. While the disassembled pump appears complex, it is really nothing more than two back-to-back diaphragm pumps.

One of the diaphragms is mounted in each of the two end covers. The centers of the diaphragms are connected by way of a lipped cylinder. The cylinder is driven back and forth by the yoke of the operating lever, which converts up-and-down pedal motion to in-and-out diaphragm motion. The strong operating spring returns the pedal to its up position after being depressed.

The inlet and outlet nipples act as manifolds, supplying and collecting water from the pairs of inlet and outlet valves so that water is ejected on both up and down pedal strokes.

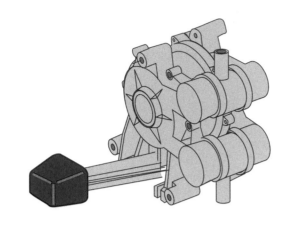

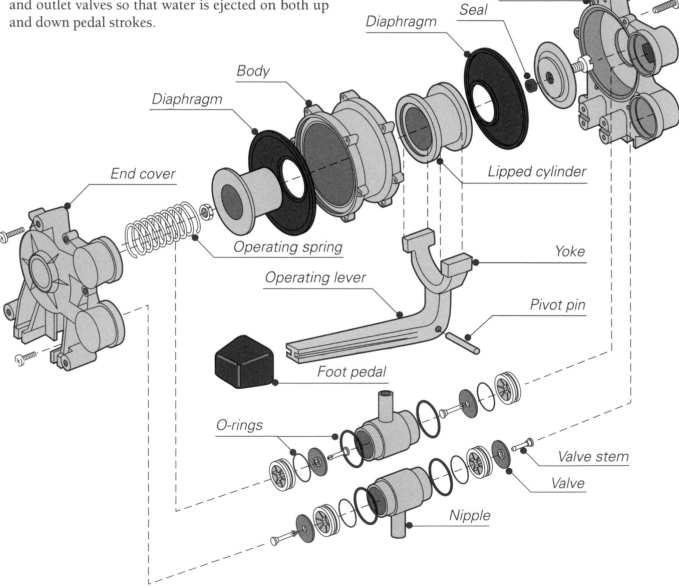

Jabsco Par-Mate Electric Diaphragm Pump

The Par-Mate water pump is designed for RVs and boats having multifixture water systems. The pump starts and stops automatically with the opening and closing of a faucet or other water-consuming fixture.

Similar to several other 12 VDC pressure pumps, the Par-Mate is a double-acting diaphragm pump in which the diaphragms are actuated by an electric motor. Gears inside the motor housing translate rotary motion into alternating strokes of the plungers and centers of the attached rubber diaphragms. The diaphragms are only about one inch in diameter, but the rapid action produces a flow of about 2.5 gallons per minute.

A third diaphragm inside the valve housing pushes, under pressure, against a spring (see pressure switch assembly). When the water pressure reaches an adjustable upper limit, the distended diaphragm presses against a microswitch, turning the pump off.

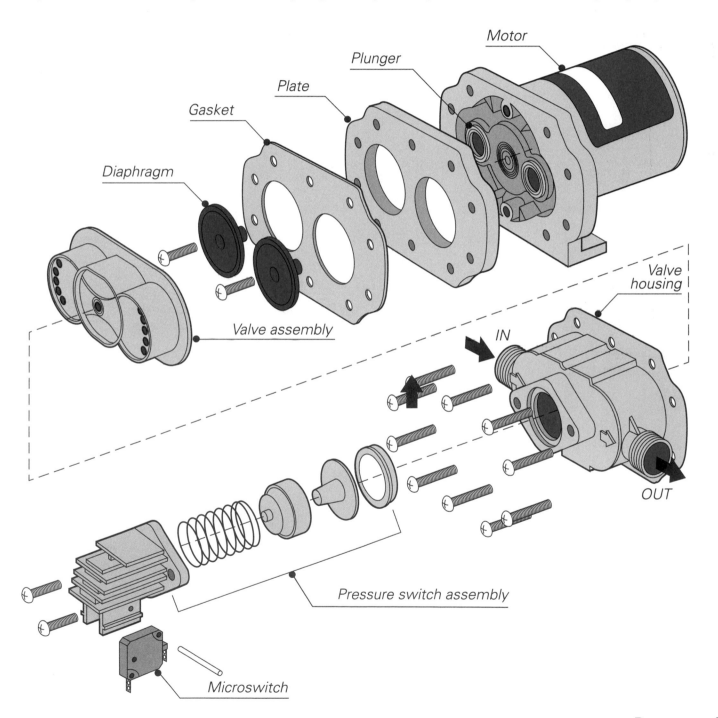

Motor

Plunger

Plate

Gasket

Diaphragm

Valve assembly

Valve housing

IN

OUT

Pressure switch assembly

Microswitch

Water Systems

The Raritan Galley Flow water pressure system is an excellent example of a complete freshwater system for boats.

Water may be supplied directly under pressure from a dockside water hookup or drawn from the ship's freshwater storage tank. Water drawn from the ship's tank is pressurized by a flexible diaphragm pump (see facing page). A small accumulator tank attached to the pump helps prevent rapid on-off cycling of the pump. For less cycling, a larger expansion tank may be installed on the downstream side of a check valve.

Both accumulator and expansion tanks contain captive-air bladders. As the water is forced into the tank by the pump, the air is compressed. When the pressure reaches its upper limit, the pump stops. As water is drawn from the tank, the air pressure drops to the low limit of the pressure switch, triggering the pump to recharge the tank.

Cold water is drawn directly from the expansion tank. Hot water is supplied by a 6-, 12-, or 20-gallon water heater, which may contain an engine-coolant heat exchanger, as well as a 110 VAC heater element for running on shore power.

The engine-coolant heat exchanger is a coil of copper tubing inside the water heater tank. The freshwater coolant is diverted, on its way from the thermostat to the engine's heat exchanger, through the water heater exchanger, imparting some of the engine's heat to the water heater tank.

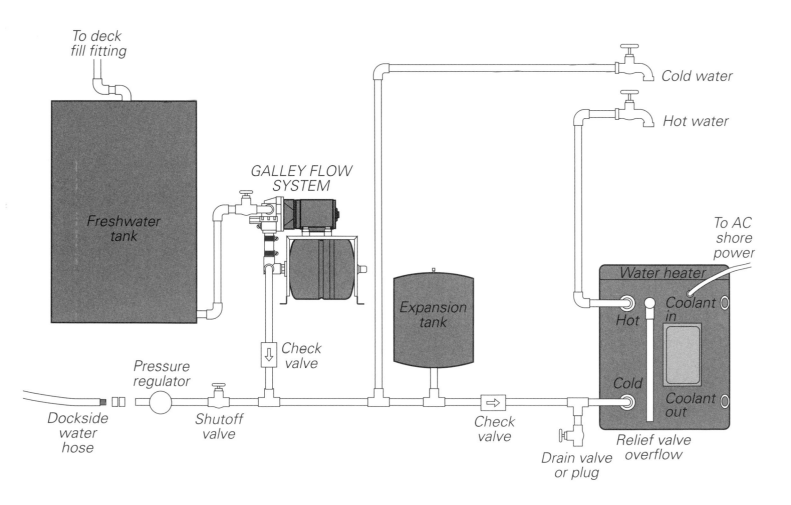

Raritan GMPT Galley Mate Pump Assembly

The Raritan Galley Mate pump is similar in operation to the Jabsco Par-Mate double-acting diaphragm pump shown on page 153, the major difference being its use of four diaphragms instead of two.

Due to the rigidity and membrane-like construction of boats, mechanical vibration anywhere in a boat is readily transmitted throughout the boat. Diaphragm pumps convert rotary motion to back-and-forth piston motion, generating low-frequency noise. For this reason, Raritan has switched to a much quieter flexible impeller pump in its Super Galley Mate system.

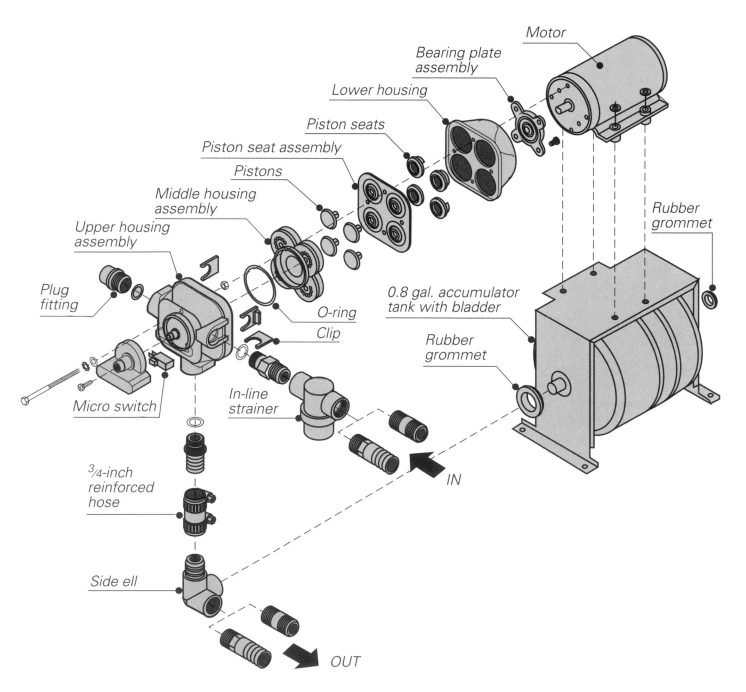

Marine Toilets

The discharge of untreated sewage is prohibited in U.S. waters within the three-mile limit. Inside three miles waste must be either treated before discharge or directed to a holding tank by a secured Y-valve.

The Raritan LectraSan MC (microprocessor control) is a Coast Guard–certified Type I marine sanitation device (macerator/chlorinator) for vessels 65 feet or less in length. It can treat and discharge waste in all areas except EPA-designated No-Discharge Zones. When operating in such areas you must employ, a holding tank (see bottom illustration). To be certain, check the regulations in force in your boating area.

The macerator is usually installed with the top of its treatment tank below the toilet discharge. If the tank is at or above the toilet discharge, a vented loop is installed in the waste line with the vent terminated outside the hull.

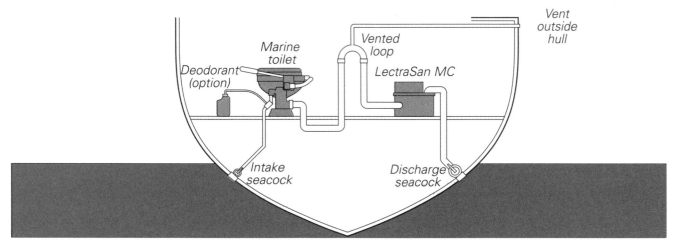

Marine toilets installed above the waterline are less prone to siphoning, and thus their intake lines don't need a vented loop.

Vented loops serve to introduce air into pipes terminating below the waterline. Otherwise, water might siphon into the vessel, flooding it. Installation of a toilet below the waterline requires a vented loop in the discharge line. A treatment tank below the waterline also requires a vented loop between the treatment tank discharge and the thru-hull. The tops of vented loops should extend at least 4 to 6 inches above the heeled waterline and the vents should terminate outside the hull. The intake loop is not vented, but allows cleaning of the raw-water strainer without closing the intake seacock.

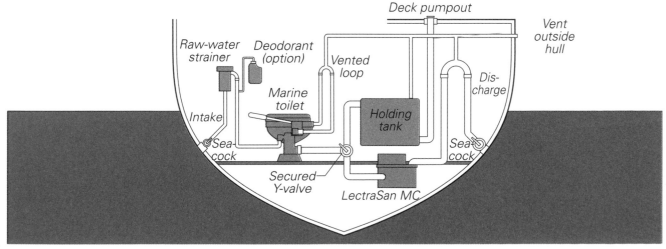

Toilets installed below the waterline should be fitted with vented loops in both the intake line and the discharge line.

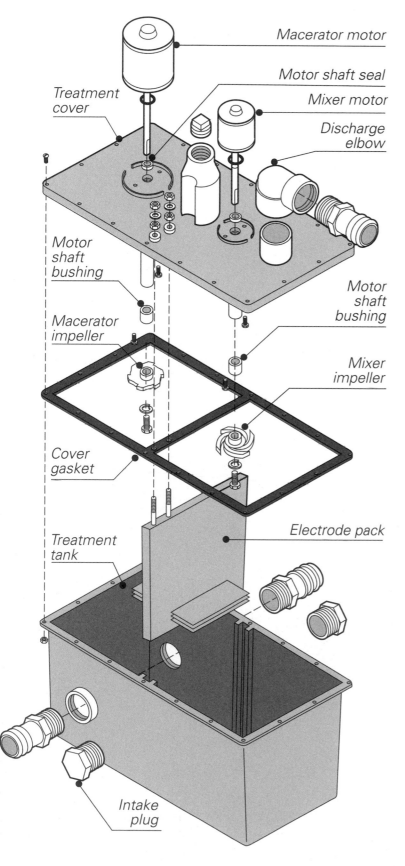

Macerator motor

Motor shaft seal

Mixer motor

Discharge elbow

Treatment cover

Motor shaft bushing

Motor shaft bushing

Macerator impeller

Mixer impeller

Cover gasket

Treatment tank

Electrode pack

Intake plug

The LectraSan MC

When the head is flushed, the wastewater flows into the first chamber of the treatment tank, displacing overboard wastewater that has been previously treated.

The new waste is first macerated (ground into a fine slurry) while an electric charge is applied to the electrodes in both chambers for several minutes, converting the conductive saltwater solution into hypochlorous acid. The acid destroys most viruses and bacteria before reverting back to salt water.

A mixer in the second chamber comes on every time the toilet is flushed to prevent the accumulation of sludge in the tank.

Note that the system requires salt water to generate the acid. Vessels operating in freshwater can install an optional salt-feed tank, which automatically siphons salt solution into the toilet discharge with each flush. A less expensive option for the weekend sailor is a handy container of salt and a spoon with which to add a spoonful with every flush.

Raritan PHII Marine Toilet

A single piston pumps both inlet water and waste. To let water into the bowl, the intake valve handle is turned counterclockwise to the "open" position. Pushing the handle and piston down pulls water past the intake ball valve into the top of the pump housing. The following upstroke forces the water out of the freshwater discharge into the bowl.

At the same time, the piston acts to empty the bowl of waste through the bottom of the pump housing. On the upstroke waste is drawn from the bowl into the pump housing through the rubber flapper valve. On the following downstroke the flapper valve closes and the waste is forced from the pump housing out through the joker valve.

The intake valve must be either in the fully open (flush) or fully closed (dry) position—never in between. The fully closed (dry) position allows the bowl to be pumped dry.

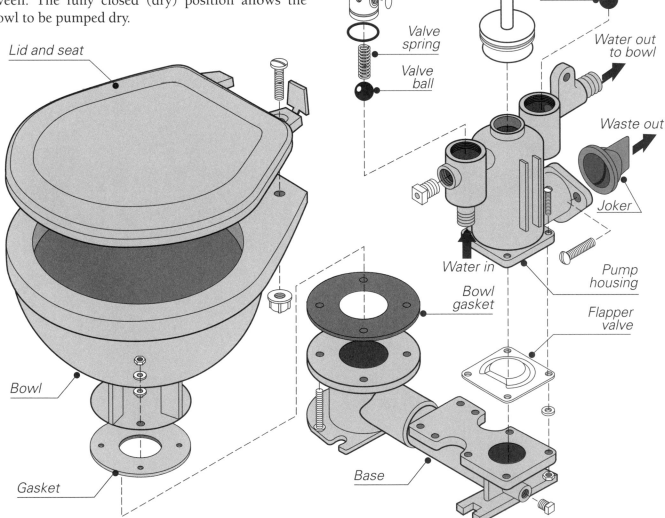

Some manufacturers recommend flushing a quart of vinegar through the system once a week to prevent the buildup of calcium (calcification), particularly in the discharge lines.

PHII Electric Conversion Kit

The PHII Marine Toilet may be converted to the PHEII Electric Marine Toilet by the simple addition of a motor-drive kit. The kit's gearbox housing bolts to the toilet base between the bowl and the pump.

When the unit's push button is pressed, the motor turns a worm, engaging a worm gear. The gear reduction slows the worm gear to about 100 rpm and increases the torque exerted on the gearbox output shaft.

The shaft is pinned to a short link arm that drives the connecting rod. As the link rotates, a pin in the slot at the bottom of the connecting rod forces the rod up and down. The top of the connecting rod is bolted to the piston rod yoke, so the piston is forced up and down. The toilet can always be converted back to manual operation by disconnecting the connecting rod from the piston rod yoke and replacing the handle.

The motor drive relieves the operator from pumping the handle but not from operating the toilet's inlet valve.

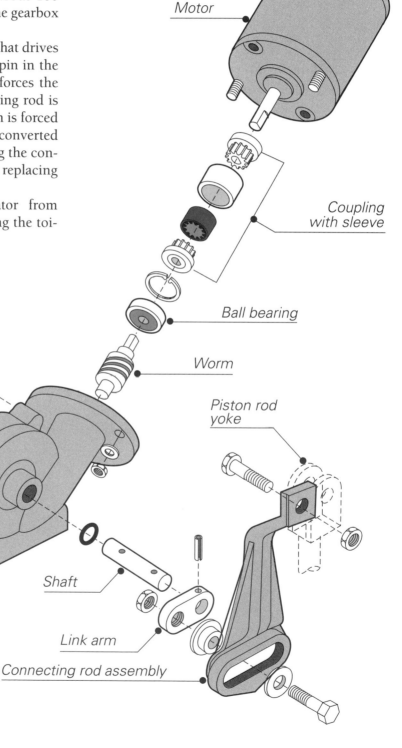

Motor

Coupling with sleeve

Ball bearing

Worm

Piston rod yoke

Gearbox cover

O-ring

Worm gear

Gearbox housing

Shaft

Link arm

Connecting rod assembly

Tapered-Plug Seacocks

The traditional bronze seacock consists of a tapered bronze plug fitted inside a matching bronze body. The plug may be across the body (as in the rubber plug seacock on the following page) or in line with the body (as shown at right).

The plug has a large through-hole, either across its diameter or axially and out the side. In either case, when the handle lines up with the seacock's discharge, the hole is in line and the seacock is open. Turning the handle a quarter turn closes off the hole. Whether the seacock is open or closed is, therefore, obvious.

The plug is held in the tapered hole by a keeper ring. The plug should be greased liberally and the keeper tightened only enough to prevent leakage. Excessive tightening simply squeezes out the grease and makes the seacock hard to operate.

Bronze seacocks are metal components immersed in seawater. Due to the potential for galvanic corrosion, they are often bonded to the ship's DC ground. For a discussion of whether to bond seacocks, see page 137.

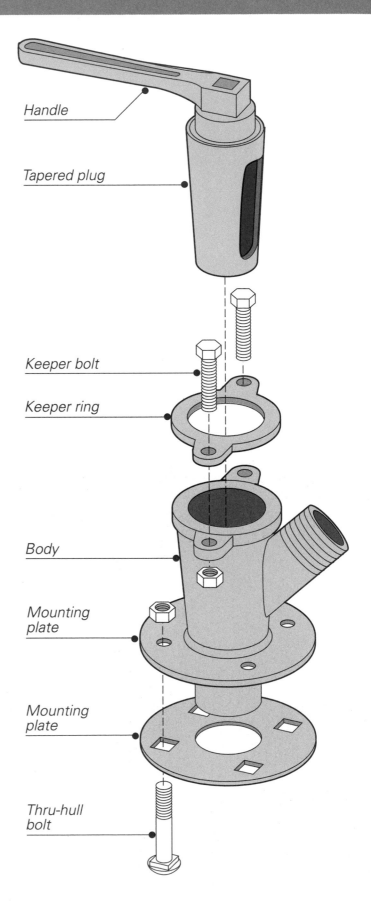

Handle

Tapered plug

Keeper bolt

Keeper ring

Body

Mounting plate

Mounting plate

Thru-hull bolt

Expanding-Plug Seacocks

Traditional seacocks were all bronze. Two factors have led to their increasing replacement by alternatives: expense and susceptibility to galvanic corrosion. One such version is the expanding rubber-plug seacock.

The plug is a rubber cylinder with a large hole at a right angle to the cylinder axis. A handle is fitted to an extension of the plug. With the handle in line with the bronze seacock body, the plug hole lines up with the seacock inlet and outlet. With the handle crossways to the seacock body, the hole in the plug is blocked and the seacock is closed.

The seal between plug and body is effected by compression of the rubber plug. The plug fits between a metal seal disk and a metal keeper ring. The keeper ring is bolted firmly in place, then a wing nut is screwed in to tighten the seal disk against the plug. Being rubber, the plug expands radially to seal against the body.

The wing nut should be tightened only enough to stop leakage. To operate the valve, the wing nut is first loosened to allow easy turning, then retightened.

If the wing nut is overtightened, the rubber bulges into the inlet and outlet holes in the body and takes a permanent set, effectively destroying the plug. The rubber can also be damaged by petroleum-based lubricants, so the plug must be lubricated with silicone-based waterproof grease.

Due to its susceptibility to damage, this type of seacock has fallen out of favor.

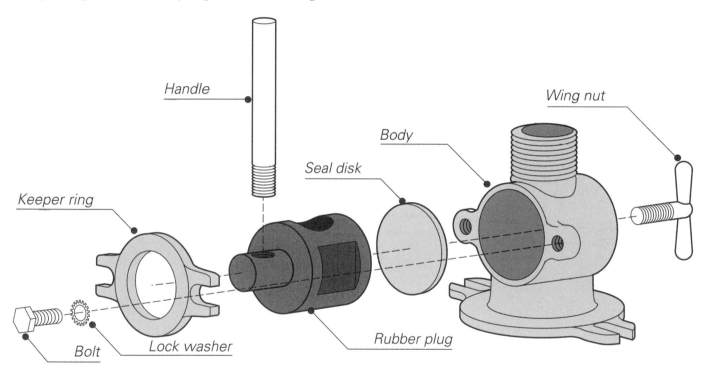

Handle · Wing nut · Body · Seal disk · Keeper ring · Bolt · Lock washer · Rubber plug

Ball-Valve Seacocks

Ball-valve seacocks have long been the favorite of plumbers and are becoming more popular on boats. With bronze or stainless balls and Teflon seats, and with minimal sliding contact area, these valves require no annual maintenance yet remain easy to operate.

The principle is the same as that of the plug-type seacock, except that a ball is substituted for the cylinder. A ball with a concentric thru-hull is trapped between concave top and bottom seals. When the hole lines up with the center holes in the seals, the valve is open. When the ball is turned 90 degrees by a stem fitting into a slot, the valve is closed.

Stops molded into the valve body limit the handle travel from fully open to fully closed. Again, the valve is open with the handle in line with the body.

Plastic versions of this seacock are growing in acceptance. Not to be confused with household-plumbing PVC valves, marine versions are molded of glass-reinforced, high-strength plastics. While they are immune to corrosion, plastic seacocks still must be operated and lubricated regularly. If they do stick, you can't take a hammer to the handle as you could in the past with the all-bronze versions.

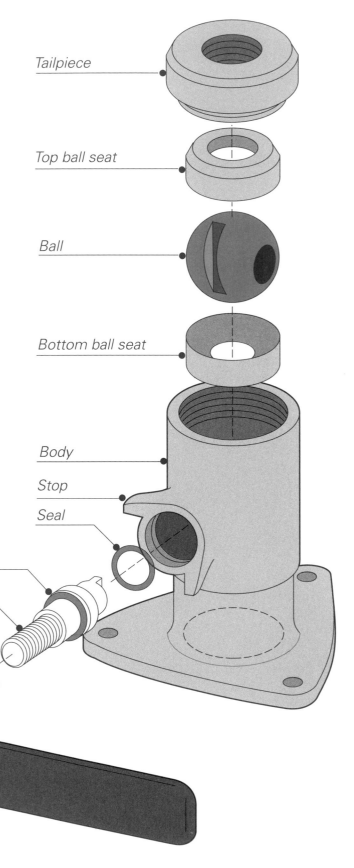

Tailpiece

Top ball seat

Ball

Bottom ball seat

Body

Stop

Seal

Seal

Driver

Packing nut

Handle

Stem handle nut

Y-Valves

The Y-valve is designed to connect one or the other of two inlet ports to a single discharge port. Since direction of flow is not critical, it can also be used to direct the flow of a single input to one or the other of two discharge ports.

The cylindrical valve body has three equally spaced ports. A rubber plug resembling a half cylinder fits into the valve body. In one position of the handle, two of the ports are connected through the missing half of the plug, while the other port is blocked. In the other handle position, the open and blocked inlet ports are reversed.

Y-valves are commonly used on boats to divert sewage either to a thru-hull for immediate overboard discharge or to a holding tank for later discharge or pumping out. When used for this purpose, the valve should have a means of padlocking the handle so it cannot unknowingly be switched to overboard discharge. Older Y-valves lacked this provision. Many newer models have holes in the handle and body for a padlock. If yours doesn't have the padlock provision, the Coast Guard has been known to accept a sign posted near the valve instructing that it be in the non-overboard-discharge position at all times within the three-mile limit.

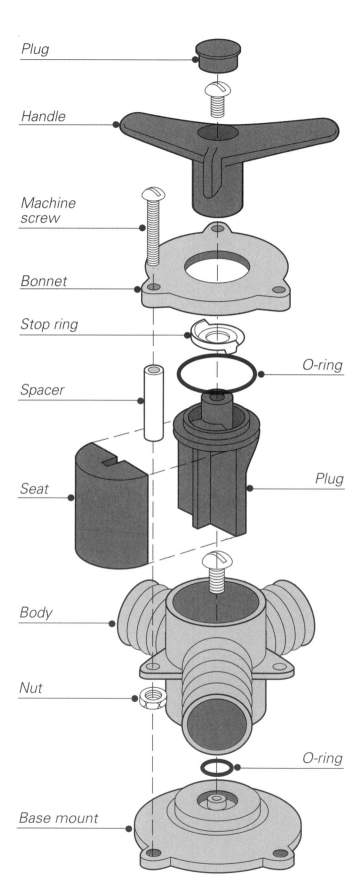

Plug

Handle

Machine screw

Bonnet

Stop ring

O-ring

Spacer

Seat

Plug

Body

Nut

O-ring

Base mount

Refrigeration

If you know that water boils (turns from liquid to gas) at 212°F at normal atmospheric pressure, but that its boiling temperature rises at higher pressure (such as in a pressure cooker), and that the evaporating water absorbs a lot of heat, then you are on your way to understanding how a refrigerator or air conditioner works.

The boiling point of water is much too high to use it as a refrigerant, but other fluids boil at temperatures below the freezing point of water! One such refrigerant is ES-12a (see graph at right), one of many refrigerants developed to replace R-12 Freon, now banned due to its adverse effect on the earth's ozone layer.

At atmospheric pressure (15 psi), ES-12a boils (evaporates) at about –26°F. If we compress it to a pressure of 150 psi, however, it boils at about 110°F. Since this temperature span approximates the range from freezer temperature to maximum atmospheric temperature, ES-12a may prove useful.

In the refrigeration system on the facing page, the refrigerant is sucked into a compressor. The piston compresses the gas to about 150 psi, in the process raising its temperature to about 120°F.

The hot, compressed gas then flows through the discharge line to a condenser—a heat exchanger—where it is cooled to below its condensation point and turns to a liquid.

From the condenser the hot liquid first passes through a dryer, which assures no water contaminates the refrigerant, then on to an expansion valve.

The function of the expansion valve is to control the release of the hot liquid into the low pressure of the evaporator coil. When the fluid emerges from the expansion valve, the dramatic drop back to near atmospheric pressure causes it to boil (evaporate) at about –25°F, absorbing heat from the evaporator coil. The evaporator coil is the frost-covered tubing you see in an older refrigerator or freezer.

From the evaporator, the now cool gas is again sucked into the compressor, and the cycle is repeated.

Now for some details.

Condenser

Efficient operation of the condenser requires that heat be quickly and continuously removed from the tubing. Air-cooled condensers utilize metal fins on the tubing and air flow over the fins to remove the heat. The efficiency of such an arrangement depends on both the temperature of the air and the

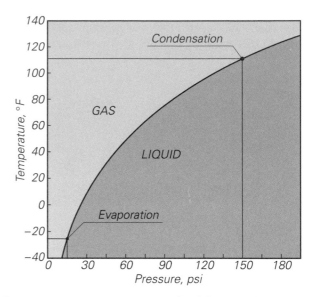

Pressure-temperature curve for ES-12a refrigerant. At temperature and pressure combinations above the curve, the refrigerant is a gas; below the curve it is a liquid. Condensation and evaporation occur at points on the curve.

rate of air flow. A stuffy engine compartment is obviously not a good location for the condenser.

Evaporator

The evaporator shown has very little heat storage capacity. As a result, the compressor will cycle on and off every few minutes. A lot of energy is lost starting the compressor, so the efficiency is relatively low. A better system encloses the evaporator coil in a small rectangular tank (a holding plate) filled with liquid having a low freezing point. The compressor runs until all of the holding plate liquid freezes. The holding plate then functions much like a block of ice. Properly sized for the refrigerator box, a holding plate system requires running the compressor just once a day for an hour or so. By running such a system only when the engine is running, all of the considerable load is removed from the boat's batteries.

Controls

A small temperature-sensing bulb on a capillary tube is attached to the suction end of the evaporator coil. The pressure (temperature dependent) in the tube controls the rate of fluid flow through the valve and thus the temperature of the evaporator coil.

When the temperature of the refrigerator box rises, a thermostat switches the compressor on to move and compress refrigerant, cooling the box.

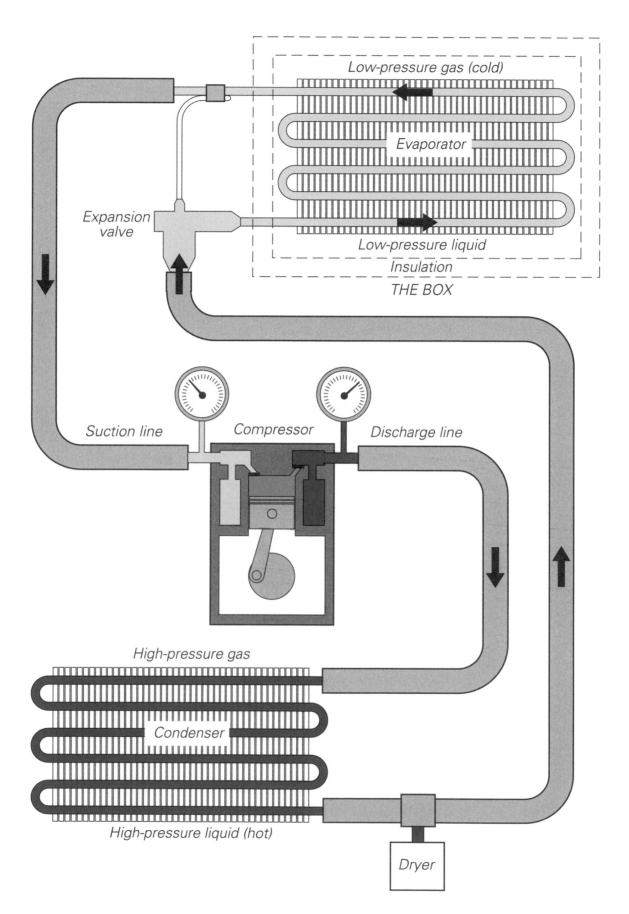

Low-pressure gas (cold)

Evaporator

Low-pressure liquid

Insulation

THE BOX

Expansion valve

Suction line

Compressor

Discharge line

High-pressure gas

Condenser

High-pressure liquid (hot)

Dryer

Adler Barbour Cold Machine

The introduction of the Cold Machine revolutionized small-boat refrigeration. Until that time refrigeration systems involved belt-driven compressors, meticulous and tricky purging and charging operations, and constant monitoring of system temperatures and pressures. You literally had to be, or hire, a refrigeration technician to make ice aboard.

The Cold Machine is supplied as a kit with a precharged and hermetically sealed compressor. Other than constructing the insulated box, installing the Cold Machine involves only running the copper refrigerant lines, connecting the quick-connect couplings, finding a well-ventilated space for the compressor and condenser, hooking up to 12 VDC, and plugging in the phone-jack thermostat.

That being said, the efficiency of the air-cooled condenser and simple evaporator box is relatively low, so Adler Barbour now offers the Super Cold Machine, which includes a more efficient water-cooled condenser and a holding plate.

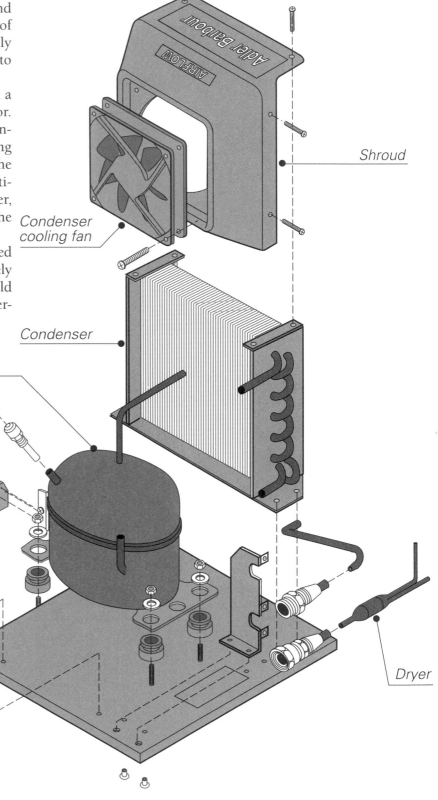

Shroud

Condenser cooling fan

Condenser

Compresser

Controller

Dryer

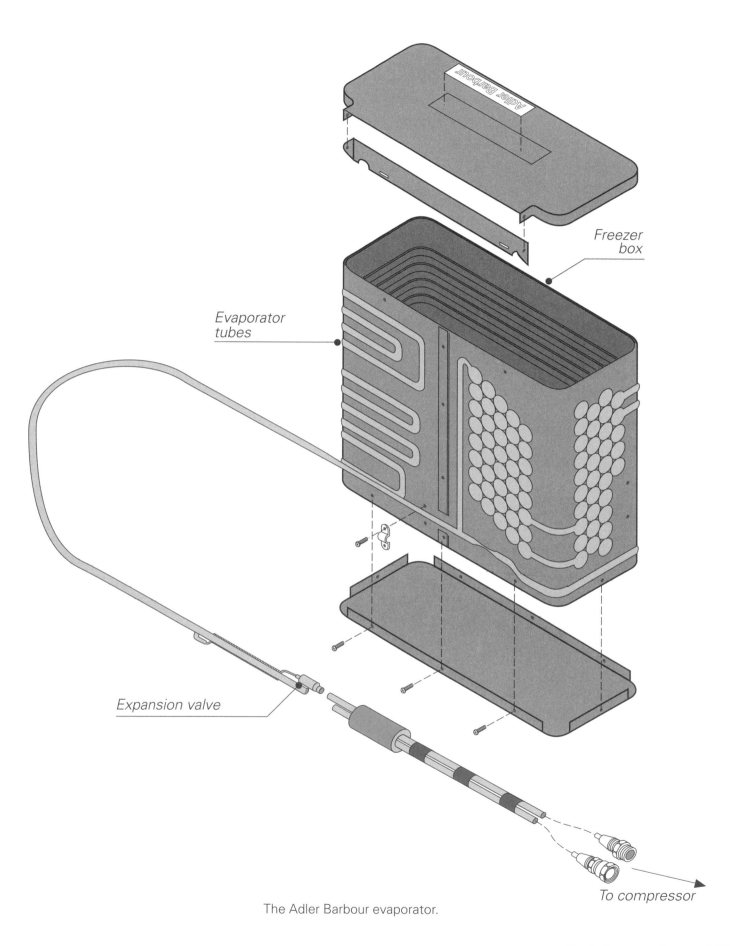

Freezer box

Evaporator tubes

Expansion valve

To compressor

The Adler Barbour evaporator.

Diesel Stove and Heater

The Dickinson Atlantic is representative of diesel pot burners, which are a favorite among fishermen and long-term liveaboards because the fuel is:

1. inexpensive
2. available worldwide
3. the same as that used in the engine
4. of low volatility

Fuel is pumped up to a "day tank" at least 12 inches above the metering valve. The stove burns only 1.6 gallons per day on low heat, so a 2-gallon tank is adequate. From there fuel flows by gravity to the metering valve, which feeds fuel to the bottom of the pot burner at a controlled rate (see illustration on facing page).

The fire is started in a small priming pool in the pot bottom, aided by a combustion-air fan. After the pot heats up, the fuel vaporizes and burns cleanly above the burn ring without need of a fan.

The cooktop is the cast-iron surface immediately above the flame. Flue gas normally flows over the top of the oven, heating it to 300 to 350°F on low heat, but pulling up the oven bypass damper forces the flue gas under the oven, increasing oven temperature.

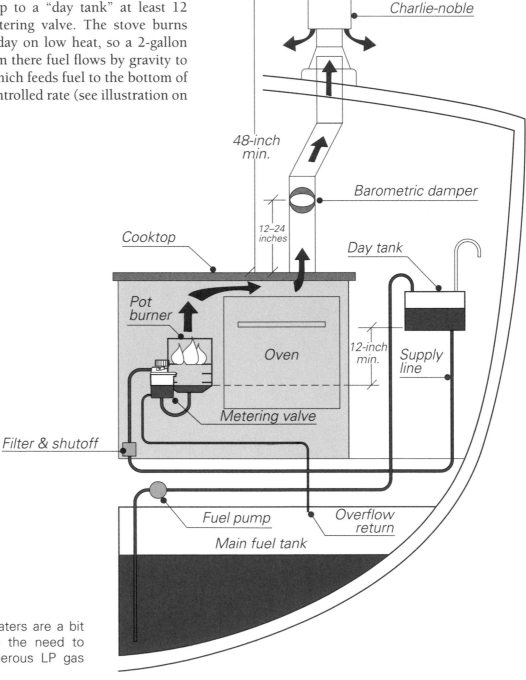

Diesel stoves and heaters are a bit messy, but eliminate the need to deal with more dangerous LP gas (propane).

Dickinson Fuel Metering Valve

The fuel metering valve controls the rate at which diesel fuel is fed to the burner—and thus its heat output—and it limits the level of fuel in the pot regardless of the burn rate.

The fuel is supplied by gravity to the metering valve inlet. Just inside the inlet fitting is a fine-mesh brass screen to filter out any particles that might clog the needle valve. The body of the valve contains a pool of fuel and a pivoting foam float. When the fuel reaches the desired level the float rises, pushing the valve needle up into its seat, shutting off the flow. By this means a constant level of fuel is maintained. A backup overflow tube spills excess fuel to a bottom fuel return fitting, from which the fuel returns to the main tank.

The rate at which fuel flows to the burner is determined by the control knob. The bottom of a setscrew, threaded through the knob, rides on an inclined surface. Turning the knob forces it and its attached metering stem up and down.

A vertical slot is machined into the bottom of the metering stem. With the knob fully clockwise, the knob and stem are at their lowest point, and the slot is fully below the hole in the metering stem guide, so no fuel can flow to the outlet. As the knob is turned counterclockwise, the metering stem and slot rise past the stem guide hole, and fuel flows at an increasing rate into the hole, down the slot, and out to the burner.

The metering valve is calibrated for No. 2 diesel fuel at room temperature. Other fuels and temperatures alter the fuel viscosity and resulting flow rate. The metered flow rate can be adjusted by loosening the locking nut and turning the Allen setscrew a half turn at a time. Turning the Allen screw clockwise raises the knob and stem, increasing the flow rate.

The Dickinson fuel metering valve is low tech, but a model of reliability.

Locking nut
Setscrew (Allen setscrew)
Control knob
Filter screen
Inlet
Valve seat
Valve needle
Overflow tube
Float pivot
Foam float
Body
Fuel return
Metering stem guide
Outlet to burner
Spring
Washer
Metering stem
Circlip
O-ring
Metering slot
Fuel level

LP Gas Installations

For cooking convenience and comfort aboard, nothing beats LP gas (propane). The only problem is that LP gas is heavier than air. Gas leaking anywhere within the hull enclosure may settle and build up in the bilge. If the concentration becomes great enough, a spark may ignite the gas, literally blowing the boat apart. For this reason LP gas equipment should be installed in accordance with the ABYC Standard A1, LP Gas Systems.

The gas cylinder(s), pressure gauge, regulator, solenoid valve, and all supply hose connections (except at the appliance) must be located within a vapor-tight locker. The locker must open only from the top and directly to the outside atmosphere. The top cover must be gasketed and latched tightly. The

locker must be vented from the bottom with a ½-inch minimum thru-hull and hose, sloped continuously downward (no low points to trap a water seal) and outboard to a vent that is above the waterline and at least 24 inches from any opening to the boat's interior or engine exhaust. All exiting hoses and wires must be gasketed to be vapor-tight.

Tanks may be of steel or aluminum (preferred), must meet Department of Transportation standards, and must be recertified every twelve years in the U.S. They must stand upright and be firmly secured to the compartment. The main valve should be turned off whenever the boat is left unattended. (It is also a good practice to turn off the valve between uses even with a solenoid control installed.) Assuming no

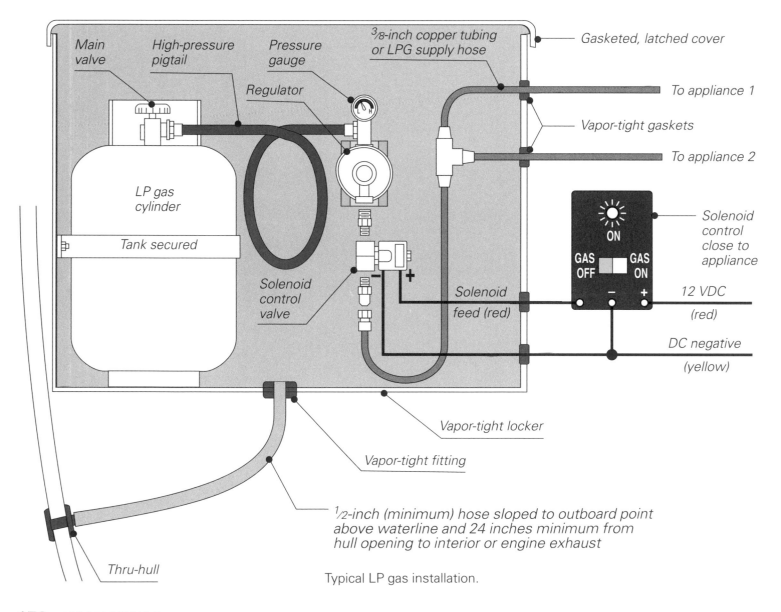

Typical LP gas installation.

cabin heater, average usage when cooking three meals a day on a stove with an oven should be 1 pound of gas per person per week. A 20-pound tank should thus last four to five weeks.

Although not mandatory, a 300 psi pressure gauge is an important safety feature, allowing testing for system leaks. The pressure gauge must be installed immediately after the main valve. It can be mounted directly on the bottle or installed on the locker wall and connected to the bottle with a supply hose pigtail.

Note that the gauge does not indicate the amount of fuel in the tank; you must weigh the tank to determine that. The single purpose of the pressure gauge is to allow testing of the entire system for leaks.

To test for a gas leak:

- Open the main valve.
- Turn solenoid valve on.
- Turn off all appliances.
- Note the pressure gauge reading.
- Turn off the main valve.
- After fifteen minutes read the pressure gauge again.

Any drop in pressure indicates a leak in the system.

A regulator drops the gas pressure in the tank from about 150 psi to about 0.5 psi. A tank-mounted marine regulator has a built-in pressure gauge and connects directly to the main valve. A wall-mounted regulator connects via a short, high-pressure hose assembly. Regulators are available with inputs from two tanks, allowing for simple switchover and replacement of empty tanks.

A solenoid control valve inside the tank compartment allows the gas supply to be turned on or off from the galley or some other point near the gas appliance. Although no more effective than manually turning off the main valve at the tank, considering human nature, it is a far more reliable method. The solenoid opens the gas flow only when the control panel is "On." Thus, if power fails, or if you leave the boat and turn off the battery switch, the gas is automatically turned off.

When you're not using the gas you must switch off the solenoid control panel. Some solenoid control panels incorporate a gas "sniffer" in the bilge. If gas is detected at 10 percent of its lower ignition limit, the solenoid is turned off and a warning light and/or alarm is activated.

The hose, if any, between the tank's main valve and the pressure gauge or regulator must be a high-pressure pigtail. (Some regulators and pressure gauges mount directly on the main valve, eliminating the pigtail.) Any hose from the vapor-proof compartment to an individual appliance must be continuous. Thus, if there are multiple appliances, the individual supplies must be taken from a T-fitting or a manifold inside the compartment.

The runs can be either of LPG supply hose (a reinforced rubber hose rated at 350 psi working pressure) or of $3/8$-inch copper refrigeration tubing. Tubing should be secured at least every 18 inches and protected against pinching, bumping, flexing, and abrasion. Points where tubing passes through the hull or bulkheads should be sealed.

Index

secondary fuel filters, 26, 29
seizing (knots), 85, 87, 97
self-tacking jibs and staysails, 102–3
servopendulum windvane, 70–71
shaft alignment: after rig tuning, 80; importance of, 13, 46
shaft couplings, 12, 13, 46–47
shaft seals, 12, 49
sheet bend (knot), 92
shock absorbers, 121
short splices, 86
shrouds, 78, 80–82
Simpson Lawrence Sea Tiger 555 two-speed windlass, 119
Simrad Tillerpilot, 69
single anchor (anchoring), 122
single-braid rope, 84
snatch block, 98
snubbers, 121
spinnaker controls, 110–11
splices: end, 87; eye, 87, 88–89; long, 85; short, 86
spreaders, 78
square knot. *See* reef knot
Sta-Lok swageless fittings, 76, 77
standing rigging: fractional rig, 79; masthead rig, 78; swaged fittings, 75; swageless fittings, 76–77; tuning, 80–82; wire rope, 74
starter motor, 23, 41
staysails, self-tacking, 102–3
steering cables and levers, 58
steering, inboard: dual-station hydraulic, 61; single-station hydraulic, 60
steering, outboard: hydraulic, 62; rack-and-pinion, 59; rotary, 59
steering, sailboat: chain-and-wire drive, 63, 66; pedestal, 63–67; quadrant drive, 63, 67; rack-and-pinion, 63–65, 68; radial drive, 63, 67
stern tube, 12, 45
stopper knot, 97
stray-current corrosion, 134, 137
stuffing boxes, 12, 13, 48
swaged fittings, 75
swageless fittings, 76–77

T
tackles. *See* block and tackle
tapered-plug seacocks, 160
tautline hitch, 95
thermostats: freshwater system, 36, 37; refrigeration, 164, 165, 166; seawater system, 35
three-blade, feathering Max-Prop propeller, 51, 55
thru-hulls, 134, 135, 137, 160
timing gear, camshaft, 19, 20

timing gear housing, 16, 22
toilets, marine. *See* marine toilets
transmissions: planetary, 44; Yanmar KM2-A, 42–43
travelers, 112–13
trochoid pump, 34
trucker's hitch, 96
turning block, 98
twisted rope, 84
two anchors off the bow (anchoring), 122
two-blade, feathering Max-Prop propeller, 51, 54
two half hitches, 94

V
valve adjust screws (engine), 21
valve cover (engine), 16, 24
valves, 160–63
vane pumps, 148
voltage regulator, 131, 143
Volvo MD31A alternator, 144

W
water heater, 154
water pumps. *See under* pumps
water system, 154–55
watt-hours (WH), 130
wet-acid batteries, 128, 129, 131
Whale Babyfoot Pump Mk. 2 diaphragm pump, 151
Whale Flipper Pump Mk. 4 manual piston pump, 150
Whale Gusher Galley Mk. 3 diaphragm pump, 152
Whale V Pump Mk. 6 pump, 150
whipping (rope), 84, 87
winches, 114–15
windvane, servopendulum, 70–71
wire rope, 74; crimping, 88. *See also* rope
wire rope eyes, 88
wire rope fittings: swaged, 75; swageless, 76–77

Y
Yanmar fuel filters, 27, 29
Yanmar KM2-A transmission, 42–43
Yanmar 2GM diesel engine, 16; air intake and breather, 25; camshaft, 16, 20; cooling system, 35–40; crankshaft, 16, 19, 24; cylinder block, 16, 17; cylinder head, 16, 21; flywheel housing, 23; fuel system, 26–32; horsepower rating, 15; lubrication system, 33–34; pistons, 18; starter motor, 41; timing gear housing, 16, 22; valve cover, 16, 24
Y-valves, 163

Z
zincs, sacrificial, 35, 134, 137. *See also* galvanic corrosion